THE PURSUIT OF
INEQUALITY

PHILIP GREEN

THE PURSUIT OF INEQUALITY

PANTHEON BOOKS · · · NEW YORK

Library of Congress Cataloging in Publication Data
Green, Philip, 1932-
The pursuit of inequality.

Includes index.
1. Equality.   I. Title.
HM146.G73   305   80-8661
ISBN 0-394-50676-6

Designed by Joy Chu

Manufactured in the United States of America
FIRST EDITION

CONTENTS

ACKNOWLEDGMENTS

This book is the first volume of a two-volume work on the topic of equality. The project out of which it has grown was inspired by a suggestion from the late Eli Chinoy and from Peter Rose, both of Smith College, and was continued with the help of a grant from the National Endowment for the Humanities.

Earlier versions of Chapters 2, 3, and 4 appeared in *Dissent* in the spring, summer, and fall 1976 issues, and are reprinted with the permission of that magazine. Those earlier versions benefitted inestimably from the editorial attentions of Edith Tarcov and Michael Walzer of *Dissent*, as well as of Dorothy Green. My understanding of some of the technical issues surrounding the discussion of IQ was greatly enlarged by Janet Grenzke and Patricia Y. Miller of Smith College. I should also thank Andrew Zimbalist of Smith College and Robert Paul Wolff of the University of Massachusetts for their knowledgeable comments on my discussion of the division of labor in Chapter 4.

Chapter 5 was originally presented in a somewhat different form to the Project on Women and Social Change at Smith College in the summer of 1979. I am deeply grateful to all the members of that project for their invaluable comments on and criticisms of that paper, and especially to Susan C. Bourque, Kathryn Pyne Parsons, Diedrich J. Snoek, and Kay B. Warren. In addition, Martha A. Ackelsberg and Donna R. Divine of Smith College, Thomas M. Divine of Northampton, and Suzanne Marilley of Harvard University gave me their very helpful insights on the topics discussed in Chapters 6 and 7.

Christine M. Torre of Smith College assisted in the preparation of the first draft and of the index; her intelligent comments and bibliographic work were of tremendous help. Julia A. Erickson, also of Smith College, not only provided additional research assistance but also read and commented on the entire final draft; her incisive suggestions were absolutely invaluable. The Committee on Aid to Faculty Scholarship of Smith College deserves thanks for supporting the work of both of them. I am also deeply grateful for the expert labors of Mrs. Pauline Walker of Leeds, Massachusetts, who typed the final manuscript; and of Jeanne Morton of Pantheon Books, who did the final copy editing with clarity and insight.

Above all, the knowledge and commitment of Philip Pochoda of Pantheon Books were crucial to the completion of this project. I would like to be able to say in the usual fashion that he bears no responsibility for all my errors of commission and omission, but that would be to underestimate his contribution: for better or worse, this book would not exist in its present form but for his encouragement and collegial effort.

A final note: it would also not exist were it not for the much more important existence, in the United States, of an intellectual community of egalitarians that is still, despite all the attention now being paid to the ephemeral "new conservatives," the only truly vital intellectual community we have. I am very happy to be a part of it.

THE PURSUIT OF
INEQUALITY

CHAPTER

1

INTRODUCTION:
THE EQUALITY DEBATE

In the past century and a half the advance of capitalism has everywhere deepened the social division of labor and thus inequality on the one hand, and inspired and broadened the search for more equality on the other.

The ethos of capitalism is systematized inequality. From cradle to grave we subsist in a world of unequal incentives and rewards, of sharply stratified and omnipresent hierarchy. Very early we recognize that a satisfactory life will consist, for most of us, in fitting into some slot or other which is specifically defined as one rung on an ascending ladder of rewards and opportunities. Not to fit into that structure is to claim, literally, the status of misfit, a status likely to be unpleasant even for those whose only realistic alternative is the bottom rung of unskilled labor.

Moreover, even those who suffer from it the most do not easily oppose or rebel against the system of inequality. As long as our social reward maintains us at a level at least of subsistence, that subsistence easily becomes an attractive bird in the hand compared with the hypothetical two in the bush promised by proponents of radical reform. At any given moment the alternatives for most people are likely to seem either a continuation of the system in which they are surviving—even if uncomfortably—or a probable plunge into chaos if demands for a different system of reward and authority are taken too seriously. Just as at the particular level even the strongest trade unions may be daunted by management's threats to close down operations if they persist in their demands, so at the general level the well-being of everyone is clearly endangered by the threats of the managers of capital to export it, or disinvest in it, should reformers or revolutionaries persist in their demands for "more." Unless the demand for equality is fueled by a natural tendency of the system toward growth (as in periods of general economic advance), or by real despair (as in periods of major depression), its fulfillment always lies in a future to which no road from the unequal present appears to lead very simply or directly. Indeed, in more frequent periods of inflationary advance or of general but uneven economic development, segments of the working class are easily turned against each other in the name of protecting those marginal differences in position that distinguish them. In short, inequality as the predominant feature of capitalism comes to seem an inescapable necessity of life.

It is because what is seems at any given moment to be what is necessary that, as Marx wrote, "the ideas of the ruling class are in every epoch the ruling ideas." But although the ideas of the ruling class are the ruling ideas, they are not the only ideas. Furthermore, the ideas by which a ruling class justifies itself to society as a whole somehow must also seem to speak to the needs of society as a whole if the ruling class is to be allowed to continue its rule. In short, the ideas of an epoch always contain their own contradictions.

Thus the system of material production (and relationships of material production) we call "capitalism" is also historically associated with a political and social system we call "liberal democracy." Whereas the ethos of capitalism per se is inequality, the ethos of liberal democracy is equality. Despite vast economic divisions we learn that we are all citizens and in some sense equally citizens; that every citizen should count for one and none for more than one; that government is supposed to be of, by, and for the people; and that the system promises worldly "success" to all of us who are not incorrigible idlers: every man (if not woman) can be a king. Authority is alleged to result only from merit, not from wealth, and wealth itself is justified as only a reward for serving an important social function.

From the perspective of capitalist reality, liberal-democratic "equality" must appear to be a set of illusions, a pleasing façade hiding ugly but necessary truths. But from the perspective of liberal democracy, capitalist "reality" comes to seem a fraud, a betrayed promise, even if everyone knows that the promise was never intended seriously. "Equality of opportunity," though a truth for some, remains clearly a myth for many; as such, it becomes a source of cynicism. Incredible disparities of income and power do not dwindle over time, or dwindle only slightly, no matter how hard those at the bottom of the ladder work to overcome them; wealth and power are flaunted in displays that have no conceivable relation to any vital social function. Born from that sense of betrayed promise, waves of egalitarianism, of demands for "more equality"—populism, socialism, or merely the inflationary demands of organized labor—periodically break upon the capitalist shore. In no capitalist nation can the public philosophy be described simply as either inegalitarian or egalitarian; the balance between the two moods always depends on which leaders or parties are prepared to press which demands at a particular historical juncture.

Since the legitimate capacity to make public policy stems, however tenuously, from the egalitarian institution of universal suffrage—majority rule—the actions of governing apparatuses partake of the same dual quality found in the public philosophy. Recoiling from the depressing fact that nothing ever seems to change—that income remains distributed with immense inequality, that progressive tax systems are not really very progressive, that governing elites are usually oligarchies rather than aristocracies, that corporate power seems untouchable—we can easily fail to notice the reverse tendencies in capitalist societies. Since the introduction of universal manhood suffrage at least, in all capitalist societies those who control the state justify their actions sometimes in the name of more equality, sometimes in the name of equal growth in well-being for all—but hardly ever in the name of inequality. If a tax break is advocated for corporations or for the wealthy, it is said to be done only in the name of increasing economic growth for the benefit of all. Special advantages for economic elites, as in the United States tax code, are introduced *sub rosa*, never proclaimed out loud. No one defends legislation by suggesting that the better class should be rewarded more and the inferior class less (except where members of the inferior class are alleged to be idle spongers); no legislator who hopes to advance in political life ever announces that his goal is to permanently maintain existing inequalities because some people naturally deserve more than others and it is morally right that they get it. Business elites in most capitalist societies spend a good deal of time and money vociferously denying that they exercise any independent power at all, political or economic; and even the most unregenerate opponents of social reform actually suggest that if only the right (i.e., laissez-faire) policies were followed, the gap between rich and poor would in the long run narrow rather than widen: this is the homage that vice self-consciously pays to virtue.

By and large, the only exceptions to these generalizations are to be found in those few situations where an entire working class has been subjected to direct coercion (e.g., Nazi Germany), or where ruling classes have managed to exercise coercion against a scapegoated segment of a fragmented working class (e.g., the American South). For at least a quarter of a century, however, in virtually every advanced capitalist society political debate has followed the pattern outlined above, conservative parties being distinguished from liberal, social democratic, democratic socialist, or communist parties chiefly by their insistence that "what is good for General Motors is good for the country," not by any overt justifications of inequality.

In his controversial and influential work, *A Theory of Justice*, John Rawls proposed as a fundamental principle of justice (in a democratic society) what he called "the Difference Principle": "that social and economic inequalities, for example inequalities of wealth and authority, are just only if they result in compensating benefits for everyone, and in particular for the least advantaged members of society."[1] Hostile anti-egalitarian critics treated Rawls as though in announcing this principle he had deserted the traditions of liberal democracy for some kind of menacing revolutionary doctrine. In fact, however, it was Rawls who was properly representing the liberal tradition, and his critics who were deserting it. And since liberal egalitarianism at times begins to shade over into reformist policies that loosen the grip of capitalist inequality (as in movements for worker self-management in Sweden and Norway), and at other times generates more radical demands precisely as its illusory nature becomes too painfully evident to too many people, the demand for more equality is always potentially on the agenda of liberal capitalist politics. Even in periods of retrenchment, policies favorable to the continuation of capitalist inequality are never adopted without a struggle. The Rawlsian promises made by the parties of inequality during those struggles ("we'll all be better off in the end if only we tighten our belts now") offer hostages to the future and thus lay the groundwork for future waves of egalitarian agitation.

It is in the light of these considerations that we must view recent "neoconservative" arguments that it is not "the people" but only elitist members of "the new class" who want more equality.[2] At the conceptual level, of course, the argument is ludicrous. The "new class" is simply the "knowledge class": the class that writes and talks about ideas, institutions, and processes instead of just working at ordinary production or clerical jobs. It follows quite evidently that if members of the "new class," so defined, are responsible for the spread of egalitarian doctrines, they are also responsible for the spread of inegalitarian doctrines, or of any doctrines at all. If "neoconservative" theorists want to adopt the notion that elitist intellectuals cunningly persuade elements of the masses—or each other —to adopt their private notions of egalitarianism, they must explain how it is that the billions of dollars' worth of antiegalitarian communications dispensed each year by those rather more substantial elites who own and control the mass media simply fail to overwhelm the comparatively muted egalitarian chorus.

The most obvious explanation is that large numbers of people have inchoate ideals and beliefs which are more or less receptive to egalitarian persuasion. There is ample empirical evidence for that explanation, too: public-opinion polls even in the relatively "conservative" United States show substantial support for such symbols of the case for "more equality" as national health insurance, price controls, the Equal Rights Amendment, and even, to a growing extent, some public control over corporate power. If we define "equality" in the utopian sense of absolute equality and an end to the social division of labor, then no doubt most people will reject it; the idea makes neither practical nor intellectual sense given the way most of us willy-nilly lead our lives. But to deny that the majority of people would like to lead lives that offer them, and their children, prospects for material satisfaction and political influence much less sharply inferior to those of existing economic elites is to fly in the face of all the historical, behavioral, and rhetorical evidence available to us.[3]

The real significance of the knowledge class, then, is quite different from that imputed to it by anti-egalitarian polemicists. The effect of inegalitarian institutions, in a secular and at least partially democratic social order, necessarily is to set classes and groups against each other; only some kind of mass acceptance of a notion that we are all part of a hierarchical "great chain of being" could mitigate the divisive effects of institutionalized inequality. Given even partially democratic processes, moreover, no way of life can be stable for long if a majority does not either actively support it or passively accept it for want of an alternative.

Since the most fundamental inequality in capitalist society is between the many who, owning no means of production, must work in order to live and the few who own means of production and thus need not work in order to live, political conflict will focus on that inequality, unless it can be somehow deflected. Those who think that the cause of equality will gain from the confrontation attempt to persuade the less politicized majority that their real enemy is the economic elite: "big business," or "capitalists." Those who wish to deflect the conflict may attempt to persuade this same majority either that their real enemy is located abroad, in which case all classes would have a common interest in overriding their class differences; or that their real enemy is some other social group, a minority against whom they would do better to ally themselves with the business interest; or both. In effect, these are the two major, permanent alignments in any capitalist society, whatever names they go by at any moment and however well organized and well represented they actually are. Even when, as in the United States today, the egalitarian tendency is barely represented in one of the only two organized political parties, its lingering effects still offer about the only distinction between those parties. In this perennial conflict, members of the knowledge class—those who specialize in public writing and public talking—must necessarily play the major part on *both* sides: they must present the arguments for and against more equality. Within that class the ideological contradictions of capitalist society are therefore played out.

The substance of these arguments, of course, varies with circumstances; fashions in debate vary as do fashions in everything else, and perhaps for similar reasons. Little more than a decade ago, most intellectuals, journalists, and political activists assumed that the conditions inhibiting an approach to more equality were structural and thus in principle subject to attack. In a reformist tradition containing such diverse figures as Marx, Mill, Dewey, R. H. Tawney, Gunnar Myrdal, and Franklin D. Roosevelt, the instrumentalities of government were seen by most people as the logical weapons for that attack. Opposition to egalitarianism centered on the alleged inefficiency or utopianism of nonmarket or cooperative economic practices, as well as on the notion that the autocratic communist societies of Eastern Europe demonstrated both the unlikelihood of achieving real equality and the terrible dangers inherent in making the attempt. On the other hand, home-grown theories of egalitarianism (e.g., the "New Left") were undergoing a rebirth in the United States, Great Britain, France, and several of the West European social democracies. These theories forswore the East European model and emphasized instead the decentralization of polity and economy as the most appropriate path to more equality. Moreover, throughout the capitalist world, popular (if not mass) movements were inspired and activated by the new egalitarian doctrines. In that sense, both an academic and a political debate were truly joined during the 1960s, and at least the argument that egalitarianism was simply utopian seemed much less compelling than it had just a short time before.

At that time it would not have been necessary to write a book such as this one. The arguments we will be concerned with in the essays that follow address questions different from whether a cooperative, humane society of equals is compatible with what we have come to think of as a "high standard of living," or with political liberty, or with industrialism in general. Instead we will be asking, much more mundanely, whether the average person is capable of making a contribution to society that is deserving of an average social reward; whether people in general are capable of managing their affairs democratically; and whether public authority can or ought to be used to rectify maldistributions of wealth, privilege, or power. For the traditional argument that the complications of large-scale industrial society render perfect equality utopian—an argument advanced by Max Weber and by the functionalist school in sociology, and in political science by the theorists of "democratic elitism"—has been replaced by potentially much more devastating arguments.[4]

It may not be a coincidence that the closer the issue of equality came to being on the agenda of practical political action, the more social scientists began to provide arguments supporting existing elites and the maintenance of gross inequalities. Precisely at the height of the earlier debate about equality, and perhaps incited by threats from popular movements against racial, sexual, and class inequalities, there was a resurgence of interest in the Victorian "science" of biologically rooted inequality, which at least in the United States had usually been only an underground current in the intellectual and academic worlds. Now biological inegalitarianism has again become one of the major strategies adopted by intellectuals wishing to justify the maintenance of things as they are. At the same time, and in large measure in response to unrelenting demands for racial and sexual equality, American intellectuals and politicians who once thought that the use of public policy to bring about more equality was limited only by practical exigencies began to retreat from the whole idea of public political action and of social reform. Instead, more and more of them argued, and continue to argue, that egalitarian public policies are by nature unjust and oppressive even when they bear no visible relation to the communist model or to utopian projections. These two streams of thought fit together quite logically, the one claiming that egalitarianism is socially destructive and the other that it can accomplish nothing anyhow because of biological limitations. Thus during the 1970s the intellectual party of inequality gradually came to dominate the American dialogue, and this party opposes not only perfect equality but any further advances toward equality at all.[5]

To a great extent, of course, that shift was a response to domestic and international developments adversely affecting the comparative wealth and power of many Americans as part of a national group and as individuals. But in some measure also the shift was heralded, inspired, and continually promulgated by the academic intellectuals whose works are inspected in the following pages.

This book is addressed to those members of the knowledge class who directly or indirectly, wittingly or unwittingly, have been the attentive audience of those works. In the first group of essays, Chapters 2 through 5, I analyze those sociobiological arguments which have attempted to persuade us variously that blacks *naturally* cannot be the equals of whites, nor women of men, nor the poor of the well-to-do. In those arguments immutable genes or hormones have been substituted for the divine will that was once said to predestine human souls to damnation or salvation, but the reasoning used to justify privilege or group superiority remains the same. Chapter 2 discusses the general approach to social analysis of sociobiologists whose implicit message is that major change is impossible because of our genes. The specific focus of this chapter is on the question of the genetic influence on intelligence, which has provoked one of the major intellectual controversies in recent American history. Chapter 3 deals, more narrowly, with Arthur Jensen's notorious argument that their genetic structure renders American black people, on the average, inherently less equipped to reason abstractly than American whites. It is in the arena of race that the most significant egalitarian initiatives were attempted in the 1960s, with what are still very ambiguous results; the potential uses of a deterministic genetic theory in offering a rationalization for the shortfall between policy and outcome are all too obvious. That is true also of Richard Herrnstein's associated argument, considered in Chapter 4, that egalitarian policies aimed at eradicating poverty can merely rigidify class lines and thus must have the unintended effect of producing a permanent class of the genetically as well as socially poor.[6]

Jensen and Herrnstein between them dominated one whole side of the intellectual dialogue of the 1970s, in which perceptions of the "difficulty" or "impossibility" of planning for major social change—a kind of rejuvenated Burkeian conservatism in which the *ancien régime* always seems "natural" because as of yesterday it was still there—replaced liberal or radical optimism as the most pronounced component of the American temper. Steven Goldberg, whose work on gender inequality is discussed in Chapter 5, has been less influential (perhaps because his version of the essential sociobiological argument is even more vulgarized than Jensen's or Herrnstein's). However, his work still is of great significance as a compendium of the arguments that characterize the antifeminist backlash and that have slowed, at least temporarily, the drive for sexual equality which characterized the 1970s as much as the drive for racial equality did the 1960s.[7]

These arguments, taken together, might be called the weak version of inegalitarianism. Though pernicious or even potentially vicious in their effects, they are ultimately weak because, as we shall see, they are intellectually corrupt; they have managed to attain currency only because various people found it profitable to accept them, not because there is anything intrinsically compelling about them. Indeed, implicitly the arguments of Jensen, Herrnstein, Goldberg, and their sympathizers repudiate the entire ethos of liberal democracy; their appeal is designed for a time of crisis, not for the long run.

However, all these biological arguments operate to confer the authority of "nature" on existing social arrangements and thus militate against demands for significant social change. As such they fit in quite well with the more general antireform mood of recent years, a mood dominated by those members of the educated middle class who see the further extension of the welfare state, egalitarian social reforms, or truly democratic political institutions as imposing a social cost that they are being unfairly asked to pay. In the second group of essays, Chapters 6 and 7, I shall consider the neoconservative arguments made by certain representatives of that class, that the Rawlsian principle of demanding a justification for inequalities, and of requiring a shift in the direction of more equality when inequalities cannot be justified, should be replaced by an individualist ethic that rejects the use of public power to achieve egalitarian ends.

Individualism is certainly as central to the ethos of liberal society as is egalitarianism: the greatest of all liberal philosophers, John Stuart Mill, was both an individualist and an egalitarian, after all. Thus the arguments discussed in Chapters 6 and 7 might be called the strong version of inegalitarianism, in that they appeal to principles that, in the United States at least, are thought by most people to be a basic part of the democratic ethos.

The two aspects of liberal individualism that will be discussed in those essays—the principle of equal opportunity for individuals and the principle of limiting government interference with the "free" market—might at first glance seem to be unrelated to each other; certainly many people who uphold the first of those principles would repudiate the second unqualifiedly. But in practical fact they are deeply related. Each makes *individual* well-being the source as well as the criterion of social justice, and considers versions of the good or the just which define them collectively as factually and morally false. Each too, we shall see, proceeds by the almost unnoticed expedient of accepting past assertions of collective good while opposing any attempt to extend them to present-day groups who were excluded from the benefits of the past.

The essays themselves focus on two separate but related substantive issues, which have been central to recent controversies about "big government" and its alleged interferences with individual free choice: the issue of the rightfulness of affirmative action, or "reverse discrimination" as it is called by its critics; and the more general issue of the rightfulness of using the tools of governance to redistribute income or regulate business. In both cases, intellectuals have discovered supposed grounds in ethical or political principle that have the same practical effect as the biological arguments discussed in the earlier essays: they make planned social change seem in some sense wrong, against nature.[8] The clear implication of both these sets of arguments, in other words, is that the halting steps toward greater equality that have been taken within the framework of liberal capitalism should be arrested, or even rolled back: that instead of pursuing equality, we should pursue inequality.

The unchecked individualism which the new ideologues of inequality express and justify is false to the experience of most people, as the arguments that justify it are false to our knowledge of history and social relationships. But as an ideology which most people also accept from time to time it is still extremely potent; after all, billions of dollars are spent every year to propagate it. For example, almost all "socially conscious" movies or television productions conclude with a heroic *individual* accomplishment, and leave us with the good feeling that some specific individual has come to a happy or at least cathartically tragic ending. To criticize the ideology of the new individualism, therefore, is in part to swim against the stream—but with the intention of recalling people to a different version of social reality which, when they stop to think about it, they will know to be true.

The concrete interests of various groups that in Marx's terms ought to be experienced in political unity are instead perceived as opposed by members of those groups themselves, not only in the United States but almost everywhere else in the industrial world. Essays written for an intellectually trained audience can hardly change that condition; interests are what they are and will be what they will be until powerful actors on the political stage can bring about a change in the conditions that produce the opposition of interests. My more modest purpose is to demonstrate that the arguments of the new individualism, whether biological or ethical, are factually worthless, conceptually inadequate, and morally indefensible. If that demonstration is persuasive, it should suggest that once again it is time to turn our attention away from arguments that justify inequality, and to think harder about the possible ways in which we can achieve more equality.

PART ONE

THE
RATIONALIZATION
OF
INEQUALITY

CHAPTER

SOCIOBIOLOGY AND INEQUALITY

It is useless to ask what is the source of natural inequality because that question is answered by the simple definition of the word. Again, it is still more useless to inquire whether there is any essential connection between the two inequalities; for this would be only asking, in other words, whether those who command are necessarily better than those who obey, and if strength of body or mind, or virtue are always found in particular individuals, in proportion to their power or wealth: a question fit perhaps to be discussed by slaves in the hearing of their masters, but highly unbecoming to reasonable and free men in search of the truth.

JEAN-JACQUES ROUSSEAU,
A Discourse on the Origin of Inequality

I. From the very moment that the idea of a natural science replaced reliance on Holy Writ, the intellectual center of gravity in the defense of inequality against demands for social change began to shift from divines to natural or behavioral "scientists." Although the Victorian period saw the height of the version of the defense that I have called biological inegalitarianism, recent years have witnessed startling new peaks, as scientists once again rise to defend the existing distribution of the good things in life.

The specific content of biological inegalitarianism is the science (or rather, the alleged science) called hereditarianism. From its beginnings, in the work of the racist and elitist eugenicist Francis Galton, to the present day, the procedure of hereditarianism has always been the same. A scientist (most often working outside the area in which he has done his most serious work), convinced that civilization is in danger of cultural pollution from external or internal causes, finds that the source of the danger —feeble-mindedness, subnormal intelligence, crime, homosexuality, mental illness, alcoholism, drug addiction—lies in the faulty genes of *some class of people other than that to which the scientist himself belongs.* A pseudoexperiment or observation, usually involving either nonhuman animals, prisoners, or a small number of pairs of human twins, is arranged to prove the charge and "save" the culture. Every canon of scientific procedure is flouted in these experiments or observations: randomness of and controls on test samples are ignored, and obvious intervening variables that might suggest a different relationship are carefully ignored or misreported; farfetched mechanisms of inheritance are suggested by way of explanation (among the favorites are "incompletely penetrant" genes and *outré* theories of "survival of the fittest"). Instead of behaving like real scientists and testing their own pseudohypotheses, the biological inegalitarians zealously set out to undermine all alternative (usually much simpler and more obvious) explanations by whatever means necessary. When the contrary facts roll inevitably in, suggesting overwhelming support for environmental or interactive explanations of human social phenomena, they simply move on to some new field in which they can play the game all over again.[1] Even when confronted with overwhelming evidence (as was recently the case with one of the most famous studies of human heredity) that the results of a crucial observation have been deliberately falsified, they press on, ignoring the evidence or calling for "further research." Never does it occur to them that the proper course of action is not to do further research on a suspect hypothesis that depends on cooked data, but rather to dig into the so-called other evidence to which they always refer, to see whether it too is contaminated. They never doubt themselves but only the "enemies" who have so embarrassingly exposed them; hardly ever do they comment at all on follow-up studies that call their work into serious question.[2] In the end, the response of one hereditarian to the documentation of fraud in the most famous twin study speaks for them all: "I could not care less. I do not need any statistical evidence to recognize the validity of inheritance."*

Biological inegalitarianism is more than misapplied "science," however; it is a political strategy, simple and easily recognizable. It always proceeds through the study of some outgroup which is held to be inferior in some important way. The shortcoming of this outgroup, be it a racial or ethnic minority, a "lower" social class, or the female sex, is held to be natural or innate to the group. In other words, victims of social discrimination fail, not because of repression by the powerful, but because they are genuinely inferior. Their particular badge of inferiority —their evident lack of some social good which the observer's group or class obviously possesses—is not man-made: the sources of differential human behavior and achievement are biological. That being the case, the assignment of high and low status to various groups is nothing more than the recognition of their *true* nature. Thus science, or what is claimed to be science, serves to reinforce commonplace stereotypes about others: blacks are less intelligent, women less aggressive, the poor less energetic. Since on the premise described here the only thing that would help people change their status relative to others would be a change in their biological constitution (which cannot be "redistributed" except by means of an unconscionable interference with the very blood and tissue of individuals), the biological inegalitarians offer what seems to be an impregnable support for the status quo. They make whatever is appear natural and therefore right.

There are, of course, many grounds on which it is possible to oppose redistribution through public policy; many theories of moral behavior, obligation, and political rationality call it into question. Moralistic and political objections to redistribution,

---

*Thus, the notorious and worthless "studies" of the Jukes and the Kallikaks are still referred to by hereditarians and still appear in high school biology texts; and Edward O. Wilson speaks approvingly of the discredited studies which purported to show that men with XYY chromosomes are more predisposed to criminal behavior than biologically more ordinary men.[3]

however, have the helpful feature that the social interests from which they proceed are usually clear. Those who seek more equality and have already opted for redistribution in some form or other, therefore, are unlikely to be persuaded by such arguments against it. The biological argument is different, though. With it, the alleged authority of "science" is placed squarely behind the notion that it is not just politically questionable but practically futile to propose collective social action to eliminate or attenuate the major inequalities that divide us; to redistribute social goods.

The biological inegalitarians, in sum, explain every crucial cultural response as being the result of a biological stimulus. If one group behaves differently from another, that is not because the two have different historical experiences, but because their genes are different. If general patterns of domination and subordination are found worldwide, that is not because the same kinds of people have sought power successfully, but because our genes or our hormones or our glands demand domination and subordination.

At this writing, despite the frauds, errors, and false starts of the past, this kind of thinking has gained new credibility with the intellectual public under the rubric of "sociobiology." In the midst of the acclaim for sociobiology one is almost hesitant to point out that no sociobiologist has ever yet produced any actual evidence of a biological determination of human culture. A human geneticist can point to the gene for, say, Down's syndrome and show us how distortions in a normal gene produce the deadly effect. No one has ever isolated a gene for any form of cultural behavior, nor even suggested what group of genes could affect just one instance of it. But how could they? Human society is culturally, linguistically, symbolically, organizationally, and ethically so complex and diverse that nothing about it can possibly be explained by the existence of uniform genetic and physiological processes in individuals, modified only by ecological variation (as is the case with nonhuman animals). Prima facie, any attempt to reduce to mere variations on a biological formula the extraordinarily diverse interactions humans have with one another, with their various natural environments, and with their man-made additions to and modifications of those environments must force us to ignore or de-emphasize the obvious *socialness* of so much of the human world we participate in and see around us. Every day we see people, including ourselves, respond to their surroundings in ways that unquestionably relate to the nature of those surroundings. We also see ourselves developing different ideas (about such things as "equality") that cannot be related merely to the kinds of individuals that we are, unless we understand that the individual and the social world are inextricably part of each other. Given the richness of the interaction between individuality and socialization, indeed, the only conception of human genetics and human biology that makes sense is that, as opposed to other animals, humans are equipped to create cultural worlds. These initial acts of creation often foster further creativity and invention (both for better and for worse), so that "human nature"—the interplay between self and others —takes off from its origins in a unique, often indecipherable, and yet clearly observable manner.*

In the face of the wealth of information we have about this aspect of human social interaction, and without any evidence at all for a determining (in the sense of limiting) biological input, hereditarians cannot show any link between biology and culture except via the crudest kinds of statistical correlation, that "rude and slovenly mode of generalization" which Mill called "the mode of simple enumeration." Count up as many aggressive men, high-IQ Orientals, or domestic women as one wants, only a prejudicial search for a "hard" science of human behavior can

---

*These critical remarks about the sociobiological approach are only meant to be applied to those examples of it which result in the making of comparative statements about different human groups, or different norms of social behavior (e.g., egalitarianism versus inegalitarianism). Those sociobiologists—none of them well known to the public—who mean by "social biology" simply the attempt to understand how humans *originally* became different from other higher mammals and prospered because of the difference, as well as what the difference entails, are engaged in a fundamental inquiry that every serious social theorist from Plato to Marx has engaged in at some time or other. In addition, there is obviously a great need for ecological analyses of human culture—for studies which investigate the crucial interaction between culture and physical environment. Since that interaction will often be describable in terms taken from the biological sciences, even from mathematical biology, the rubric of "sociobiology" can also be used to comprehend such studies. However, that would be a sociobiology that made little or no use of the concept of genetic determination that Wilson, Lionel Tiger, Raymond Dawkins, and others have associated with "sociobiology" in popular discussion.[4]

justify the substitution of mystifying and deterministic hypotheses about unobserved genes or hormones for explanations based on the much more palpable social structures and relationships that we are able to observe.

Even a careful, cautious, and relatively unprejudiced hereditarian like Edward O. Wilson, whose recent work *On Human Nature* has been received with respect, can only invent fanciful hypotheses and offer arbitrary assertions about the influence of heredity. Invariably, his nicely phrased and superficially plausible contentions about human society lack even one persuasive concrete example. Thus his introductory statement, "Biology is the key to human nature, and social scientists cannot afford to ignore its rapidly tightening principles," is followed by several chapters of patently inaccurate generalizations; secondhand accounts of marginally interesting studies that have never been replicated; casual references to popular prejudices about the sexual division of labor, hierarchy, and so forth; the imposition of sociological categories on animal behavior, which, having been incorrectly described as though it were human, is then made the source of comparative statements about human society; and the elaboration of circular arguments (based on such helpful inventions as genes for "conformity" or for "spite") to explain away the persistence of and variation in those human social behaviors, from altruism to murderous aggression, that are so clearly inexplicable as any kind of "natural selection."[5]

Only an understanding of the social realm will enable us to explicate the behaviors and institutions that take place within it, but the relegation of the social realm to a secondary status is exactly what the hereditarians propose (even when, like Wilson, they deny having that intention). Thus they legitimate, among other ideological constructions, notions of the naturalness and irremediability of human inequalities. In abstracting the study of the causation of (or relationships between) human behaviors from a social matrix, they make it seem as though that matrix were only a side-effect of biological "causes." Our bodily processes, in their view, lead us to respond to a world that is presented to us—but nothing is said to explain how "our" world came to be the way it is, so utterly different from the world of some other "us" centuries past or centuries in the future. Instead, we are given such noninformation as Wilson's (inane) assertion that "cultural change is the statistical product of the separate behavioral responses of large numbers of human beings who cope as best they can with social existence."[6] What produced and continues to reproduce that "social existence" which we have had to respond to and cope with, other than sheer random chance, remains a mystery; though it is no mystery that we are being told we can do little that is constructive about changing it. History and sociology as attempts to understand the way we behave socially disappear from the world-view of the hereditarian, to be replaced by the simplistic view, long ago demolished by Hume and Mill (and related directly to "the mode of simple enumeration"), that a statistical correlation between the occurrence of two phenomena shows that one must have "caused" the other.

In this kind of social study, therefore, the misconceived "science" and the hidden (or not so hidden) ideological agenda are always conjoined, as a hypothetical example will show. Suppose we were to note, as we certainly should, that everywhere in the industrial world people who do factory work tend overwhelmingly to set off to work in the early morning. The only available sociobiological explanation of this phenomenon is that there is a "natural" metabolic or diurnal cycle which makes most people want to go to work no later than a few hours after sunrise, and that *therefore*, in response to this natural phenomenon, factories open when they do. If we adopted this explanation we would then not merely be failing to notice the possibility that (in the language of the statistician) there is an "intervening variable" we had neglected to take into account; we would in addition be carefully obscuring the facts that a particular human agency, wielding powers that came into being in a particular way at a particular time, *forces* people to go to work in the early morning, and that the people themselves, much less their genes, never were allowed to express any real choice in the matter. But as we shall see, this imaginary example of sociobiological analysis is no more absurd than several which have gained notoriety and respectful public attention in recent years. It is, in fact, but a variant on a common theme: the exercise of power by some over others is necessarily mystified when we do not allow ourselves to see it as a conscious expression of self-interest, but observe it only as a "natural" relationship. This, of course, is the other side of the argument that blames the victims for their victimization.

II. The denigration of social structure as a causative factor in human affairs thus obscures both the role of human agency in the past and present and the possibility that it may play a different role in the future. For the real social world in which the man-made components of inequality among groups are all too visible, biological inegalitarians substitute an invented world in which human differences are "innate." To repeat, none of this is accidental. They pursue spurious or meaningless correlations in order to make a show of "scientific" knowledge where we actually have no hard knowledge at all. And they attempt to persuade us to suppress the only educated ideas we do have about the determinants of cultural variation, so that we may be dissuaded from pursuing those social changes that would make these ideologues uncomfortable.

In recent years this strategy has been nowhere more evident than in the public discussion of genes and IQ or "intelligence," a discussion initiated over a decade ago by Arthur Jensen and Richard Herrnstein. Jensen and Herrnstein are not usually identified in the public press as "sociobiologists"; this appellation is usually reserved for sociobiological theorists and popularizers such as Edward O. Wilson, David Barash, Lionel Tiger, or Robert L. Trivers. But Jensen's and Herrnstein's discussion of the inheritance of intelligence is precisely sociobiological; to come to grips with that discussion is to understand fully the implicit linkages between sociobiology, hereditarianism, and inegalitarianism.*

That individuals are not identical in their various capabili-

*Most well-known sociobiologists have avoided discussion of Arthur Jensen's propositions about genes and intelligence. None that I know of has disavowed him, however, though he is clearly working in their field; and Wilson has written: "Genetic studies based on the comparison of identical and fraternal twins suggest that *primary mental abilities* [italics added] and perceptual and motor skills are the most influenced by heredity, while personality traits are the least influenced." Jensen and Herrnstein would surely have to be forgiven if they take that statement to heart—nor can we doubt that their work deserves to be called "sociobiology" when it is, as here, received as authoritative by the author of the term himself.[7]

ties is a truism; and that for each of us the limits of our various capabilities are set to some extent by our genetic inheritance is an almost equally reasonable supposition (though it is still nothing more than a supposition, Wilson *et al.* to the contrary). Nothing is implied by our acceptance of these two claims except the acknowledgment that some people will always be able to outperform other people in various ways. That simple, even self-evident statement becomes a basis for inegalitarianism only if we add to it the further assertions that the nature and extent of the visible differences among people at the present time reflect *primarily* genetic and ineradicable inheritance rather than environmental or interactive influences; and that the visible differences in accomplishment among various discretely discernible *groups* within a single society result from differential, inherited, and ineradicable predispositions that are somehow genetically common to those groups and that are passed on by group inbreeding. Those are exactly the assertions that Jensen and Herrnstein have made, and their argument is thus a guide to the program of the new, "scientific" inegalitarianism.

According to Jensen, "success" in American (or any modern) society is legitimately a function of a particular kind of intelligence that might best be called "conceptual" intelligence or "cognitive ability"—the kind of intellectual skill needed to make complicated technical decisions or do essential scientific research. This particular kind of intelligence is allegedly encapsulated in various intelligence or IQ tests (which have in common that their results, for a given individual, tend to show a high rate of intercorrelation). Also according to Jensen, the kind of intelligence measured by these tests is largely *heritable;* that is, the difference between the average IQs of any two groups of people with different average IQs can be much more easily accounted for, statistically, by positing a genetic rather then an environmental influence. Jensen reaches this conclusion by reviewing a series of studies of genetically related persons, ranging from mere siblings to one-egg (monozygotic) identical twins, who from birth or a very early period in their lives have been reared apart (there are also a few studies of unrelated children reared in the same home). Jensen postulates that by separating the environmental influence on these children (their place of residence and the people bringing them up) from the genetic influence (their actual blood ties), and then comparing their IQ scores, one can estimate the genetic influence—the heritability —quite accurately. Thus we can put a hard number to the old argument about "nature" versus "nurture."[8]

Estimates of this heritability figure, by people who have followed Jensen's procedure, range from a low of 0.25–0.35 (that is, 25–35 percent as a proportion of the statistical variance between two different IQ sets accounted for by postulating a heritability factor) through a midrange figure of 0.50 to a high of 0.80 (Jensen's estimate, which he justified chiefly by discounting almost all studies but those involving identical twins and adopted foster children, and by ignoring necessary caveats about interpretation of the data that other authors have pointed to).*

If the postulated heritability factor indeed exists, and is as high as he claims (or close to it), certain unpleasant conclusions seem to follow, according to Jensen and Herrnstein. We cannot easily close the intelligence-as-IQ gap that already exists between different classes or groups by educational effort or other environmental interventions, and we are doomed to the continued existence of a society based on real, "naturally" transmitted, and thus permanent group differences: that is, a "naturally" inegalitarian society. ("Doomed," to be sure, is my own word; one does not get the impression that the sociobiological inegalitarians see the matter in that light at all.) And of course, a widespread acceptance of the general notion of heritability in this sense would quickly lead many people to conclude that whatever our norms with respect to equality, they are beside the point: genes (if not blood) will tell.

---

*In the language of statisticians, the standard deviation of a series of measurements is discovered by taking the sum of the squares of all deviations from the mean, dividing that figure by the number of deviant measurements, and then taking the square root of that figure to get the standard deviation (SD). E.g., in the series of measurements -2, 4, 6, 7, 10, the standard deviation (SD) equals 4, since the squares of all deviations from the mean measurement of 5 add up to 80 and, there being five deviant measurements, one-fifth of 80 is 16, of which the square root is 4. As for the *variance* of a series of measurements, that is given as the square of the standard deviation, which in this case would be 16. Statistical analysis, then, tries by various methods to find the "cause" of that total variance —i.e., why all measurements were not 5, and how much of the deviation from 5, that is, how much of the total variance of 16, is caused by one factor or another.

And yet, Jensen's and Herrnstein's use of the notion of the heritability of IQ is clearly and unequivocally defective. The nature of its defectiveness, moreover, tells us something important about sociobiological reasoning.

As I noted earlier, no gene for intelligence or any other social phenomenon has ever actually been observed. "There is no single gene for the measure called IQ, let alone for the broader construct of intelligence." One educational psychologist has summed up what we do know about the inheritance of intelligence more precisely:

> From the point of view of the user of an intelligence test the most important reason for not defining intelligence in terms of a genetic substrate is that a given person's standing with respect to genetic factors cannot be inferred from a test score. The test measures acquired behavior. Independent assessment of the genetically determined biological base is presently possible for only a tiny portion of the human population, e.g., phenylketonuria. Some few of the acquired organic differences can be independently assessed, e.g., certain of the birth "injuries." Experimental control is lacking in studies of human genetics so that it is even impossible to draw conclusions about the relative contribution to the variance of genetic factors in an analysis of variance design. . . .
>
> While a biological substrate for intelligence is made necessary by biological knowledge, the construct cannot at the present time enter into testable hypotheses in any except the most general fashion. Any given organism may have an innate capacity for the development of its intelligence, but the limits of this are very nebulous indeed. This capacity, furthermore, is not necessarily fixed at a given level throughout the life span. . . . It is safe to conclude that no amount of training will transform a chimpanzee into a human being intellectually, or a Mongoloid into a genius, but present data do not allow much more specific inferences than these.[9]

How is it, we might wonder, that a subject about which we are told hardly any "specific inferences" can be drawn can be the topic of Jensen's confident assertions about the "heritability factor" in IQ, and thus about the underlying reality of what IQ purports to measure? Studies of the "heritability" of IQ can impart no information about the actual inheritance of intelligence, or of the qualities that make up our responses to IQ tests. Those studies are merely sets of statistical observations—the "mode of simple enumeration"—and they can only (if accurately reported) tell us what is happening under particular social circumstances. Such studies cannot possibly tell us what *can* happen under *all* circumstances; only a theory linking observations to produce a universal law can do that. As we observe Jensen (and Herrnstein) trying to generate such a theory, we are observing a classic case of the substitution of social prejudice for social science.

III. The "heritability" of a trait refers to the extent to which variations in measurement from the average value of the trait may be traceable to genetic variation in the measured population. For a population that has regularly inbred to the exclusion of outsiders, a heritability of, say, 0.80 would mean that four-fifths of the total variation from the mean would be accounted for by genetic differences in the population. But that figure is not, as Jensen has erroneously implied and as inegalitarians wish to believe, a function of the "innateness" of the trait being measured. In fact, "heritability" and "innateness" have nothing logically to do with each other.

At the beginning of his original presentation of the "theory" of the heritability of IQ, Jensen tells us:

> The average correlation between phenotypes and genotypes for IQ is about .90 in European and North American Caucasian populations, as determined from summary data presented later in this paper. . . . [He refers to the twin, sibling, and foster-children studies.] The square of this value is known as the heritability—the proportion of phenotypic variance due to genetic variation. . . .

"Phenotypes" are the obtained measurements of the actual expression of a gene or genes—in this case, allegedly, IQ scores for individuals or groups; "genotypes" are the actual genetic constitutions of individuals. That is, Jensen tells us we are seeking correlations between test scores and genetic makeup. But how can we possibly know the latter if the exact nature of the genes (if any) for intelligence is unknown and individual genotypes are therefore unmeasurable?

Jensen's answer to this question is as follows:

> Unrelated children reared together [i.e., foster children] . . . have no genetic inheritance in common, but they are reared in a common environment. Therefore the correlation between such children will reflect the environment.

He adds shortly thereafter:

> The conceptually simplest estimate of heritability is, of course, the correlation between identical twins reared apart, since, if their environments are uncorrelated, all they have in common are their genes. The correlation . . . in this case is the same as the heritability. . . .[10]*

Now the problem in this kind of work is not simply the reliance on statistical studies; it is not necessary to be a scientific philistine to protect the integrity of the human subject. After all, we often gain knowledge of the human condition through statistical measurements—as long as we can believe in good faith that what we are inferentially measuring really exists. However, if personal or social prejudice is the only ground for giving credence to our indirect measurements, then the tools of statistics merely erect a rickety structure of nondata balanced crazily atop the original prejudice. That is the case here. To take one blatant example, it is by now certain that the most celebrated twin studies, those of noted English psychologist Sir Cyril Burt, were

---

*That conclusion is false, since in statistical operations one always *squares* the raw correlational figure to get the technically correct measurement. By refusing to do so, Jensen inflates the alleged heritability figure, since the square of a fraction is always smaller than the initial fraction (of less than 1). In an appendix to one of his books, he explains why he made this obvious error, but the explanation is based on the massive conceptual confusion discussed immediately below.[11]

faked. Burt, "knowing" as a good inegalitarian would that intelligence must be both genetic and unequal, simply made up IQ scores and variances for his subjects. (Those readers who find it hard to credit this well-documented charge of fraud on the part of a major scientific figure can reflect on the response to the exposure of Burt's fraud, quoted on page 17 above.[12]) But sheer fakery is the least of our problems here.

The other studies Jensen relies on were presumably conducted with honesty, but they had something else in common: the bizarre and biased notion of "environment" that is visible in the quotations from Jensen. We can allow Jensen his assumption that monozygotic twins have completely identical genes. We do not know that this fact has anything to do with their allegedly similar IQ scores unless we know beforehand that intelligence-as-IQ has a genetic character, which is exactly what we are trying to prove by establishing its heritability in the first place! For all we know, the correlation between IQs of the separated twins (if there actually was one) is satisfactorily explained by common factors of diet, education, discipline, and so forth in their separate but not wholly dissimilar environments—and none of it is explained by their genes. How can Jensen assert otherwise? Only by asking us to believe the impossible: that their environments had *nothing* in common—were "uncorrelated." Certainly a much likelier hypothesis, and one borne out by reinvestigations of these studies, is that the adoption agencies tried to place the separated siblings in roughly equivalent "environments." Jensen thus moves us into a world of sheer fantasy in which the lives of merely separated people can have literally nothing important in common: can be "uncorrelated." As if that were not bad enough, when dealing with foster children he stands the fantasy on its head. Not only do separate homes have *nothing* in common, but the *same* home presents *everything* in "common," as though adoptive parents always treated their foster children exactly like their biological ones (or, for that matter, as though biological parents treated their second biological child exactly like the first). So that we, like Alice, can be asked to believe *three* impossible things before breakfast, Jensen also implicitly asks us to accept the further hypothesis that their *pre*adoptive environments had no ultimate effect on the foster children who eventually moved into the adoptive homes where they had "everything in common" with their adoptive siblings.[13]

Two more recent studies (not of separated twins), which have attempted to control background variables more carefully, highlight Jensen's error. One, based on the largest sample of twins ever studied, comes to the conclusion that "the data are generally consistent with a substantial influence of the genes in accounting for individual differences in these domains, but they imply a substantial influence of the environment as well—indeed, they do not altogether exclude a completely environmentalist position." The qualification is justified by the speculative but not implausible assumption that environmental factors unobserved by the experimenters were having some effect. The second study begins dramatically with the assertion that the data "demonstrate the unmistakeable contribution of genetic factors to individual differences in intellectual ability, interests, and even prejudices," but concludes with the remark that "when a child's environment is basically humane, we find that genetic background plays a larger part in accounting for individual differences." The authors of these studies seem unaware of the conceptual confusions that stand behind their own inability to be unequivocal—seem unaware, that is, that every time they arbitrarily redefine "environment" (and our decision as to what to put under the heading of "environment" must always be arbitrary) they also necessarily change the heritability figure they are trying to isolate. But they both implicitly make the point that though the heritability of intelligence is probably real in some sense, numerical *measures* of it are derivative, for one of the things built into all such measures—whether the experimenters realize it or not—is assumptions about the environmental influence that sociobiologists disparage.[14]

Jensen, by contrast, is able to go so hopelessly awry because he does not actually understand the concept of heritability. This he seems to have in common with all those sociobiologists who insist on transferring observations directly from the animal kingdom to the human realm. As developed by geneticists, the concept of heritability was intended, not as a means for solving metaphysical conundrums about man's nature, but rather as a means for making experimental work in genetics easier. The heritability of a trait is nothing more than the possibility of breeding true for that trait *if and only if* all nongenetic influences are controlled; it is

> the extent to which variation in successive generations is predictable in terms of *genetic control* and is therefore *subject to selection in straightforward fashion.* ... Highly heritable traits are easily subject to effective selection; slightly heritable ones require intense selection to provide significant genetic progress.[15]

Thus geneticists who are trying to breed true a certain trait in a plant, an animal, or an insect—who are applying the notion of "heritability" in its truly biological sense—are not trapped in a vicious conceptual circle that forces them to make distinctions between the indistinguishable. They simply (not always so simply, to be sure) *control* for the environment of their breeding population. After having come to some conclusion, based on observation and experience, about the relevant environmental effects on a particular trait, they then eliminate or hold constant the impact of those effects. Trial and error will eventually produce a fit between the estimated heritability value of the trait and the degree to which it is actually manifested in the breeding population's descendants. If this does not result, then the experimenters will know that they probably did not control for all relevant aspects of the environment, and must try again. Fortunately, Jensen cannot arrange for people to have identical twins one of whom will be removed to a home which is exactly unlike the other's home in every important respect.

Of course, if we had some antecedent reason to believe in good faith that intelligence-as-IQ is inherited—that is, if that hypothesis were based reasonably on observation and experience—then we still might consider these pseudostatistical studies, even though it had been manifestly impossible to control them in any scientific sense. Interestingly enough, we do know a fair amount about the genetics of what seem to be more strictly biological traits in both animals and humans. Among domestic animals, for example, the heritability of traits having to do with size at birth is generally quite low, even though those are economically valuable traits. How then can we be asked to believe that reasoning capacity in humans, which no one is trying particularly to breed true, is of a more rigidly genetic character than the birth weight of domestic sheep, which by comparison have been born of parents living in idyllically controlled and uniform environments? In other words, it is not simply that Jensen's reasoning is circular and the assumptions it is based on absurd, but that the nature of its absurdity is tendentious: the notion of "correlated" and "uncorrelated" environments can be held only by a sociobiological fantasist who begins by refusing to acknowledge the diversity and power of human culture and social order.

The problem of this kind of sociobiological reasoning is more than merely empirical. Even in a totalitarian dream world we could not "hold the environment constant" while studying our own genetic determinations, because, as human beings, we cannot draw any verifiable boundary between the two any more than we can pick ourselves up by our shoelaces and suspend ourselves in midair. The "we" that is trying to separate ourselves from some "otherwhere" is a we that does not even exist except as part of the otherwhere, in response to it, and as a determinant of it. It is not that it is difficult to conduct a proper scientific experiment which will determine how much of an influence is "innate" or "genetic," how much "environmental," and how much "interaction between the two"; rather, the distinction makes no sense. We are not trying to find out whether the chicken or the egg came first; that metaphor is inappropriate here. Personality is both personal *and* social; the way we interact with "society" is personal; neither exists without the other. The pseudoscientific dream of a sociobiologist like Jensen is to find some characteristic measurable with definitive statistical accuracy at the moment the infant comes out of the womb. Such characteristics may indeed exist—blood type, pigmentation, certain chromosomal or hormonal deficiencies. But other than specific organic malfunctions, we know of none that determine the way people behave socially. None could, for people cannot behave socially until they live in society, and there is no such thing as a social "behavior" except as others have weighed, judged, or measured it. This version of the sociobiological method is, to repeat, not merely a methodological fallacy but a theological heresy (or orthodoxy, depending on one's creed): the idea of inherent and eternal damnation or salvation.

IV. Consequently, the notion that a conscious, sentient, active being can study, "scientifically," the influence of genes on its own intelligence (or its aggressiveness or its social capacity) is worthless. Even more crucial, so too is the notion that it is of any great moment that there exists a statistically demonstrable "gap" between one group's or individual's manifestation of a trait and another's. Even if we could know the extent to which a trait is biological in its initial determination, we would still be much more interested in knowing whether manifestation of the trait is subject to deliberate environmental and social intervention. When Jensen and Herrnstein assert that the "heritability" of intelligence gives cause for concern, they are obviously suggesting that the more the statistical variance for a given trait is traceable to genetic differences, the more difficult egalitarian social intervention with respect to that trait must be. Jensen goes so far as to say directly:

> The degree to which equal conditions of teaching or instruction will diminish individual differences in achievement *is* [his emphasis] inversely related to the heritability of the "teachability" of the subject in question, and various school subjects probably differ considerably in heritability. . . .[16]

This syllogism is simply fallacious. He has assumed that to the extent that a trait is statistically heritable it cannot be environmentally influenced. In fact, all a given statistic of heritability tells us (also assuming its accuracy, which cannot be assumed for any statistic in this field) is how much or how little observable and measurable environmental influence there has been *until now*. It does not tell us anything about the prospects for success in attempting to overcome a deficit in a trait that appears to be heritable: the two things have nothing to do with each other.

It is indeed true that if we offer a piece of information only once to an entire group of pupils and do not repeat it for the benefit of those who failed to get it the first time, then the genetically slower learners (as well as the poor attenders) may never catch up with the faster ones. Since Jensen is not stupid, we must assume he did not mean to be simple-minded. Clearly he means rather that heritability equals irremediability. He is, again, badly wrong. We cannot help but think, given the obviousness of his error, that the mistake is based, again, on sheer ideological willfulness.

We can see how willful and tendentious Jensen is by looking at a trait that is without doubt of a strongly biological nature in humans. One of the things we mean by saying that twins are "identical" (that is, monozygotic or from one fertilized egg) is that they are of identical height (technically, length) at birth; if that were not true, we would decide that we had been mistaken in thinking them identical. This is an indication of our belief that height in humans is subject to a strong genetic influence. Of course, such beliefs can be wrong, as the history of various sciences from astronomy to medicine demonstrates. In this particular realm we will be certain of our belief if we have actually isolated in humans (or at least in animals) a gene for height and observed what happens when it is tampered with. Or, we may decide that our belief is worthy of being considered knowledge because observation over many years and of many cases has told us beyond doubt that (roughly speaking) short people have short children, grandchildren, and so on, and tall people the reverse.

On the other hand, we are also aware that height in human *adults* is not genetically determined in the same sense as is the height of humans at birth: the average heights of different human groups (that is, inbreeding populations) change over time, and even change relative to each other over time.

With respect to the first point, if we starve (relatively) one of a pair of identical twins throughout its infancy and childhood while the other is helped to flourish, the two will grow up to be of different heights; to attain the limits of our physical possibilities we require not only the right genes but decent nourishment. Knowing this, though, we still think that the genetic influence on human height is strong. If we take two pairs of identical twins, one of which we think has genes for being relatively tall and the other genes for being relatively short, and we "starve" one twin in each pair, then eventually one twin in each pair will be shorter than its otherwise "identical" sibling; but, we expect, the short twin in the "tall" pair will usually remain taller than the short twin in the "short" pair. This hypothetical case suggests both the meaning and the limits of the notion of genetic determination in individuals. Because we must go to such extremes to make any pair of identical twins grow up to unequal heights, and because (in many cases) what we think of as the normal genetic relationship between "taller" and "shorter" will still obtain even after we have done this, we think of individual height as something that, though subject to environmental influence, is fairly strongly determined by genes.

Conversely, with respect to the second point about height in human adults, we have reason to believe that genetic determination in the relative height of human groups is very weak. Over the centuries, changes in patterns of human consumption and life-style in Europe have brought about sharp increases in the average height of men and women, and the pattern of increase continues to be visible. Furthermore, the differences between various populations have shrunk even within the twentieth century, as changes in diet and health care have normalized (by our standards) the average height of several peoples (such as the Japanese) who only a brief while ago were considered relatively short.[17] To take an even less ambiguous example, thyroid deficiency brings about various symptoms of physical and mental retardation in infants; it is clearly genetic in origin. But if the genetic condition is known, the effects of it can be obviated by giving a putative mother massive prenatal doses of artificial thyroxin. Even when the condition becomes known only at birth, if it is detected soon enough postnatal adjustments of the infant's body chemistry are possible, and all effects can again be obviated. The genetic inheritance will remain, and may still be capable of being passed on to a later generation, but no actual harm will have been done.

Similarly, susceptibility to tooth decay (caries) through softness of the dentine is a genetic trait. "Bad teeth," in this sense, are both heritable—as Herrnstein at one point remarks—and endemic. Yet simply adding a goodly amount of fluoride to all water supplies, plus the general inculcation of good dental habits, would virtually wipe out caries within one or two generations: this Herrnstein neglects to mention. All our previous "measurements" of susceptibility to tooth decay, its incidence and variations in incidence, would become of no importance, though the trait indeed represents an "innate" disposition—surely much more so than does "intelligence." Moreover, it would be possible to arrange things so that "bad teeth" as a condition would seem to be carried ethnically or racially: we need only eliminate all fluoride (including "natural" fluoride) from our water supplies, give fluoride pills in copious amounts to members of the dominant social group only, and prohibit dentists from treating members of subordinate social groups in any way. Within a very short time our "statistics" would show that children in the first group "inherit" good teeth from their caries-free parents and children in the second group "inherit" bad teeth from their caries-ridden parents. On the other hand, in a more egalitarian society it would not matter if there actually were qualitatively different genes for susceptibility to tooth decay, unlikely as that eventuality is. It would not matter, because fluoridation would attenuate or eliminate that condition whatever the genetic predisposition.

Thus, simple reflection upon matters of common knowledge tells us that from a policy standpoint the only important question about differences in manifestation of a trait is not whether those differences (and by implication the boundaries of expression of the trait itself) are "caused" genetically but whether the trait itself is *malleable*, and whether we are willing to deal with it on that basis. There are, to be sure, highly heritable traits that are almost totally unmalleable: blood type, for example. There are also acquired traits that, once widespread, are virtually unmalleable: habits and customs can endure for millennia despite strenuous efforts to erase them. Most important for our purposes, however, is that there are traits, highly heritable in all populations, that are thoroughly malleable and in some cases quite easily so.

V. There are actually two different points raised here. We want to know not only whether a given trait is malleable by conscious environmental intervention; we are also interested in knowing whether the existing expression of a trait prior to any deliberate intervention is the unmediated outcome of a genetic predisposition. Only if we think that the malleability of intelligence as measured by IQ (or any other performance tests) is slight or nonexistent, *and* that the measurements of "intelligence" we do have truly represent the unmediated outcome of a genetic predisposition, can we put forth in good faith a belief in the genetic determination of intelligence. Yet to make either of those assertions is to commit an evident absurdity.

As to the meaning of the IQ scores or other measurements of "intelligence" or "cognitive ability" with which we are familiar, we cannot doubt that when people take intelligence tests of any kind, their performance is determined more by their whole life experience than by their "innate capacities." Although Jensen continually works to cast doubt on it, that proposition is beyond any doubt. (Binet himself, who should have known, said specifically that intelligent thinking was an art that improved with practice, and with the opportunity to practice.)[18] We must never forget that test scores in themselves are in no way a direct outcome of the organism's characteristics, whether genetically or culturally induced. Rather, they represent a translation of the relevant characteristics by some mediating behavior, whether purposeful or not. And behavior, of course, is based not merely on the innate ability to perform a task but also on one's momentary ability to perform it according to instructions, and on the (conscious or subconscious) willingness or desire to perform it.

What *all* IQ-type tests, whatever their apparent and superficial dissimilarities, have in common is that one must be tuned in to the idea of abstract testing behavior, which includes the existentially arbitrary notion that one ought to finish tests quickly and as specified by authority in order to do well at them. *All* the tests are abstract in the sense that none of them involves solving a concrete life problem. They all require that the subject treat competitive paper testing as a legitimate institution that makes sense and to which energetic attention ought to be paid, for a lengthy period of time. The "intelligence" they measure, then, like all but a few human traits, is socially constrained if not defined. It consists to some degree in (1) the ability to understand conceptually abstract questions; (2) the ability to answer conceptually abstract questions speedily and as commanded; (3) the ability to answer conceptually abstract questions for existentially abstract purposes speedily and as commanded; (4) the *willingness* to answer, the *interest* in answering, or *physical ability* to answer conceptually abstract questions, speedily, and as and when commanded, for existentially abstract purposes.

Of those subtraits, only (1) has to do with what we might mean by genetically transmitted "intelligence." The others are all the results of transactions between the tested individual and that individual's experience, culture, environmental background, hopes, and fears.

All such measurements, that is, give us only a more or less faithful reflection of the way people live, and can therefore tell us little or nothing about how individuals or groups "really" or "innately" differ from each other—if such a conception is even meaningful. Once again, in this general idea that we can discover, isolate, and measure the "innateness" of a human capacity that is never expressed except for social purposes, under social pressures, and in a social milieu, we see the sociobiological fallacy in its purest form. The "rapidly tightening principle" we ignore at our peril is that people are constrained, not by their biology, but by the material and cultural world they grow up in, the pressures it imposes on them, and the opportunities it presents them.

As to the question of the malleability of "intelligence," that can only give us difficulty if we ask it in such a way as to preclude an optimistic answer. That is, if we ask the question "Can the genetically imposed limits on an individual's capabilities be modified by human intervention?" the answer will of course be "no." But that kind of question, the kind which Jensen likes to ask and answer, depends for its numbing effect on the fact that the conclusion is already contained in the question's phraseology. If we remain agnostic (the only posture the evidence allows us) on the prior question, which is whether genes impose restrictive intellectual limits on all of us, then we can deal with the real matter at hand: Do we think the learning of new skills, or the improvement of basic skills, is possible for human beings? Is individual improvement through education possible?

It would clearly be fatuous to take that question seriously; what kind of behavior could we possibly adopt on the basis of a negative answer? Even Jensen does not dare go that far. In the first place, he claims that IQ, which supposedly stands in for "innate conceptual ability," is not modifiable. His most notorious statement to this effect occurs in the opening sentence of his initial *Harvard Educational Review* article: "Compensatory education has been tried and apparently it has failed." On this count, the evidence we have, for what it is worth, shows him to be wrong both in general and in particular.

As to the general question, there are many well-known and documented instances (with which he is quite familiar) of significant advances in IQ levels for specific populations, whether targeted experimental groups or broad masses of people such as rural Southern blacks moving to the urban North. Jensen, who is indefatigable in his pursuit of egalitarian arguments, has never answered the statement by two students of this subject who, summarizing all the available data, conclude that *"improvement in the social environment of groups at a marked disadvantage can bring about a substantial improvement in IQ levels and a decline in the frequency of mild mental retardation."*[19]

On the particular count, Jensen's remark about the Head Start programs of the 1960s, made before the dust had even settled on them, is typical of the inegalitarian's rush to judgment in believing that nothing could come of social reform anyway, so why wait for the evidence? Follow-up studies of Head Start a decade later have indeed discovered a decided improvement in the academic performance of children from almost a dozen of those programs, when they are compared with children of similar background who were not involved in Head Start.[20] Other recent studies have found definite correlations between scholastic improvement and such simple matters as faithfulness of school attendance (a very strong correlation with suggestive policy implications) or the college background of schoolteachers. A carefully focused analysis involving "data from a total of nearly 900,000 pupils spanning 70 years' research in more than a dozen countries" concluded (a surprise to no one who has ever been a teacher) that class size has never heretofore shown up as a critical variable in pupil performance only because the differences between the schools being studied, with respect to average class size, were marginal. However, when average class size is cut dramatically, as from thirty to fifteen, equally dramatic improvements in pupil performance come to light. Concurrent observations of specific schools which managed the same kind of reduction have borne out the analysis of the more abstract "data." Another study recently concluded in Great Britain found striking differences between "successful" and "unsuccessful" schools dealing with the same kinds of children, "success" having to do with the ethos of a school, the commitment of its teachers, and its retention of a fair share of "high ability children."[21]*

Alternatively, Jensen argues that whatever else compensatory education can do, it cannot *equalize* IQs, or intelligence. He is not the only person to have made that claim, of course. Christopher Jencks, in his first major work on inequality, concluded that "the evidence suggests that equalizing educational opportunity would do very little to make adults more equal"; and the authors of the British study referred to above are careful to point out that the "successful" schools they observed still do not "equalize" pupil performance.[23] Pupils who entered those schools with a "good" intellectual background improved their skills as much as did those with a "poor" intellectual background, and over all the children of professionals remained ahead of working-class children. But two things need to be said about these conclusions. First, "equalizing opportunity," which both Jencks and the British investigators studied (in effect), is precisely not "compensatory." Compensatory education would consist in the devotion of massively greater amounts of educational and social resources to children from backgrounds conducive to poor intellectual performance than to children from intellectually privileged backgrounds. In that real sense, compensatory education exists in neither the United States nor Great Britain; in the United States, indeed, to the extent that "compensatory" treatment is offered, it is most often overcom-

---

*Moreover, even these studies deal only with conventional schooling in the social welfare (capitalist) state. The sort of work that these schools and programs by and large do not engage in is illustrated in an anecdote from the experience of a psychologist working with Eskimo children:

> Evon was badly damaged when he was born unexpectedly at a fishing camp with no one to attend his mother. He has cerebral palsy as well as some intellectual retardation. The question is how best to teach him in a two-teacher school with no special equipment except interest and concern. A later visit proves that those were the essentials; and a careful, patient teacher aide (with a ninth-grade education) is working a minor miracle with Evon, who now can stand almost straight, can talk in sentences, can count and recognize colors. . . .[22]

Evon's, of course, is a much more severe case of intellectual deficiency than that afflicting most low-IQ children.

pensation for the already advantaged. People living in well-off communities, whose children are already advantaged by most indices, benefit from a richer tax base and are therefore able to spend more money on education than people living in poor communities—just as for generations the South supported the education of whites more generously than that of blacks, or as upper-class Protestants had special access to private schools providing considerably more social opportunity than the parochial schools available to working-class Catholics. Today, even leaving such comparisons aside, "tracking" systems in many jurisdictions regularly guide middle-class children toward college and the professions, and lower-class children toward vocational training and skilled or semiskilled labor.

Of course, neither American society nor any other industrial society is socially immobile; far from it. But the most the American educational system accomplishes as an equalizing force is to provide threshold resources for everyone capable of taking advantage of them. Above this threshold ambition, aggressiveness, and sheer luck (as Jencks notes) will, in an expanding economy, carry some of the system's beneficiaries upward: enough, in the past, to fuel the ideology of "equal opportunity." But many children are not equipped to take advantage of the resources of public education and other social support systems; many who are lack the right kind of ambition, aggressiveness, or "luck." Little is done, or ever has been done, actively to counteract the effects of class or racial stratification. To make judgments about whether we can compensate through "compensatory education," or training, or social reform, or whatever, we at least ought to have tried.

More fundamentally even, Jensen sets up an egalitarian straw man to burn down, and completely distorts the issue at stake. No one cares, nor should care, whether all people could be made to have the same "IQ," or the same real "intelligence." (In fact, since "IQ" is a wholly relational measure, people must always differ on those tests so long as we take them seriously —otherwise there would be no reason to give them.) Intelligence, to be sure, is not like susceptibility to tooth decay; there truly are some people who behave in a way that demonstrates what we call "genius," and others who seem to have what we call "high intelligence." No one would assert that all human beings could or should be "educated" to function at one of those levels. But "equality" and "uniformity" are not synonyms, though anti-egalitarians like to pretend they are. Equality of treatment simply means that everyone receives the best treatment they can get, given available social resources and the kind and extent of treatment they need. Egalitarians believe nothing more extreme than that all non-brain-damaged human beings can probably function at least at a socially useful, moderate level of intelligence such as is necessary to do jobs deserving of an average social reward. It does not matter whether some people have lower IQs than others as long as all can develop their capabilities to their widest limits. As to that, there is not the faintest reason to believe—and certainly Jensen gives us none—that we have even begun to explore all the potentially fruitful avenues for improving human intellectual capabilities. To take the limits as defined by what we do now, rather than as elastic and open, flies in the face of everything we know about the development over time of human culture and human behavior.*

VI.

There may be all sorts of reasons, from scarcity of resources to lack of political will, why we cannot dramatically reallocate the resources we spend on formal and other types of education, including on-the-job training. It may also be that schools as we know them are a relatively inefficient educational instrument, and that we have not yet discovered what a better one would look like. Almost certainly, education in the formal sense will never accomplish what it could as long as it remains as now, detached from any realistic commitment to the provision of fulfilling job opportunities for all. But the biological intransigence of the human material is a myth. As with most human traits—certainly with those that are properly classed as dispositions or potentialities—our best guide is still the commonsense observation that whatever the natural limitations of our various intelligences, their force can be and has been greatly attenuated by concerted human action. The attempt to make of sociobiologi-

---

*It is a separate question whether the jobs people do, and thus their social rewards and satisfactions, must be related to "intelligence" at all. On this point, see Chapter 4 below for a fuller discussion.

cal reasoning something more than mere speculation about an aspect of our humanity that we will almost certainly never be able to measure, let alone formularize for policy purposes, results in the substitution of sheer prejudice for science. In order to show that biology has consequences for the pursuit of equality one must be, as we shall see, a dedicated inegalitarian to begin with.

CHAPTER

RATIONALIZING INEQUALITY: RACE

I. In the previous chapter, I have treated first sociobiological reasoning in general, and then the Jensen-Herrnstein thesis about the inheritance of "intelligence" in particular, at the level of abstraction. At that level it is easy enough to point out both the logical inadequacy and the sociological meaninglessness of that kind of reasoning. The force of the sociobiological metaphor in all its diverse forms, however, is not abstract but concrete: concrete, that is, in the way the doctrine of biological inequality has been applied to social groups which many people are already prepared to believe are in some way "inferior." Indeed, it might not be an exaggeration to say that the recent interest in sociobiology stems from its previous concrete applications in scholarly discussions of race, class, and gender, rather than the other way around. It will not do, then, to dismiss assertions about the inferiority of certain social groups simply on the grounds that the sociobiological reasoning on which those assertions depend is muddleheaded and ideological; it is general acceptance of the assertions that vindicates the reasoning. It is those assertions we must consider, then, in order to understand how certain intellectuals have been rationalizing inequality in recent years, and to be able to respond definitively to the question whether they should have been given as much credence as they have received so far.

In the political logic of the era, we must begin with the subject of race. In the United States today arguments for and against egalitarian social change invariably turn on the subject of race—not surprising in the only major industrial nation built on a legacy of domestic slavery. At the intellectual level, reformist social thought since the 1960s has been forced to confront repeatedly the fact that significant elements of the American black population remain in an intransigently depressed condition despite all the social welfare and antipoverty programs that have come and gone, from the New Deal through the Great Society. Whereas both reformists and revolutionaries, in their different ways, see this circumstance as an incentive to try harder, or as an implicit criticism of previous efforts for being niggardly and half-hearted, conservatives view each new policy failure as further proof that government programs in general cannot improve the position of millions of black people. It is but a short step from this kind of resignation to the conclusion that not merely social policy but black people themselves are somehow at fault. To try harder is thus to throw good money after bad.

At the level of mass political movements, the racial problem has had the same or even a greater impact. It is superficially puzzling that as middle-class opposition to the American welfare state seemed to grow in strength, arguments that the bloated defense establishment or the cozy relationship between government and big business are responsible for inflationary statism made little headway. But those arguments were aimed at targets that have no deep emotional affect attached to them; they are impersonal and institutional, and difficult to put in political focus. In contrast, every practicing politician was aware that in the 1970s American opposition to government was primarily opposition to welfarism; opposition to welfarism was primarily white opposition to what was viewed as the further expansion of expensive or intrusive government programs aimed at helping black people. It is beside the point that the kinds of welfare programs blacks benefit from take up a disproportionately and almost irrelevantly small share of the total of government expenditures; what matters is their visibility and the over-all situation in which they have come to be perceived. (It is, for example, of great significance that a majority of American opinion-makers

live in two cities, New York and Boston, in which the economic
and social costs of having to deal with a largely black underclass
are greatly magnified.) The general egalitarian commitment of
white Americans has always coexisted with widespread racial
inegalitarianism, with the balance struck between them at any
period determined, at least in part, by the nature of political
leadership, the policies of the major parties, and the general
state of the economy. In the 1970s, the capitalist economy fal-
tered worldwide, and showed particular weakness in the United
States. Political leadership responded by moving sharply to the
right. Although mass responses were more ambiguous, the unwillingness of government and big business to do anything
about economic amelioration for the general public, coupled with
their pious verbal (and occasionally programmatic) concern for
the black minority, had the effect of worsening race relations.
Thus, despite the fact that most poor or working-class Americans are not black and that most American black people are not
poor, racial attitudes are the cutting edge of egalitarianism and
inegalitarianism in the United States.[1]

In this context the specific content, the timing, and the reception of Arthur Jensen's version of biological inegalitarianism
must be seen as a political act, just as the earlier spate of pop
sociobiological works about human aggression must be seen as
incidents in the Vietnam War (as contributions to American foreign policy, so to speak). It was in 1969 that Jensen first made
public his claim that it is "a not unreasonable hypothesis that
genetic factors are strongly implicated in the average Negro-
white intelligence difference." Two years later, Richard Herrnstein, in the *Atlantic Monthly*, argued forcefully that owing to
the genetic determination of intelligence, there always must be
a lower class of inferior intelligence in any technologically complex society.[2] Although Herrnstein carefully did not endorse
Jensen's remarks about race, his article had the effect of popula-
rizing Jensen's "hypothesis" that intelligence, as measured by
IQ tests, is largely determined by our genes and that discrimina-
ble social groups may innately have more or less of it. In almost
no time at all, that notion had captivated the public (or at least
the media of public communication) and at the same time had
become a prominent feature of academic discourse in several
professional disciplines. Few ideas manage to attain both public

notoriety and academic respectability; that this one was so successful suggests that it was an idea whose time had come once again. In Britain the notion that the "lesser breeds" are genetically inferior had always been received complacently. There, Sir Cyril Burt, the most famous British human geneticist, had already prefigured Jensen's and Herrnstein's arguments; and the Belgian-born psychologist Hans Eysenck had made a career of moving from one discredited claim about heredity to another.[3] In the more pluralistic United States, that kind of behavioral "science" had been driven underground by World War II and its aftermath, although from time to time such writers as Henry Garrett, Audrey Shuey, Nathaniel Weyl, and the Nobel Prize-winning physicist William Shockley had asserted that blacks were genetically inferior to whites with respect to intelligence. (Weyl, in his massive compendium of racial stereotypes, offset that conclusion by noting that black people were "naturally" more musical than whites.[4]) On the other hand, the revival of interest during the 1960s in a hereditarian account of man the naked killer—or rather, the *creation* of interest in that account through use of publicity—showed that the politics of hereditarianism (still the politics of imperialism and inequality that it was in Victorian times) was again acceptable to intellectual elites. What Jensen and Herrnstein brought to this discussion, then, was an apparent technical sophistication that it had never had before; the contemporary revival of biological inegalitarianism really stems from their work.

Now, it appears, a significant part of the American intellectual class was ready to turn its back decisively on egalitarianism. Although the left challenged Jensen (often with a passion equal to his own), it is more striking how influential mainstream intellectuals and academics received his dual message about genes and race. A few with the technical knowledge to do so, like Christopher Jencks, questioned Jensen's inflation of heritability figures and thus his estimate of the extreme difficulty facing programs designed to improve the education of blacks. In the heartland of academic liberalism (and conservatism), however, his comparative statements about race were hardly challenged; rather, they were received with caution as an interesting and potentially very important point about which no further comment could be made by an uninformed person. Almost everyone recognized that Jensen's work on heritability must be controversial; hardly anyone outside the community of educational psychology (and not many within it) set out to investigate his claims about *race* with the same scholarly enthusiasm. The standard response to Jensen was "More work needs to be done"—more work, that is, on the proposition, already accepted as an empirical and testable proposition, that black people are inherently inferior.[5]

This reception by many intellectuals, or at least their complacent inattention to the new doctrine, combined with the assiduous cultivation of publicity by Jensen, Herrnstein, and Shockley to produce a virtual monopoly on public attention. A decade later, this attention still persists in an attenuated form. Dozens of books and articles have been written in the intervening period demolishing both the "factual" and the theoretical bases of Jensen's and Herrnstein's work.[6] None of the criticisms, however, has received the kind of front-page newspaper publicity and large-circulation magazine build-up that the original claims did. Now, moreover, the message of genetic determination has once again been carried forward by Edward O. Wilson, again with maximum publicity for the original assertion of the doctrine and only minimal exposure for its critics. As an ultimate irony, though both Jensen's and Herrnstein's work was (as we shall see) theoretically incompetent and factually false, and though the incompetence and the falsity were integral to the genetic determinism they proffered, it was (and perhaps still is) considered scandalous and anti-intellectual to say outright that such work should be rewarded with neither research funds nor professional tolerance.

That is, pseudoscience has been turned into a weapon against the real thing, so much so that a distinguished scholarly publishing house like the Free Press is not ashamed to announce in its "preview" of Jensen's latest work that he has successfully refuted his critics, and to quote with pride an advance review which says that the new book "is likely to spark the most explosive debate yet over race and IQ"—meaning, not to put too fine a point on it, a debate over the proposition that blacks are mentally inferior to whites. Despite the fact that, as we have seen, hereditarianism is an intellectual wasteland, it is still necessary to come to grips not merely with the general genetic argument for inequality but with the particular argument that there is a genetically based inequality in "intelligence" among distinct human groups, which is passed on by group inbreeding.

What, then, is the nature of these claims about race? We have already noted Jensen's ascription of the IQ differences between individuals, or average IQ differences between groups, to "innate" biological rather than environmental causation, and his further assertion that IQ tests really do measure the most useful and important kind of intelligence for a society such as ours. If the results of these indicative tests are then summarized for certain population subgroups, it turns out that there are marked differences in the average scores obtained by some of them. Most notably, class, race, and certain other ethnic statuses tend to be predictors of IQ level. *On the average,* the lower one's social class by the usual census indicators, the more likely one is to have a below-average IQ and the less likely to have an IQ well above average; the same is true for blacks as opposed to whites.

> On the average, Negroes test about one standard deviation (15 IQ points) below the white population in IQ, and this finding is fairly uniform across . . . 81 different tests of intellectual ability. This magnitude of difference gives a median overlap of 15 percent, meaning that 15 percent of the Negro population exceeds the white average.[7]

If all the assertions we have discussed in the previous chapter were true, then these figures would seem to indicate that black people are somehow intellectually inferior to white people *by birth.* Jensen and his supporters, to be sure, have denied that this message is in any way "racist"; rather, they urge, he is simply trying to ensure that black children will receive an education relevant to their special problems and needs. But the real core of this message is revealed most tellingly in a passage in which he denies uttering it—in which he expounds the concept of "associative intelligence" (more simply, the ability to learn by rote) as a more constructive level of intellectual understanding at which to approach and teach black children, on the average.[8] Since he has just finished telling us that *conceptual* ability is the cornerstone of true success in our kind of technologically advanced society, and since "associative" (rote) ability clearly fails to reproduce, in his description, the important types of intellectual linkage ascribed by him to conceptual ability, the hidden prescription that low-IQ blacks and their descendants should be adjusted to a permanently secondary social role becomes manifest.

At first glance there is something odd about Jensen's single-minded deductions from the statistics of IQ distribution. In order to advance the "hypothesis" of innate biological causation, Jensen had to discard the contrary thesis of environmental causation; yet on the face of it, this dismissal of environmental causation should have been unconvincing even to those who failed to understand the logical disconnection between heritability and environmental influence. After all, it is not difficult to specify with some plausibility the nongenetic components of the black/white average IQ difference. If we begin by considering merely the most obvious facts about race in the United States, it is clear that we would expect average black IQ scores to be lower than average white IQ scores in some unpredictable but noticeable degree. That is true if for no other reason than that, despite the fact that most poor people are whites, blacks are *proportionately* much more likely than whites to be found among the poor, the marginal, the excluded. They will be among those who, in other words, have little reason to approach tests of abstract reasoning ability with high morale or any interest at all, and who can get little coaching from their parents of a kind specifically aimed at developing testable intellectual skills.*

Nor, of course, is "interest" or "morale" all that is in question. The instability and penuriousness of family life add their effects, as does the greater susceptibility of the poor to chronic disease (often undiagnosed), their poor nutrition, poor prenatal and obstetrical care, and all the other components of the ill

---

*Though Jensen's summary of the IQ data is generally correct, he at one point makes the situation of blacks look much worse than it really is by comparing the very unrepresentative "failure" rate of *Southern* blacks on the Armed Forces Qualification Test with a *national* sample of whites, and by also neglecting to mention that draftees were not necessarily representative of the two total populations in the same way. Though Jensen suppressed this "mistake" in his later writings, he has never as far as I know apologized for it, though it was called to his attention by a colleague, Jerry Hirsch, whose work he knows well.

health of the poor. Even the simple lack of enough sleep is an important element in this life-style. To think that these conditions might have no effect on an organism's performance is clearly absurd.

To be sure, millions of upward-mobile children of lower-class parents "succeed" in conventional terms much better than many children of middle-class parents. Equally certain is that millions of children of lower-class parents have higher IQs than many children of middle- or upper-class parents, and that the psychosocial pressures on many middle- and upper-class children are disastrous. But we are only trying to explain an *average* differential in what is, after all, a purely relational statistic (IQ scores). Moreover, there are various more substantial reasons why we should again expect average black IQ scores to be lower than average white IQ scores, again in some unknown degree. For the disproportionate injury done to blacks in America is not merely what we would expect to be imposed on just any group of below-average social status. The concepts of class or status (the latter term referring more to perceived social position than to measurable economic position) are not in themselves sufficient to enable us to compare, even crudely, black and white *achievement*. In the United States, black people have also constituted a separate *caste*, that is, a group of persons marked off from the rest of society by special, and in this case discriminatory and restrictive, treatment.

It is true that in another notorious apology for racial inequality of the late 1960s, the social scientist Edward Banfield argued that black people no longer constitute a caste but are now discriminated against "only" because of their lower-class life-style.[9] His own data, however, showed that even non-lower-class blacks suffer from immense discriminations. Moreover, he also provided plentiful evidence that discrimination against blacks was definitely caste-oriented in its origin (how could it be otherwise, since we are talking about ex-slaves?), and the expectation that one will be mistreated because of one's race cannot be sloughed away overnight, especially when such mistreatment continues in many ways, overt and subtle. Although it is true that in recent decades millions of blacks have attained middle-class or skilled working-class status, in the end what Banfield depicted as "lower-class" life is still reserved disproportionately for blacks in this society. In fact, Banfield was able to convert his powerful account of the "hidden injuries" of caste and class into a rationalization for racism only by insisting that "class" (more appropriately, "life-style") is something one chooses for oneself—in the case of the "lower" class, by their refusing to make appropriate efforts to change it. Like Jensen, he blamed the victims for their victimization, thus relieving whites of the onus for the depressed condition of blacks. (One is reminded of the remark made by the bandit chief in the film *The Magnificent Seven*, that "God must have wanted the peasants to be shorn, or he would not have made them sheep.") Nor are the theories of genes and of individual "choice" incompatible. After all, if some people voluntarily "choose" a "lower-class" life-style, there must be some reason why they are so benighted compared with the rest of us. The genetic theory of intelligence will explain this misuse of intellect as well as any other: genes can generate our propensity to be unemployed in the same way as they generate our propensity to do badly on IQ tests. Banfield's notion that there is a "culture of poverty" indeed lacks the power of Jensen's genetic theory, the total surrender to fate which Jensen justifies, because it offers no real theory of causation. The idea of a "culture of poverty," devoid of any structural account of how people get trapped in that culture, begs for some further explanation: if there is no structure of white oppression, then black inferiority is the only available alternative. That may explain the greater popularity of Jensen's work which, passing itself off as "science" rather than as mere sociological metaphor, gives a more self-satisfying account of why "we" are superior to "them" and thus implicitly stands behind every existing inegalitarian theory of racial differentiation, including Banfield's.

In either case, of course, people's accurate perceptions of the way they are being treated are attributed to their "irrationality" or "lack of conceptual reasoning ability," thus hiding the truth that "class" *or* "caste" as systems of social organization are also systems of power and are ways of describing who can do what to whom. (One commentator has written an extended and telling article demonstrating that throughout his career Banfield has written about marginal groups in diverse societies without addressing the issue of the truth of their perceptions.[10])

It is true that many of the comparative difficulties of black life in the United States are difficulties deriving from class rather than (or as well as) caste, and so are shared with other distinguishable subgroups of the American population. It remains important to insist that although there are similarities in the fates of the various ethnic (immigrant) groups in the United States, we have not accurately described the comparative deprivation of American blacks until we have noted the equally important differences between their collective fate and that of the others. The major difference is fundamental: conscripted slavery is hardly similar, psychologically or sociologically, to voluntary emigration motivated by hope. Over the generations black people, in contrast to other "immigrant" groups, have correctly perceived American society as unremittingly closed, tyrannical, and hostile. (That one must put the word "immigrants" in quotes when referring to American blacks itself indicates almost everything we need to know about the difference.) That hostility can be and often was implacable, perhaps most dangerously so after the abolition of slavery. Thus even middle-class blacks trying to make their way in America, especially in the past, have had to expend excessive energy in avoiding destruction, figuratively and literally. White society still has not wholeheartedly repudiated the attitudes that made self-defensive and evasive behavior a much more logical response to the world for blacks (on the average) than for whites, whatever Banfield may suggest to the contrary. Put another way, Banfield's analysis, as much as that of any Marxist, shows graphically that capitalist economy, in both its period of growth and its period of stasis, demands the existence of an underclass consisting largely of the unemployed, the unemployable, and the hopeless. Is it possible to imagine that in the twentieth century this role could have been played more regularly by any other ethnic group than that consisting of ex-slaves and their descendants?

For all these reasons, we must remember that it is only very recently that significant numbers of black parents of any social class have either been able to think realistically of preparing, or have been encouraged to prepare, their children for a career in professions that make the intellectual demands most apparently associated with IQ-type tests. In addition, there obviously was no tradition of such careers either in slave society or in the preslavery African communities. Children generally imitate the behavior of adults around them, and thus the general intellectual talent of black people has tended to flow elsewhere; differential expectations will clearly dictate differential behavior as supply adjusts to meet demand.

Furthermore, by virtue of their encountering exacerbated conditions of frustration (being prevented, in effect, from becoming "Americanized"), as well as disabilities of various kinds, black children are often (by comparison with whites, on the average) less well prepared than they might be for constructive interaction with a structured learning environment. The schools themselves, confronted with a relatively ill-prepared and stigmatized population suspicious of their intentions, very often perceive this population as a social problem to be "dealt with" in a merely custodial way, rather than as a human resource to be nurtured and encouraged. The education of black children tends to be taken less seriously than that of whites; it is made clear to them that the credentialing function of the schools will not work for them as predictably as it would if they were white, and that even when it does, it will be less meaningful to their futures. Just in case there are teachers or principals who take their educational function seriously and refuse to give that message (as of course there are many thousands), there is the much more immediate lesson to be derived from the average experience of their parents and acquaintances, which so often makes the apparent point that their chances in the professional job market are poor and their doing well in school will not be very useful; they should channel their energies elsewhere. Though a great number of black children overcome all these handicaps (or, being genuinely middle-class, never face many of them in the first place), it should come as no surprise that an above-average number of children learn to look elsewhere for satisfaction. One thinks of the Harlem youth quoted by Banfield, who, on being asked why he didn't "go downtown and get a job," replied that he could make in one day of selling marijuana what it would take him a week to make doing unskilled labor—the only other "job" he was qualified for.[11] The feeling that one is limited to that kind of alternative (or to simple unemployment) has to make the kind of planning for the future that encourages serious attention to one's education seem futile. Thus is produced the well-known result that the performance of black children on the average *declines* with attendance in school, relative not only to that of whites but to the level of potential suggested by their first-grade performance.*

In every way, black children as a group have been more removed than the average white child from the cultural mainstream and thus from a realistic sense of mastery of its most important intellectual artifacts. Jensen insists at one point that American blacks have not been subjected to "extreme" negative environmental conditions—by which, it turns out, he means total sensory deprivation! That comment merely highlights his social insensitivity. An environment does not need to be "extreme" in his peculiar sense to have a chilling effect, any more than black children need be actually caged or beaten on exhibiting creative intellect for their exhibition of it to be inhibited. It is not necessary that the developmental environments for behavior be "extremely" different but only that they be different in relevant ways; there can be no doubt that they have been for many black children. Furthermore, the condition of being especially subject to disadvantageous social circumstances has always been perfectly apparent to black people of all ages. Perhaps even today —when, in conventional terms, the "successful" black middle class is much larger than it has ever been before—a style of life that at key moments substitutes the "affective blockages" of anxiety, defensiveness, withdrawal, and suspicion of "white institutions" for more securely rooted behaviors may remain a seemingly realistic option for black children in much greater proportion than for white children. This certainly has been the case in the past, during the pre-1960 period from which most of our IQ studies date. We hardly need look further to explain the shortfall of American blacks in average IQ scores.

These considerations are strengthened by the fact that "in-

---

*In the late 1970s the Educational Testing Service of Princeton completed a six-year study which concluded, according to a report in the *New York Times*, that "disadvantaged" children "enter school with a broad range of abilities and as much self-esteem as any other group but that the process of schooling may hamper these traits." All the conditions mentioned here can be summed up by saying that "disadvantage," however defined and caused, puts children in a position where they will be more likely to receive negative rather than positive messages from both testing and schooling.

telligence" in its various measurable aspects is far from being the only indicator of comparative social welfare. When we look at other apparently unrelated indices we discover, for example, that an almost exactly similar relationship obtains with respect to the relative life expectancies of blacks and whites (at age one year) as holds for IQ. No one has ever thought to explain life expectancy genetically, since a genetic explanation would be so far-fetched and an environmental explanation is so obvious. In the Republic of South Africa average life expectancy is about sixty-five years for white males, fifty for black males. One wonders if anyone would attempt to explain that disparity genetically, or to argue that American blacks live longer than South African blacks because their genes are superior?

The same is true for IQ scores. Despite his impressive apparatus of studies in statistical genetics, Jensen's genetic hypothesis was ultimately unnecessary and misconceived for explaining the racial IQ gap. Indeed, given the history of race in the United States, what needed to be explained was not why the gap is so large but why it is not even larger.

Now, to be sure, a decade after Jensen first dropped his bombshell, the average educational attainment of blacks has continued to increase sharply to the point where it nearly equals that of whites, and in some sectors, the wages of professional black men and women have virtually attained parity with those of white men and women. However, owing to the much heavier burden of black unemployment, the lack of wage parity in many occupations, the overrepresentation of blacks in low-paying sectors of the economy, and the still greater-than-average size of black families, the comparative wealth of the black community as a whole shows no progress in that period, and extreme and unrepresentative conditions of social pathology remain.[12] By the 1960s at least, none of what I have said above about the social condition of blacks would have been startling to Jensen or anyone else; the description offered here is not novel or even arguable. Even were we to join Banfield in blaming poor and marginal blacks for not engaging in the extraordinary act of will necessary to adopt his rules for upward social mobility, the facts about how the black community got where it was then still stand: they shout. Jensen himself, as we shall see, conducted a testing exercise during which he revealed more than half of the black average IQ gap to be illusory even though he controlled for only some of the severe caste disabilities from which American black people have suffered. How then could he have asserted with such certitude that environmental differences did *not* account for that gap, but that its explanation was to be found rather in the "science" of human genetics; and how could he have persuaded so many otherwise thoughtful people that he had made a serious critique of egalitarianism?

II. Jensen cannot have believed only that intelligence is measured directly by IQ tests, that IQ values within and between populations are heritable, and that heritability equals irremediability. All of these dubious propositions could be true, and yet the particular racial IQ gap in the United States still could be caused by the obvious differences in the average social environments of American blacks and American whites.

The root of Jensen's racial inegalitarianism must therefore be sought elsewhere. It is found, to be precise, in his alleged empirical demonstration that, all such theoretical questions aside, the environmental differences between blacks and whites do *not* account for the average IQ difference.

Jensen's attempt at empirical demonstration consisted of two parts. On the one hand, he tried to show that particular negative environmental conditions (such as those discussed above) do not affect IQ performance, whatever other effects they have. On the other hand, he tried to prove that blacks (or nonwhite "races" generally) in the "same" social position as whites still do not perform, on the average, as well as whites on IQ tests. The two strands of reasoning together led him to conclude that whether or not IQ represents a malleable trait, *interracial* IQ differences at least are not socially malleable.

This alleged empirical demonstration must finally bear the entire weight of Jensen's case. If there is no significant difference between the average IQs of those members of the two races who live in roughly similar social environments, and if those environmental conditions bearing on them unequally when they live in dissimilar environments can be linked directly to IQ gain or deficit, then there is nothing further to explain. The whole theoretical apparatus of genetics studies—comparisons between separated twins, for example—will then be irrelevant to the subject of race, whatever its scientific merit or (as I have argued) demerit. Jensen must establish the two empirical arguments I have attributed to him; he must refute the two counterpropositions I have suggested immediately above in this paragraph. If he cannot do that, then the work geneticists have done may still be thought to be suggestive about the importance of genes in determining some proportion of the apparent differences in intelligence that exist among *individuals*. But the attempt to demonstrate the same phenomenon for racial or ethnic *groups* will deserve no further attention and will eventually be remembered only as a scandalous contribution to the lore of the pseudoscience.*

Yet it is doubtful if a supposedly serious intellectual argument has ever before been based on a more uncomprehending use of genuine data and a more wholehearted reliance on utterly spurious "data." If we look at Jensen's most central empirical "demonstrations," we see that his view of what constitutes "evidence" is idiosyncratic, his presentation meretricious, and thus his claim to have demonstrated the genetic ineradicability of the IQ gap utterly false. The notion that biology accounts for the greater part of the average IQ difference between American blacks and American whites indeed turns out to be a footnote in the history of pseudoscience.

We shall look at Jensen's two propositions in turn: first, that environmental conditions usually thought to be detrimental to the normal development of the human organism do not have a major effect on IQ (or "intelligence"); second, that the IQ gap persists even as the average environmental conditions of black people more closely approach the average situation of American whites.

With respect to the first kind of argument, Jensen purports to review the literature that suggests dysfunctional prenatal, natal, and postnatal environments may have a debilitating effect on intellectual performance and may thus account for much of the IQ deficit of blacks, who on the average suffer from these kinds of dysfunction much more than whites. In several chapters

---

*See Appendix A for a further discussion of the irrelevance of heritability "data" to the interracial comparison.

of *Educability and Group Differences,* Jensen attempts to attack the notion that unequally distributed conditions such as reproductive casualty, malnutrition or poor nutrition, lead poisoning, or chronic disease are implicated in the racial IQ difference. In some cases his arguments are self-contradictory, as when he tries to bolster his genetic "hypothesis" by offering evidence that the "prolongation of infancy," from which black children allegedly suffer, leads to later intellectual stasis (chapter 16 of *Educability*). How the prolongation of infancy can be anything but cultural Jensen cannot explain, and his tortured discussion of this point gives the impression of nothing so much as a man wrestling himself to a fall. In other cases he flagrantly misuses simple statistical notions to avoid the clearly environmentalist implications of his own evidence.* But on the whole his efforts in this vein are of little interest, even if the best face is put on them.

Jensen's invariant procedure is to argue that the environmental condition he is discussing can have a significant effect on the average IQ of a deprived group only if it occurs with much greater frequency and intensity than it does in the United States. His estimates of the frequency of occurrence of these phenomena are often idiosyncratic, but that hardly matters. None of these conditions may have a significant effect on the average IQ by itself; if all the deprivations that blacks suffer from more than whites had such an effect, the IQ deficit would be 30 or 40 rather than 15 points. It is enough that each of the postulated conditions—I mean the conditions educators and psychologists have *observed,* at one time or another, to have a depressing effect on intellectual performance—more often makes some small negative contribution to the lives of blacks than to the lives of whites.

Moreover, most often two or more conditions will be operating together: slum living and lead poisoning; poor nutrition and chronic disease; lack of sleep, parasitism, and the results of birth complications. It is not possible to "test" the results of each of these relative deprivations in the sense that Jensen would like us to test them: isolating an experimental group and a control

*See Appendix A.

group for each variable, and determining the discrete effects. Only an absolutely totalitarian state, devoted to nothing but testing theories of social causation, could arrange the conditions for a "proper" test. On the other hand, it is absolutely unnecessary to pursue so relentlessly the chimera of a "pure" behavioral science, for in fact the environmentalist proposition has already been successfully tested—by Jensen himself. In his original essay on race and IQ, he reports a difference of 8 to 10 points in the IQ scores of a group of black children in a standard pretest situation where no attempt was made to overcome fear, racial distrust, and resistance and in a final test situation that he supervised very carefully with an eye toward overcoming those external constraints. He denies that the difference indicates a change in "ability," and of course he is correct: but it never occurs to him that the reason "ability" had not changed is that "ability" was not being measured in the first place. It is quite obvious, given what we know about our social world, that we should attribute the difference to his having mitigated, by his personal intervention ("environmentally"), the inhibitory effects of some of the factors discussed above. His report, furthermore, replicates the findings of a twenty-five-year-old study by another psychologist who was able to produce even more dramatic changes in the measured IQs of "disadvantaged" children by using trust-inducing techniques that did not have nearly so great an effect on the test efforts of middle-class children.[13]

The cumulative impact of their various relative deprivations, for black people as a whole, is the totality of being black in America and thus disproportionately poor, excluded, and oppressed. Jensen mocks those who, unable to establish a strong correlation between any particular aspect of the poverty syndrome and low IQ, insist that the syndrome itself is the chief contributor to the poor performance; that environmental damage, depressed economic and social status, and a psychic orientation limited by low or simply nonprofessional aspirations all fit together to make up a relatively low-performance intellectual life-style. But of course the effects of that syndrome have been measured: by IQ tests! Not being standardized for differential racial or ethnic group performance (as they are, for example, standardized to make sure that the performance of the sexes is generally equal), IQ tests reflect well the differential impact our

kind of social environment has on people who are able to participate more, or less, in its most characteristic institutions. Child
psychologists who use IQ tests diagnostically, in an individual-
ized therapeutic setting (the only legitimate use for such tests),
have always known that it is impossible to make generalized
comparisons using a measuring instrument that has been standardized according to the norms of a particular population or
subpopulation (such as white Americans). The real meaning of
the oft-heard criticism that IQ tests are "culturally biased" is not
merely that bias inheres in the language, or in the specific questions asked, or in the expectations of what constitutes a "right"
answer—though there is certainly much of that.[14] The fundamental bias is in the more general, and foolish, notion that children will approach the tests at an equal level of physical and
emotional morale.*

---

*Recently Jensen published another collection of essays on IQ called *Bias in
Mental Testing*. The several hundred pages he devotes to an attempt to show
that tests are "not biased against native-born English-speaking minorities" is
one of the most monumentally wasteful diversions of scholarly resources on
record. For the most part he argues that the tests are free of statistical bias (that
is, that their results are internally consistent): an assertion which, if true, would
suggest that they are a reliable measuring instrument, but would have no
implications as to the nature or causes of whatever it is they are measuring.
When he actually does address the subject of cultural rather than statistical bias,
the result is embarrassing. A typical Jensenian statement is the following: "Cul-
ture-reduced items are usually those that are nonlanguage and nonscholastic
and do not call for any specific prior information for a plus-scored response." He
then contrasts geometric figures with pictures of buildings to illustrate his point.
The notion that two-dimensional abstractions are somehow more "natural," less
"cultural," than pictures of social realities is as bizarre as it is undefended by
Jensen. Much worse is the assumption that we have modes of response to
cultural artifacts, such as geometric figures, that are somehow from ourselves
entirely and not constrained by the culture: a proposition defensible only on the
assumption that each of us has a soul, "essence," or some such entity that exists,
inalterably, prior to our interaction with culture (in the womb?). Anyone may
believe that, of course, but since it is the very proposition that Jensen is trying
to *establish* by his endless statistical correlations, the kindest thing we can say
is that he has engaged in the worst of all the fallacies of reasoning: assuming
what is to be proved. Apparently (perhaps willfully) he cannot understand that
propositions about "cultural bias" are not and cannot be subject to statistical
proof or disproof. That is because such propositions do not order data; they order
categories of thought, ways of apprehending a social order. To say that a "test"
is "biased" against a certain group who are full-time inhabitants of a particular
culture (see the first quotation above) is no more and no less than to say that
the *culture* is "biased" against them, and that the test is an artifact of that
culture which demands normal cultural resources (if one is to do well in it) and

Jensen himself is well aware of this. At one point in an analysis depending on his use of variance models involving the mythical $h^2 = .80$, he said with patent condescension that "an environmental theory of the racial group difference must therefore posit some hypothetical factor or factors (e.g., racial discrimination) having no within-group variance to account for the between-groups difference."[15] Surely that is exactly what environmentalists "posit," but Jensen never returned to this point again. He never says anything further to belie the obvious conclusion that environmentalists "posit" that "hypothetical" factor of "racial discrimination" as the summation of all the disabilities to which American blacks are subjected, because it is so obviously the determinative factor in the IQ or any other difference. (Whether the motive for the discrimination to which black people are especially subject is racial or, as Banfield insists, cultural—because of their "lower-class" life-style—is not relevant here; either way, the posited psychic effect will be the same.)

If we started with a hypothesis of rough equality among the genetic potentials of different racial and ethnic groups, we would have no difficulty at all in explaining the shortfall of black IQ, nor would we feel a theoretical need to decompose the discrimination/poverty syndrome into its (nondecomposable) component parts. The average IQ racial differential is 1 standard deviation —one-sixth of the total range within which 99 percent of measurements fall in a normal, bell-shaped distribution: 15 IQ points in this case. That variation surely seems to be of about the same

---

distributes normal cultural rewards (if one does well in it). These are political and sociological judgments, and we test them by comparing them with our own experience: there is no other way. A person's experience, of course, includes everything that person has read as well as personally observed. But the most trivial and, in contexts such as this, useless knowledge we can have is reports of experiments that abstract from real social experience; that try to isolate social phenomena for comparison by "holding society constant." The effect on people of living a certain way within a given social order is precisely what is at issue. We can only measure the effect of one phenomenon on another by considering them as though they were separate; but society and the person cannot be considered as though they were totally separate without doing violence to the very concept of "society." That, of course, is exactly what sociobiology does: as the inane remark by Wilson quoted on page 21 above reveals, the sociobiologists "study" human society by first defining it out of existence and then limiting their observations only to the truncated statistical "individuals" who remain.

order of magnitude as the average differential in life-chances between blacks and whites, owing to such factors as life expectancy, susceptibility to tuberculosis or other debilitating illnesses, and drug addiction; to repeat, this seems to need no further explanation. Thus all Jensen's half-hearted and sometimes self-contradictory ransacking of researches into the effects of environmental deprivation is ultimately trivial.

III. In the end, therefore, the validity of Jensen's argument about racial equality rests entirely on the *second* series of comparisons, those purporting to show that even when class and caste are "held constant," average black intellectual ability does not measure up to that of whites. Without these comparisons, we might reasonably conclude that it is difficult to trace in a methodologically satisfactory way the exact causal sequence in differential IQ performance (the precise separation of cause and effect being so elusive in social research). Certainly we would find no reason to doubt the impressionistic observations of those who work in the field, that various kinds of environmental deprivation have a noticeable effect on mental alertness and performance. Nor would we have any reason to doubt that a sleepy, hungry, uninterested child will perform worse on an IQ test than a well-fed, alert, and eager one. Nor would we be impressed by Jensen's erroneous arguments that differences in intelligence between different racial groups are highly heritable, and that heritability suggests nonmalleability, even if we did not know (as established above) that these arguments were erroneous. Only because we were told (by Jensen) that the hypothesis of "rough equality" is incompatible with the data about IQ and race —that the IQ gap manifests itself even under conditions wherein all those variables are "controlled" (in "matching" differential racial groups for comparative observation)—could we begin to doubt whether IQ has been socially rather than genetically molded in the past, and whether we may by social effort develop our collective "intelligence" in a more egalitarian way in the future. *That* is the proposition which Jensen was able to offer to both the academic public and the general public almost without criticism from the mainstream.

But Jensen was wrong. *All of his assertions about such*

comparisons were false. And they were false even given his own Pollyanna-ish view of our ability to do controlled social research. The data actually show racial equality more than they show inequality.

There are, essentially, only a handful of major comparative data collections on which Jensen rested his entire case that caste and class do not affect black IQ performance. The most important of these must be analyzed in some detail if we are to understand how genuinely racist an intellectual construction "Jensenism" is, once stripped of that scientific aura given it by the appeal to biology. (In this, to repeat, it is typical of the hereditarian arguments of the past century.)

Before we consider those studies, it is necessary to look briefly at a related discussion Jensen used to justify his major over-all claim that race differences in "intelligence" (as measured by IQ tests) are generally determined genetically; for we could not take Jensen's argument at all seriously if the claim was that only between American blacks and American whites did this particular relationship hold. Thus, in order to combat the obvious conclusion that IQ tests are so culturally biased as to be worthless for interracial comparisons, Jensen quoted an Australian study comparing "Piagetian test performances of full-blooded Aborigines with those who were part Aboriginal and part Caucasian," of whom the original author says that "the children were brought up under the same mission conditions and attended the same school."[16] Jensen then reproduced a table titled "Comparison of the number of part-Aboriginal and full-Aboriginal children showing conservation" (a conception from the Piagetian theory of learning). According to this table the part-Aboriginal children showed a distinct advantage on all six of the administered tests, and Jensen concluded:

> The results appear almost as if the admixture of Caucasian genes, even so few as one-eighth, introduce mental structures otherwise lacking, that permit the individual to reach higher levels of mental development than normally occurs in the majority of full-Aboriginals.[17]

Jensen's claim, as stated, is deliberately shocking and provocative, although it did not seem to shock or provoke many readers. It is fundamental to his hypothesis of racial differences. It is also totally false; in order to be able to make that savagely racist distinction he distorted both the table and the interpretation of the data contained within it.

We could, to be sure, attribute this ugly episode to Jensen's personal malfeasance, but there is more to be said about it than that. The real point, generally, is that we must be wary of "statistical studies," based on minute bits of data collected in unlikely ways, which purport to contradict the notion of a common humanity; and specifically, that we must be aware that Jensen was unable to find *any* cross-cultural evidence for his genetic hypothesis without distorting the data. We are thereby alerted to look more closely at what he offered as evidence within the American setting—and this close attention is amply repaid.

As I have said, Jensen's bedrock argument was based on what happens when social class and caste are allegedly held constant in comparing IQ measurements. As can be seen in Appendix A at the end of this book, the study of Aborigines did not genuinely hold either race or age constant (as it must not, in order to make his point). When it comes to class (or socioeconomic status—SES, as it will hereafter be called) Jensen fares no better. A *detailed* presentation of his various treatments of SES is contained in Appendix A; suffice it here to say that quite obviously, no matter how many quintiles or deciles the population is sliced into, within or between races, there is proportionately a much larger black than white "lower class"; or rather, the black lower class effectively begins at a much higher point on the SES scale than does the white. This, of course, is only another way of saying what I have already noted, that gross "class" categories do not account for what is special about the black experience in America. (Christopher Jencks's data also, it should be mentioned, show a striking difference in the effects of "class" on IQ for whites and blacks.)

This ambiguity in the meaning of socioeconomic status, or class, whenever we speak of race in America, is crucial once we come to Jensen's ultimate justification—the cornerstone of his assumption that racial IQ differences are in need of additional explanation that only genes, only a theory of innate racial superiority and inferiority, can provide. What must be kept in mind is that these excursions into his "methodology" reveal not only a sociological but also a human insensitivity: the insensitivity of the inegalitarian intent upon turning every determinate human difference into an inalterable (and self-justifying) law of nature. At one point, Jensen was able to make himself write about an interracial comparison that "especially for children who have been exposed to three or four years of schooling, such marked differences in performance would seem difficult to explain in terms of differential experiences, motivation, and the like": just as though Banfield had not written an entire book explaining certain aspects of black life in America wholly as a function of the most obvious kinds of "differential" motivation. Jensen is a competent educational psychologist who has done excellent work with black children themselves, as we have noted, but he was and is totally oblivious to the obvious, as he must be. For whereas the approach of the biological inegalitarian may enable us to notice the simplest and most meaningless statistical correspondences, it requires us to avert our eyes from those transparently clear facts of social life that surround us wherever we go. As we shall now see, the obsessive urge to make a "science" out of "hard" numerical "facts," even if the numbers describe nothing that is real to our experience, is attuned perfectly to that other urge to find that we have more of whatever it is than other people because they aren't as good as we are. The first of these urges is incompatible with a fundamental acceptance of ambiguity in our knowledge of the social world; the second, with a fundamental bedrock belief in the over-all equal capacity of human beings. The result, however, is not merely scientific ideological or moral error: it is, more venally, the pursuit of inequality through the falsification of data.

IV. Jensen's ultimate justification is found in his statement, upon which all of "Jensenism" stands or falls in the end, that no one "has yet produced any evidence based on a properly controlled study to show that representative samples of Negro and white children can be equalized in intellectual ability through statistical control of environment and education." No one, it should be clear by now, can really hope to produce such a study, since the only appropriate "control" would be a comparison between blacks and whites living in a color-blind, racially egalitarian society; "studies" will not produce that. Jensen went on to "note the results of studies which have attempted to control for SES by actual matching or by statistical equating of groups." He put *all* the weight of his argument on the finding of a researcher named Audrey Shuey that where such studies provide the data necessary for more detailed interracial comparisons, "upper-status" blacks are invariably found to do worse than "lower-status" whites. Attacking the thesis that caste-linked cultural and physical deprivation might have a significant effect on intellectual performance, Jensen approvingly quoted Shuey: "It seems improbable that upper- and middle-class colored children would have no more culture [*sic*] opportunities provided them than white children of the lower and lowest class."[18]

It would be easy to dismiss these "studies" as pointless, on the grounds of Jensen's incomprehension of the operational meaning of class and caste in America. But the studies remain, and it is important to look at them. For though these studies, as it turns out, tell us nothing about innate racial IQ differences, they tell us much about the meaning of discrimination in the United States (or anywhere else), and even more about those very typical biological inegalitarians, Jensen and his source, Audrey Shuey.

The matching studies to which Jensen refers were collected by Shuey.[19] I have reanalyzed thirty-five of her total of forty-two cases, ignoring those reported between 1913 and 1929 as being without real credibility. The results are fascinating. In brief, the reanalysis shows that twenty-nine of the thirty-five studies were supposed to show substantial IQ differences between blacks and whites of the same SES. Of these, five revealed insignificant racial differences in IQ. Of the remainder, seventeen indeed showed substantial differentials of about the national average differential of 1 standard deviation (about 15 IQ points), but none of those actually made the faintest effort genuinely to compare black and white SES. It is clear from even a cursory consideration of them that the blacks and whites in these studies (almost all of them from the three decades before the beginning of the civil-rights revolution) could not have been socially "equal" in any real sense. The black children in these studies quite evidently partook of considerably more lower-class and marginal life-styles than the whites.

Of the studies that were more or less carefully controlled, in addition to those revealing insignificant differences in average IQ, four revealed moderate differences (about one-half an SD), and a fifth showed sharp differences in a lower-class neighborhood, but only moderate differences in a middle-class neighborhood—a finding inexplicable on the genetic hypothesis. The only two studies that were both carefully controlled to "match" social backgrounds *and* showed a significant average IQ difference were studies of adults (soldiers and college students) long since past the age of innocence about tests; thus neither of those studies is likely to tell us anything about "innate intelligence." Once we look carefully at the "control" or "statistical equating" of SES variables, we find that there are more "controlled studies" that falsify Jensen's claim than support it!

The remaining six studies reported by Shuey are supposed to bolster the assertion about "upper-status" blacks being intellectually inferior even to "lower-status" whites. That is the single most important empirical claim Jensen has ever made, and the one he has relied on most. If it is true, as he has continually pointed out, then no one in good conscience can support the hypothesis that environmental differences account for racial IQ differences.

In fact, however, none of the six studies Jensen refers to support his claim. Again, I leave a detailed account of these studies to Appendix A. Suffice it here to say that on Shuey's own interior evidence most of those studies were not remotely comparing "upper-status" blacks with "lower-status" whites, but when they were, the average IQ differentials turned out to be minimal or nonexistent. Thus these findings dramatically falsify Shuey's and Jensen's reports of the relationship between black and white average IQ. They are even less striking than those of a later study which Jensen, in *Educability*, carefully misrepresents in order to soften its impact. In that later study the "upper SES Negro" IQ mean is only slightly below that of "upper SES white," but more than 1 SD above that of "lower SES white." (Jensen also cites the "Coleman Report," in a cryptic reference, as having replicated these findings, but he must have had in mind a "Coleman Report" which no one else has ever seen, since no such data appear in the famous report that James S. Coleman produced for the Office of Education of HEW.[20])

In sum, Jensen wrote, and was well rewarded for writing,

hundreds of pages of tendentious theorizing to "explain" a set of "facts" that did not exist and thus neither required nor supported his explanation. All the studies I have summarized make the same point—and it is not Jensen's point. What they suggest, unarguably, is that it is very hard, in a racially discriminatory society, to "equate," for purposes of study, any indices of social well-being between the races. But the harder we try to do that, the closer we come to comparing the IQs of blacks and whites who actually do live like each other, the more the alleged IQ gap disappears.*

On first consideration it is incomprehensible that Jensen can have failed to see this, since he himself states that "15 percent of the Negro population exceeds the white average"—a figure that, to repeat, is just about what we would have predicted on the basis of a totally environmentalist and egalitarian theory of the differences in measured intelligence among racial and ethnic groups. Not only that, but in a passage in *Educability* Jensen remarks that "Negro grooms (in interracial marriages) were occupationally well above the average employed Negro male," and that therefore "the higher IQs of interracial children born to white mothers [rather than to black mothers, who allegedly tend to marry low-status white men] could be due to the genetic effect of the superior Negro father." How a "superior" father who but eleven pages later becomes inferior (as Shuey and Jensen assert) to "the lowest SES white group" can have that strikingly positive genetic effect is a question Jensen does not at-

---

*In general, not just in the racial context, Jensen is completely ignorant of the complex nature of culture in a pluralist society—which is not surprising in a sociobiologist. At one point he even compares the test scores attained by Japanese citizens living in Japan on a translated and modified version of an English-language IQ test with the scores attained by American blacks—as though the two groups were comparable culturally or in any other way. Even Mill would have been hard put to it to give a name to this fallacy. But through his insistent use of comparisons between various other American minorities in order to derogate the accomplishments of blacks, an intelligible strand emerges. On the basis of what we know about the way various peoples live, if there is any genetic influence on group IQ scores, the most likely genetic relationships would seem to be that whites and blacks are roughly equal in "innate intelligence," Orientals are somewhat more advanced, and Amerindians, who allegedly perform well on IQ tests despite their usually depressed environments, are a lot "smarter" than anyone else. Jensen is certainly free to believe all that if he wishes—just as Native Americans are free to wonder about the advantages of having high IQs.

tempt to answer. He could not, since any such attempts to explain away a naked self-contradiction would only highlight the fraudulence of the interracial "comparisons" that are the rock-bottom foundation of his inegalitarianism. The sad but indisputable fact emerges that as much as the race/IQ relationship reflects the realities of social division in America, so too does Arthur Jensen's scholarship.

V. What can we say in conclusion? We can hardly insist that racial equality has been "proved" any more than racial inequality has been. It is possible (anything is "possible" to an empiricist) that generations from now, when a black middle class has finally had the opportunity to develop on equal terms with the white middle class, there may still be more than marginal IQ differences between the races. And shrimps may learn to whistle.

We can, however, say several other things. First, we can point out, as I did in the previous chapter, that by any reckoning intelligence—the ability to cope with problems life sets for us or we set for ourselves—is something that can be and has been modified, taught, improved, adapted; it is in no way a primarily biological and unmalleable phenomenon like eye color, somatic type, blood type, or length of bones, so far as we can tell.

Second, one of the most noteworthy aspects of the inegalitarian argument, once we think to look for it, is that its proponents are careful never to discuss or even mention what ought to be the very first step in their reasoning; this is especially true of Jensen. If "natural" differences in some capacity or other do exist between certain human groups, what is the source of those differences? After all, if a trait is to be inherited in one way among the members of one group and in another way among the members of another group, there must be a differentiating method of selection; what could it be in the case of race?

With respect to the possibility of differential natural selection between "blacks" and "whites"—that is, Africans and Europeans—the only concrete suggestion that has ever been offered is the idea, for which the defenders of segregation in early twentieth-century America were responsible, that mostly "unintelligent" Africans had been "caught" and sold into slavery, thus bequeathing a legacy of inferiority to the descendants of slaves in the Western Hemisphere. In discussing sociobiology earlier, I noted that sociobiologists are always compelled to substitute fanciful hypotheses for actual data about the transmission of culture—though somehow that never suggests to them that maybe there are no biological "data" to be had about the phenomenon of culture. This particular piece of obvious ideological flummery is so historically and logistically ludicrous that no serious sociobiologist, Jensen included, has ever committed himself to it. Yet Jensen is actually worse off without this "hypothesis."

We could, after all, with at least a small degree of plausibility infer Africans to be better athletes of certain kinds than Europeans (but what would we say about the inhabitants of the German Democratic Republic?), on the sociobiological grounds that they have more recently been closer to a way of life that emphasized the importance of running, jumping, and exerting strength. No one has ever explained satisfactorily how this kind of trait selection can work for humans (though sociobiologists talk about it with the confidence most people reserve for processes they have actually observed), but at least we can imagine a selection process of this kind without departing from reason and common sense.

But in what way could we possibly explain what Jensen alleges to be "European" intellectual superiority over not just Africans but also Australian Aborigines, once absurd notions of how the slave trade worked are discarded? Surely not on the grounds that European civilization, as opposed to African civilization, values abstract intelligence. If anything, the last several centuries have witnessed a sharp devaluation of abstract intelligence, which in any event was never highly rewarded to begin with in the feudal world, nor in the tribal civilizations which preceded it. Unless we are all supposed to be the descendants of monks, bankers, and inventors, where is the selection of genes for abstract intelligence supposed to have come from? In actual fact, if one compares the two types of civilization, it seems to be true rather that hunting (which was still crucial to African societies at a time when it had long since become secondary in Europe) demands a much higher level of abstract reasoning ability than does any ordinary industrial or peasant pursuit. It is impossible to avoid the conclusion that Jensen and his followers simply assumed, without further question, that Western civilization is "higher" and therefore no explanation of the intellectual superiority of its inhabitants is needed. As is always the case with the biological arguments for inequality, in other words, common-or-garden-variety prejudice and bigotry—in this case, simple old-fashioned racism—are implicitly relied on when the variety and complexity of human cultural arrangements prove impenetrable to the thrusts of sociobiology's naïve determinism. We shall see further examples of this reliance in later chapters.

Finally, we can and should note the fascinating and persuasive historical circumstance, that all of the deficiencies Jensen finds in the intellectual performance of black people were found but a few generations ago in the measured performance of other ethnic groups as well. Thus one imaginative researcher, who, unlike Shuey or Jensen, has investigated what data there are, found that well into the twentieth century the disparity between the IQs of "native white" and Italian schoolchildren was on the average even greater than what now exists between blacks and whites; and he reports that the debate over "immigrant" versus "native" intelligence (or "Latin" and "Slavic" versus "Nordic" and "Anglo-Saxon" intelligence) followed exactly the same path Jensen has marked out today, culminating in the conclusion that the intellectual inferiority of various immigrant groups had been scientifically demonstrated to be genetic in origin! The instruments have changed, but the music remains the same.*

Indeed, one of the founders of intelligence testing in America asserted that of the European immigrants arriving at Ellis

---

*To be sure, one compendium on the subject of race argues that the "races" ("Europids" and "Mongolids," and to a lesser extent "Indianids") among which "civilization originated and advanced" do better on "cognition and attainment" tests than do "Negrids," who have never attained "an impressively high level of culture." The proffered explanation of these alleged differences is "morphological difference"—such as size of brain. The author is unable to account for these "major morphological differences" genetically but asserts that that does not matter, since "facts are facts." The wonderful thing about pseudoscience is that it obviates the hard work of the real thing: here a contemporary anthropologist tells us exactly what we could have "learned" from any nineteenth-century phrenologist. He also proffers a definition of "high culture" so naïve in its ethnocentrism that it would have embarrassed any educated person of, say, the eighteenth century. That Rembrandt must have had more "conceptual ability" than a skilled carver of African masks is, in the end, a notion that can be maintained only by someone who himself has a serious deficit in that very trait.[21]

Island in 1912, IQ testing showed 85 percent of the Jews, 80 percent of the Hungarians, and 79 percent of the Italians to be "feeble-minded." Another psychologist assured the House of Representatives that IQ tests were "objective" and that therefore problems of language had nothing to do with the finding that "the Slavic and Latin countries show a marked contrast in intelligence with the western and northern European group."[22]

All of these groups, as well as the Irish and others who were found to be "subnormal" at the time, have long since left behind them any vestige of their alleged inability to perform an average function in American society. To be sure, certain marginal differences between groups still remain: Italians and Jews do not have the same average IQ; Greek-Americans and Chinese-Americans do not have the same likelihood of becoming nuclear physicists. But none of these differences is of interest to egalitarians, and none of them *should be* socially consequential. Egalitarians do not assert the proposition that all people are equal in measurable "intelligence," nor anything like it. The egalitarians' view is only that human environment, the way people live and what they value, is more crucial to human accomplishment than the genetic factor, just as it is more crucial to the state of our teeth. Therefore, the more we can equalize or attenuate the impact of the most powerfully destructive environmental influences, the more likely we are to produce citizens all of whom are capable of making a useful contribution to their community in its own terms and thus deserving of reward from it.

In the next chapter I shall discuss the further question whether the existence of sharp IQ differences within ethnic and racial groups preordains a stratified class structure even were we to eliminate inequalities between groups. But as to our present topic, it is enough to note that most of the ex-immigrant groups have by now got to the point where they are able to hold their own in our society as it is constituted at present, and that they would be able to do even better in a more egalitarian society. Though differences exist, especially in the high IQ range, no one has recently argued that any of the white ethnic groups need have innate difficulty in achieving full-fledged participation in a modern economy.

Why should there be different expectations for blacks? In the absence of any data at all showing different racial intelligence when social factors are "held constant" even to the limited extent that social scientists are able to accomplish, we ought to find it conclusive that other ethnic groups from many different parts of the world have been able to make their separate ways, albeit at different rates of progress, in American society. Blacks should be inherently able to do as well as anyone else, *unless we prejudge their "inferiority" on purely racist grounds*. It is impossible to argue (or even hold a discussion) with anyone who is racially prejudiced and content to remain that way. But prima facie racism, which is the only available "argument" left to support Jensen's case, can be of no interest to those who wish to give serious consideration to the notion of social equality.

Certainly, there are compelling historical reasons why blacks, or any others who are both poor and excluded in 1980, may well have a comparatively hard row to hoe. These remaining minorities, at a time when economic growth cannot keep up with its past pace, make up a very disproportionate segment of the lower class, the lumpenproletariat of Marx's description. The American majority and American elites may well find it too costly—this is the real message of Banfield's *Unheavenly City* —to adopt the policies necessary to eliminate this final bastion of ethnic inequality. But these problems of policy and cost have nothing to do with the inherent qualities of races. From a genetic standpoint, once we have seen that the statistical "evidence" for innate black inferiority disintegrates when inspected carefully, we have no reason to doubt that blacks *could* follow the same path as the Irish, Italians, Poles, and Jews. The dramatic increase in the number of blacks receiving higher education and the shrinking of the disparity in wage rates for professional men of different races are pieces of evidence that that process has already begun, though with unforgivable slowness. In any event, the minimal egalitarian demand of "equal opportunity" for a *group* in a society such as our own, or in any society with an unequal reward structure, is easily satisfied. The jobs and leadership positions of which it has reasonably been said that they require both noticeably above-average intelligence (as measured by IQ) *and* above-average rewards—say, those of executives and organizers of advanced technical systems in this country—are not that numerous. Even now, when so much effort is still needed to equalize social conditions, there are undoubtedly more than enough highly, or potentially highly, intelligent black or brown or red people to fill such positions in proportion to their general representation in the American population. There are also more than enough people of all racial and ethnic groups capable of doing their share of the kind of work that requires training in a skill—given a strong social commitment to rethinking the way we prepare children for adulthood, to doing it on a truly egalitarian basis, and to setting up whatever compensatory mechanisms are necessary to create a tradition of entry into the worlds of professionalism and skill for those who lack it (see Chapter 6 below).* No doubt, each of us can think of many more

---

*Recently the argument has been made that American black people suffer, comparatively speaking, from being "a less modernized segment of the population." In this view, blacks are the victims not merely of racism and exclusion but of "an educational system that is unidimensionally geared to the requirements of technological and bureaucratic modernity." To the extent that there are historical "national" cultures that are independent of the experiences of caste and class in a given period, this concept offers a useful addition to our understanding of comparative group social behavior. But the argument, as presented by its author, Brigitte Berger, is itself unidimensional, in that commitment to modernity *rather than* a combination of class and caste influences is seen as the key to group differences in IQ. Berger makes this argument in the name of cultural pluralism (we should "respect" different cultures), but the argument has the effect of making their allegedly nonmodern cultural commitment an independent cause of the exclusion of blacks from the American mainstream. Like Banfield, Berger has discovered a way to hold American blacks responsible for their own exclusion. To be sure, it is superficially more sophisticated to speak of a group consciousness as being "nonmodern" rather than, in Banfield's term, "lower-class"; and it seems to be a triumph of tolerance to plead with us to reject uniformity in the way we approach diverse peoples in our educational systems. The implication of her argument, though, is the same as the implication of Jensen's "discovery" that blacks do better at "associative" than at "abstract" learning: in the name of understanding and explanation we are being told, quite plainly, that black people on the average are not going to be able to perform at the same level as whites at many of the society's most remunerative tasks. This is similar to the argument that women have a different consciousness from men (a commitment to the private sphere, to "inner space"). The conclusion that is invariably drawn from that argument is that our notions of equal justice do not demand equal opportunity for women in the public sphere, since the proportion of them willing and *able* to take advantage of that opportunity will always be considerably less than the proportion of men who are prepared to do so. The same conclusion is clearly intended to follow from Berger's argument: "Neither the elimination of racism nor (in the most extravagant egalitarian fantasies) the overthrow of the class system would eliminate the problem, for race and class (whatever else they may be) function in the area of IQ scores as carriers of 'modern consciousness' rather than as independent variables." With that remark, all programs of "affirmative action" or other attempts to achieve more

positions that we could say ought to be filled only by the highly intelligent, but remarkably few such positions lay claim to a markedly disproportionate share in society's rewards. (Jensen, casting around for examples of tasks that require a very high level of intellectual skill, mentions chess playing, piano playing, orchestral conducting, and playwriting—hardly professions or jobs earning a high level of average reward in this society.)

What is practically possible is one thing; what people may be willing to do is, of course, another. Finally, Jensen asks us to believe either that discrimination does not exist in the United States, or that if it does, it has no effects on its victims. The pattern of distortion in his researches is actually less interesting than his implicit commitment to one of those alternatives—a commitment that cannot have escaped the attention of those many of his educated readers who accepted his argument without qualms. That is what the pursuit of inequality is really all about: to deny, purely and simply and unashamedly, that inequality has attached to it costs that cannot be defended once they are stated plainly. In his zeal to hide those costs from view, Jensen's work, more than any other of the inegalitarian arguments we will review in these pages, shows us the lengths that members of a privileged intellectual class will go to in order to justify that privilege. "Jensenism," as unfriendly critics have called it, is nothing more than a hoax: the Piltdown man of social science.

What is shocking, what is truly scandalous and revelatory of the state of such a large part of the American intellectual community, is that Jensen's claims about race were received as an acceptable argument that one ought at least to think about by so many of his academic colleagues and intellectual readers —as though the squalid history of biological inegalitarianism in the past century were just water over the dam. (In Great Britain the "Jensenite" hypothesis, strongly advocated by Hans Eysenck, has had even more success, as one might expect.) No

---

equality by law go by the board for rigidly ignoring the limits imposed by "culture." Group culture in this version is as constricting as group genes, and in fact the two conceptions are very similar: if conscious action can't change the behavior which flows from a cultural orientation, then conscious action presumably didn't bring about the orientation either (in which case, what did?). For a further critique of these arguments, see Chapters 5 and 6 below.[23]

more demeaning proposition has ever been uttered about blacks than the proposition that their conceptual ability (as a human group) is innately inferior (in comparison with that of whites) *regardless* of their social condition; and that the conceptual ability of whites is *always* innately superior regardless of theirs. Few propositions about blacks have ever depended so much on the falsification and misuse of data. Yet no proposition evoked less interest from those liberal and new-conservative academics who dominate the news when the media want to know what "intellectuals" are thinking. In the end, well after his falsifications had been sufficiently publicized (if one cared to look), and despite protests and resignations, Jensen's peers elected him a fellow of the American Association for the Advancement of Science, one of the most prestigious organizations of scientists in the United States. The genetic argument on race is fraudulent, but apparently there are enough white scientists and intellectuals willing to accept the rationalization of inequality that it is possible to present a fraudulent case without incurring shame, and thus make the always uncertain prospect for racial equality that much worse. In considering that prospect for the future, we do well to remember that this, the worst damage to racial egalitarianism in the United States, was inflicted not by redneck bigots but by an honored member of the scientific community and his educated supporters.

CHAPTER

RATIONALIZING
INEQUALITY: CLASS

I. Although Jensen's allegations about race and IQ are responsible for most of the furor stirred up by the new hereditarians, Richard Herrnstein's assault on egalitarianism is actually much more grandiose (though it follows a little-noticed suggestion made by Jensen himself and by another psychologist, Carl Bereiter). Herrnstein linked the notion of the genetic determination of IQ or "intelligence" with a peculiar use of the conceptual category "social class"; he not only posited the existence of a lower class as a permanent *genetic* phenomenon in technologically complex societies but argued that egalitarian public policy would only make class stratification worse than it need be. Moreover, while he avoided Jensen's conclusions about race, his message was potentially even more painful for Americans, and especially black Americans. For if one accepted Banfield's argument that millions of black Americans were trapped in a lower-class culture from which no good could come, and at the same time accepted Herrnstein's assertion that egalitarian reform could only rigidify class lines by fixing them in a genetic form, then one seemed to be agreeing with the old formulation (albeit in a new guise) that the poor must always be with us. Clearly, if Herrnstein's argument is correct, then egalitarians are caught in a painfully paradoxical position. To rely on "market forces" or minuscule monetary relief for the poor in the form of a "negative income tax" as the only public policy toward class would be in effect to do nothing: capitalist social order demands the existence of a lower class for a variety of reasons, and without interference one certainly will be maintained. On the other hand, if to engage in seriously interventionist or redistributive policies is to find a cure worse than the disease (if Herrnstein is to be believed), "benign neglect" indeed seems to be the logical requirement of the "great society."[1]

Like Jensen, therefore, Herrnstein has been quoted regularly by conservatives fighting against the politics of social change, though probably few have read him carefully. For also like Jensen, Herrnstein offers a false—worse, a foolishly false —argument: an argument which through its intentional embrace of incoherence and falsity also perfectly expresses the drive of the hereditarian to make inegalitarian bricks out of genetic straw.

In order to appreciate the scope of Herrnstein's accomplishment, it is instructive to compare his work with the classic sociological theory from which it is directly derived: the structural-functionalist account of social order. This account, most immediately associated with the name of Talcott Parsons in the United States (but traced through him back to the European sociological tradition of Comte and Durkheim), suggests that certain tasks must be performed in all functioning societies, and that therefore every society must create some kind of hierarchical structure suited to allocating those tasks. All of the classical sociologists disagree with Marx and with anarchist theorists in claiming that one necessary function is the division of labor. Marx lists the essential variants of the division of labor (which at least in his early writings he seems to think could ultimately be overcome) as the division between mental and physical labor; between town and country; and between the sexes. The classical sociologists are less clear than Marx about what exactly was meant by the term, but the first of those variants was the one they all focus on in discussing the subjects of class and social hierarchy: some must work, and others must plan; there must be masses and elites.

In the 1950s a dispute broke out in the American sociological community which clarified the nature of the functionalist claims. Two functionalists, Kingsley Davis and Wilbert Moore, published an influential paper in which they restated the argument that every society must have a primary division of labor, and added that there must be some means of selective recruitment and differential reward in any society to ensure that the "right" people are recruited to fill the most important slots. In the wake of that paper a whole literature of "elite" studies has grown up, typified by and culminating in Daniel Bell's assertion (in 1975) that "a society that does not have its best men at the head of its leading institutions is a sociological and moral absurdity."[2]

At the same time, however, a countertradition also had developed in American sociology, and a series of assaults were launched on the Davis-Moore argument by critics who suggested that functionalism was a concealed defense of the status quo. The critics argued that Davis and Moore had simply justified hierarchy, and most especially (since Davis and Moore mention differential monetary reward as one of the means of achieving the necessary division of labor) capitalist hierarchy. To this critique Davis and Moore replied that they had made no claims about the goodness of any particular means of recruitment or any particular set of rewards; they also specifically denied that they had portrayed the institution of social classes as an eternal necessity, since social classes exist only where class position is passed on from parent to child and they had never asserted that kind of "recruitment" to be requisite.[3]

In retrospect, it is clear that Davis and Moore were at least partly correct in their self-defense; that is, the functionalist approach in sociology is not the same kind of apologia for inequality as is biological inegalitarianism. As long as every single task is not done in rotation by every single person, there will be some kind of division of labor, and though that arrangement is not in principle impossible the functionalists seem essentially justified in discounting it; even Marx, in *Capital*, turns out to be chiefly concerned about the humanly debilitating effects not of the division but of the specialization of labor (i.e., the refinement of industrial tasks to the point that workmen are limited to the performance of minutely varied, stultifying "specialities," and are never permitted to participate in over-all job planning). Moreover, as long as some jobs require more training than others, and not everyone can train to do those jobs, some means of recruitment to the training program will have to exist; and as long as the training for some of those jobs is inordinately difficult (whether intellectually or physically), the recruitment process will have to be selective. As for differential rewards, it again is hard (though not impossible) to imagine a large-scale society in which some people, whether ice-skaters or executives, are not in some way or other granted exceptional material rewards or shown exceptional honor.

Although the Davis-Moore functionalist position is certainly inherently anti-utopian (at least for complex societies), it is not in any other way as inherently "conservative" or "procapitalist" as has been alleged. It is not even necessarily inegalitarian. Critics of the American philosophy of "equal opportunity" (see my comments in Chapter 6 below) have always argued that a formally equal "chance" in life is meaningless unless all children really do start with roughly the same level of advantage conferred by social-class privilege or exposure to different cultural norms. Therefore, egalitarians have always insisted that a good deal more equality of *results* than now prevails in a society such as our own is necessary simply in order to make "equality of opportunity" real, instead of an empty phrase. What good does it do a child of the ghetto, they ask, to have the same legal chance to get ahead as Jay Rockefeller, when the latter is already "there" and the former is unlikely to get "anywhere"?

This form of egalitarianism, then, is concerned with abolishing inherited privilege and inherited disprivilege: nothing more. We can surely imagine a society in which no one's social background is so strikingly different from anyone else's as to be likely in itself to exclude them from early development of the skills and attitudes necessary to qualify for any recruitment process; in which no variety of reward conveys unchecked power over others; in which nothing considered a fundamental human good or necessity is held as an exclusive or special reward for elites, or distributed in such a skewed fashion that most people might just as well be said to have none of it; and finally, in which no such good is distributed in such a way that it can be passed on to one's own children while being unavailable to the children of others. We can imagine a society in which no small group of people, even if they possess elite skills, monopolizes any important social good; in which no large group of people is excluded from access to any important social good (including the decision-making process); and yet in which the development of particular kinds of skill relevant to the society's values and needs (not just the values and needs of one social class) is encouraged and rewarded. In short, we can imagine a "classless," fundamentally egalitarian society with a social structure that is completely fluid from one generation to the next, yet in which the "necessary" conditions of the abstract division of labor are also met. Thus when Daniel Bell rhetorically asks whether egalitarians would accept as desirable "a society in which genuine equality of opportunity did prevail, but a new form of income and status inequality based on merit resulted," the answer should surely be yes, but on the conditions that the inequalities are random, their extent limited, and that they do not constitute a form of class privilege to be passed on to children.[4]

II. According to Herrnstein, however—and in this he is only typical of inegalitarians who misuse the functionalist's insight —the arrangement I have just described is impossible. To him, the idea of the division of labor implies social classes—at the very least a lower class and an economic or managerial elite that becomes a class.[5] Without the existence of those two classes, social divisions based on reward for labor would be marginal, and would not separate people in the fundamental ways that "class" as we know it separates them. Must those kinds of classes persist?

With respect to the idea of a permanent lower class, what Herrnstein seems to have done is adopt intuitively (but without understanding its implications) Marx's notion that the division of labor by its very existence penalizes those who hold certain jobs for life. He seems to agree with Marx that certain types of work are inherently degrading to body and soul as compared with others. Marx thought that true of rural or peasant labor, of the kind of sexual "labor" in which women are nothing but domestic property, and of specialized labor in the factory. The question of sexual equality is discussed further in Chapter 5 below; as for the rest, if we ignore Marx's private notions about the idiocy of rural life but simply assimilate unskilled or factory-type agricultural labor to industrial labor, that is the sort of work that Herrnstein seems to think must be distributed by class: all the kinds of labor that in our society are considered dirty, unpleasant, stultifying, or perhaps even merely physical.

It is a commonplace technique of contemporary inegalitarianism to use Marx on the division of labor *against* the idea of equality. In his early writings, of course, Marx apostrophized the society in which one can "hunt in the morning, fish in the afternoon, rear cattle in the evening, criticize after dinner, just as I have a mind, without ever becoming hunter, fisherman, shepherd, or critic." If that kind of abolition of the division of labor is what we mean by equality, then egalitarianism is indeed utopian. But that is hardly the only notion of social equality that Marx ever offered, or that egalitarians generally have suggested as being possible; and to say that because utopia is impossible American capitalism is unchangeable is like saying that because people can't exceed the speed of light they can't fly to the moon. Indeed, considering his feelings about rural life, Marx himself surely cannot be taken as having intended that particular idyll as a realistic picture of "communist" or any other society. It is obvious, rather, from the bulk of his work that even Marx did not expect the total elimination of occupation in what he called "communist society." What he expected instead was the diminution of *the tyranny of the working day* (the notion that is at the heart of *Capital*), so that no person's living time need be totally dominated, nor his or her character brutalized, by lengthy and exclusive immersion in one stultifying job. There is nothing inherently wretched about working in a factory—Marx could hardly have thought that and still praised the bourgeoisie for its introduction of a high level of industrialization, as well as a work environment in which workers perforce must learn to cooperate with each other. It is only comparatively wretched when one is deprived of the ability to exercise all one's faculties by an extreme specialization of labor; by the deprivation of those levels of income and self-determination that opinion-makers in one's society deem worthy of respect; by the all-too-obvious association of certain jobs with an inferior and unhappy social existence; and by the exclusion of people in those jobs from having a voice in determining how they pursue their livelihood. Egalitarians above all propose a democratization of the workplace and social life, by making the workplace a community rather than an oligarchy; by breaking or weakening the strength of the association between job rank on the one hand and, on the other, income, decision-making opportunity, and access to control over one's workplace and the rest of one's environment. If that were done, it is not at all obvious that the now prestigious but psychologically difficult white-collar jobs would be more attractive than more democratically defined blue-collar work, in most people's eyes.[6]

In fact, if we think for a moment, it becomes clear that the work most of us think of as degraded and as done by degraded people is not skilled labor of any kind, but rather unskilled labor and all the varieties of physically taxing and so-called "dirty" work. One has only to raise the notion of egalitarianism in a classroom to discover that students will ask questions, not about how functional elites would be recruited in a society of equals, but rather about how "the dirty work" will get done. That, however, is a question that can seem daunting only to someone who is not an egalitarian in the first place. The logic of egalitarianism is that if any job has such an impact on those who do it as to become a degrading trap, then it cannot be a normal career line in an egalitarian society. The answer to the question, in other words, is either that no one will do such jobs (we will not have a society of equals until we have created machines that eliminate such work); or that everyone will share them out, or will do them in turn at different stages of life (e.g., teen-agers by way of national service); or that they will be done by incorrigible criminals by way of punishment (but a more humane punishment than being in prison), or by the truly feeble-minded by way of "treatment" in the community, or by genuine dropouts who don't want to do work that entails any responsibility at all. Alternatively, people are capable of collectively redefining work so that what was thought to be degrading becomes valuable and thus worth doing, or vice versa. For example, men (including Herrnstein, as it happens) have never had any difficulty in believing that due to their "innate" maternal instinct, women enjoy doing the "dirtiest" work of all: changing babies' diapers. Now that many women have begun to deny that that job ever really provided the satisfactions men claimed it did, some men are discovering that they too can find the time to change diapers (and generally engage in child-care activities), and some of those are even convincing themselves that it's a worthwhile thing to do. In an inegalitarian society there are indeed all sorts of psychological and economic advantages which those in more privileged positions derive from the existence of a lower class; getting work done which otherwise could not *possibly* be done is not one of them.

A "lower class," in sum, is something required by the intellectuals who write about these affairs, not by the necessities of social life. What about the other half of Herrnstein's inegalitarian argument? Must elites be so separated from the rest of society as to constitute a separate class with special and exclusive powers? Herrnstein puts forward the proposition associated with neoclassical economics (in the guise of "marginalism") that differential *monetary* rewards are indeed essential to a productive economy. But that very concrete version of the functionalist's abstract theory becomes an apologia when the notion of marginalism is put in the service of modern capitalism, which is marked by differences in income and wealth that are startlingly discrepant rather than merely marginal. Do these familiar discrepancies represent an eternal necessity rather than a historical artifact of our capitalist civilization? Elsewhere Herrnstein has argued that that is indeed the case: that such discrepancies exist everywhere in the industrial world, and that they are created by impersonal market forces which merely reflect the people's recognition of necessity. Neither of those propositions, however, is true (see Appendix B, section II).

To be sure, there is an income pyramid everywhere. Irving Kristol, in his attack on equality, claims that income is distributed everywhere "in the familiar form of the bell-shaped curve."[7] But that claim is false. The income-distribution curve is quite varied throughout the industrial world, most especially in its striking deviations from that shape: it is usually skewed very sharply at the lower end (there are many more poor people than rich people), and the skew is much worse in some societies than in others. Moreover, the distances between one form of income and another are strikingly disparate in, for example, a wealthy capitalist society like the United States or Sweden and a poorer state-socialist society like Hungary. However, we can hardly say that income distribution in the state-socialist societies is ideal, because they are not egalitarian either: Kristol and Herrnstein are quite right in asserting that at present no industrial society looks very egalitarian.[8]

What seems to be the case, rather, is that all modern industrial societies exhibit an income (i.e., incentives and rewards) structure in which skilled labor is valued more highly than unskilled labor; certain (but not all) professional services more than skilled labor; and managerial and leadership skills most of all. (Nationally or internationally prestigious talents that produce entertainment rather than goods or services are valued very highly in all modern societies.) We have already seen that, on the basis of technical requirements, "unskilled labor" need have no place as a "career" for normal people. As to the other categories, is it really "impersonal market forces" that have created our particular version of the labor force, with its massive income inequalities?

The obvious answer is that the existing income distributions were not created by "the people" in any sense, whether out of a recognition of necessity or for any other motive, but were rather created on the principle of "one dollar, one vote." The only way, that is, in which the "market forces" discussed by Herrnstein and other inegalitarians are "impersonal" is that they are based on money rather than personhood. But persons do not have equal access either to money or to the market. Indeed, this confusion between the market as a force representing buying power and the market as a force representing personal power is the most signal mystification of the inegalitarian apologia for contemporary capitalism.

Nor did a marketplace that allocates economic power to money rather than to persons come into existence by way of the free choice of a citizenry who thought it would be the best way to allocate resources. The "free market" was created in all European societies by the force and violence of a centralized or centralizing state, acting on behalf of an old merchant class and a new business class. It was only long after the enabling acts of this revolution had taken place that Adam Smith attempted to rationalize it theoretically; even his effort is marked by an intense suspicion and distrust of the business-class "conspiracy" against the public good (see Chapter 7 below for a more extended discussion of the history of capitalism). Only in the United States does the "free market" come into existence with relative peacefulness—if one ignores such incidents as Shays' Rebellion, the Whiskey Rebellion, the Civil War, and the history of American labor violence from the mid-nineteenth century onward. Where there were no precapitalist classes or estates that had to be dealt with by force or bought off, and where the polity was democratic to begin with, the massive effort of the new business class to implement its power through the use of state governments and the federal government as well has long since been thoroughly documented.[9] That a majority of the electorate may at one time or another have supported first Jacksonian agrarian capitalism and later the corporatism of the Gilded Age is a fact that only ideologues could use as "proof" that the political consequences of a national get-rich-quick philosophy were either understood, or desired when understood, by the same majority that went along with it. Whatever the necessarily unknown intentions of eighteenth- and nineteenth-century Americans, they certainly did not include the intention to create and justify deep class divisions and differentials; everything we know about the political ethos of those periods argues, if anything, the opposite.

Once we dispel the myth that confuses a financial market-place created by class power with a democratic "marketplace" of ideas and talents created by "the people," we can clarify how the former serves to magnify rational divisions of labor into the massively inegalitarian society of high capitalism. Chiefly, it is that *all* revenues from the sale of a firm's product are returned to the legal *owners* of that firm, to be disposed of by them and their hired managers (the two groups are often interchangeable), according to rules that they themselves have instituted. Those who espouse another of the branches of neoclassical economics, "human capital" theory, sometimes argue that workers are simply people who have failed to make a good economic investment in their own training, as opposed to businessmen and executives, and are penalized accordingly. But this too is theory as apologetics, for historically workers have been recruited (often forcibly) from among those people who, possessing no capital nor any resources beyond their capacity to work, could not bargain on equal terms, or any terms at all, about the conditions of work (at least, not until the rise of trade unions much more powerful than the nineteenth century could conceive of). In Adam Smith's very mild phraseology, "The workman may be as necessary to the master as the master is to him, but the necessity is not so immediate." Thus, workers are not who they are because they lack training; they lack training because of who they are. To see more clearly that the structural nature of class divisions is created rather than given, we need only hypothesize a situation in which *all* employees of any industry are hired in an equal, wage-labor status upon graduation from high school and are then selected for higher education and management training by lottery. In that situation we would recognize without any difficulty that people do not "choose" whether to be "trained" or not; only a lack of historical imagination prevents us from recognizing that once class divisions have formed historically, the fate of most men and women is just as much out of their own control as though it were given in a lottery. It is not just that workers are typically drawn from among people who are in too much immediate need to be able to "invest" in the kind of training that might move them into a higher social class; it is also the case that such training is kept deliberately as the purview of a relatively small number of people, so that the demand for a limited supply of managers and professionals by business enterprise will always produce a much higher price for their labor than the price of labor created by industry's demand for an almost unlimited supply of untrained workers. (The case of doctors in the United States is but the most notorious example of this phenomenon at work.)

All these intersections of "supply" and "demand," that is, are artificial rather than real, produced on the one hand by the fact that the market responds to monetary rather than human demands, and on the other hand by the fact that the supply of different kinds of labor is arranged by those with the power to institutionalize social arrangements to their own advantage—as modified by the self-defensive resistance or, sometimes, collaboration of organized workers through their unions. (Skilled craftsmen, of course, often collaborated with employers in setting and enforcing wage levels that would discriminate against or freeze out altogether less trained workers, especially women and blacks, in the hope that by so doing they could maintain their own relatively privileged position.) It must be re-emphasized that what stands behind that power is legal control (backed up, of course, by armed force) of the returns on private property in capital, a control itself initially brought into being in large part by the armed force of the state or by private armies. The social arrangements that are the distinguishing feature of industrial capitalism are that owners, managers, and workers have completely differentiated conditions of work and payment and job responsibilities; and that the conditions pertaining to owners and managers are kept much more like each other than either is like those pertaining to workers. Above all, workers historically had little effective claim on the proceeds of their work, since they had no power at all over the deployment and disposition of capital and thus the effective level of return on it; and since their contracts could be broken at the owner's will by the simple expedient of firing them. Moreover, what claim they did have and could enforce was (and still largely is) a claim to payment of a sharply different kind (hourly wages rather than salaries) for jobs so sharply delineated as to have no overlap with management responsibilities, and under working conditions deliberately arranged to keep workers ignorant, unorganized, competitive with each other, and untrained for the assumption of responsibility. The social classes of capitalism were the careful creation of human agency.*

The existence of upward social mobility for some individuals does not alter this judgment, for by its very nature the hierarchy of rewards under classical capitalism had very few well-paying jobs compared with the much greater number of ill-paying jobs. "Equal opportunity" under such circumstances meant no more than the opportunity of masses of people to compete with each other for a small number of better positions; by definition, though some could improve their relative *class* position, most could not. That kind of income hierarchy was not instituted because it was most efficient; on the contrary, "efficiency" was defined in a peculiar way by the class that benefitted from instituting and maintaining that kind of income hierarchy.

This aspect of the rise of the capitalist labor market has been amply documented by historians and economists from

---

*So carefully differentiated are class divisions, and so much are they a creation of law itself, that workers who invest in a firm by voluntarily taking a pay cut, as happens quite often, earn no interest on their investment—though that is exactly what it is. If they were bankers making a loan of exactly the same amount, they would receive interest.

Marx through Karl Polanyi to the present, though that documentation has managed to escape the notice of the new inegalitarians.[10] It is only this kind of historical accounting that will enable us to understand how it is that the chairman of the board of General Motors "earns" a million dollars or more, while a skilled craftsman in the auto industry earns perhaps twenty thousand dollars a year, paid at an hourly rate only while he is employed (a condition determined primarily by the manager, unless the union has achieved a contract that specifies otherwise). It is not that anyone in the United States, let alone a majority, thinks that the former's work is "worth" fifty times as much as the latter's; it is quite possible, if we thought about it, that we could find many more competent managers than now seem to exist if we lowered the pay but opened up the career line. Rather, the manager gets paid so much because that is the going rate in the "Fortune 500" manager market; and that is the going rate not because some neoclassical marginalist has calculated that managers add that much—or anything at all!—to the worth of the finished product, but because the manager market is kept carefully separated from the labor market. Managers reward each other in this fashion because it is in their joint interest to do so, and under the laws of capitalism no one is capable of preventing them from doing that; and they are able to behave in that way because their claim on proceeds is for all practical purposes the strongest claim—since neither owners nor workers are trained to manage. Thus we come to understand such curious phenomena as that during the recession periods of the 1970s, while average real take-home pay was falling for workers, that of top managers was rising sharply—as sharply as profits; that the managers of those divisions of major corporations and financial institutions that suffered sharp setbacks during the 1970s almost without exception were either promoted within their firms or hired by others at substantial increases in salary; that both the numbers of executives involved in passenger railroading *and* their average (real) salaries rose over a quarter-century as precipitously as passenger miles traveled were falling; and so on.

The marginalist analysis of income differentials, in sum, tells us nothing about how the basic income divisions were established in the first place: only a long chain of historical events, some accidental and incompletely understood at the time, some deliberately generated for individual and class advantages, is responsible for the broad outline of those divisions. The marginalist analysis tells us nothing about the comparative worth of the different kinds of labor ("mental" versus "physical," so to speak) because it is impossible to find a measuring instrument that works in the same way for both of them: only prejudice can justify numbers here. The marginalist analysis can sometimes tell us something about the comparative worth of different kinds of skilled labor—of the value added to output for which they are responsible—but can tell us nothing about the genesis of the various job classifications, which were usually the arbitrary result of a quite unmarginal power struggle between employers and unions. Nor can marginal analysis tell us anything about the relative rates of pay of those who provide social and individual services, since the compensation of such people (whose productivity can in no way be measured) is determined strictly by "supply and demand," and that, as we have seen, is determined by the class level of those whom they serve. (Thus a specialist in "nervous disorders" on New York's Upper East Side will "earn" much more than the GP in a small town, regardless of what anyone might think about the comparative value of the services they provide.) Most of all, no form of economic analysis can tell us anything about the desirability of giving the power to determine the most desirable division between reinvestment, returns to labor, and distributed surplus to the representatives of legal owners. Owning a corporation is not a reward for productivity, after all; being treated as though one has been productive when one hasn't is the reward for "owning" a corporation.

All of these distinctions are the outcome of power struggles and bargaining arrangements. That a general division of labor is necessary we may all concede; but the nature and especially the dimensions of the capitalist division of labor have been given historically, through the exercise of power by the powerful and resistance to it by the less powerful. They have become institutionalized as mere aspects of "the law of supply and demand," but the supply and demand of wealth and power, not of equal individuals. They have never been freely chosen by, to use the mystifying term that inegalitarians favor, "society."

III. Thus, the apologetic "free market" version of functionalism adds nothing to the argument that social classes are necessary except ideological evasions; neoclassical economics cannot be used to bolster the case for biological inegalitarianism. In fact, the opposite is true: what Herrnstein has done is use his biological determinism to bolster spurious neoclassical arguments about the impact of "market forces." According to Herrnstein, the critique of apologias for the capitalist division of labor such as I have given here is irrelevant, in that it is aimed at uncovering the hidden possibility of a social order in which inequalities are random, their extent limited, and the possibility of passing them on to one's children nonexistent. Precisely that set of conditions is unattainable, according to him. The more we strive to equalize the conditions under which people grow up and live, the more we will worsen the very situation we are trying to improve. Egalitarian reform is not only utopian, it is counterproductive.

> There will be precipitated out of the mass of humanity a low-capacity (intellectual and otherwise) residue that may be unable to master the common occupations, cannot compete for success and achievement and are most likely to be born to parents who have similarly failed.[11]

By adding a hereditarian component to the (misused) functionalist approach, in other words, Herrnstein posits the *biologically* necessary existence of a permanent lower class—and by implication, a permanent elite. The details of his case are easy to state. If, he argues, we merely concede, as we must, that there is *any* significant hereditary component in intelligence, we face a dilemma.* The more "equal opportunity" is actually realized in a society, the more the distinctions between people with re-

---

*As I pointed out in Chapter 2, the data on heritability actually tell us nothing about the genetic inheritance of intelligence; Herrnstein makes the same major error in logic as Jensen here. For purposes of discussion, though, we should assume that there is some genetic transmission of intellectual capacity of some kind: as long as we don't pretend that we can speak with any more precision than that, it seems a safer assumption than the contrary one.

spect to their capacities to perform necessary social tasks will be traceable solely to the genetic differences between them. That is the case because "postindustrial society" (Herrnstein leans heavily on the work of Daniel Bell without acknowledging it) is a "knowledge" society, in which the difficulty or simplicity of tasks that need doing is measured chiefly by the extent to which they possess an intellectual component.[12] Thus, since individuals have different genotypes for intelligence, some will be inherently capable of doing the most complex types of work; others will not. Those who are capable will *naturally* be rewarded more than the less capable or incapable. The resulting differential reward structure will be "rational" or "fair," not for the reasons given by theorists of rational choice, but because it will not be linked to the vagaries of an unequal environment. Once egalitarian reform has seized hold, if people have observably unequal capacities, it will not be because their parents could afford different kinds of education and health care but solely because they have different genetic constitutions—which reformers will not feel as free to "reform" as they would different environmental backgrounds. Then, given truly "equal" opportunity, those capable of upward social mobility will escape from the lower class (which must exist not simply because of the reasons given by economists but because of the biological "facts" of human nature). A good portion of those with intellectual capacities genetically below the competence level necessary for successful functioning in a "postindustrial" society will remain "behind" and marry each other—that is what biologists call "assortative mating by intelligence." They will thus create a class, perpetuated by their children whose intelligence also will be below competence level, and so on and on. The egalitarian drive to reform the environment so as to make it more equal for all will paradoxically but necessarily result in the creation of a self-reproducing lower class.

Let us now rephrase Herrnstein's assertion as a question. Suppose we could accomplish the goal egalitarians strive for. Suppose that we could eliminate birth (class background) as a factor in our life-chances by eliminating or attenuating the unequal and stratified effects of our present social environment, so that everyone's innate and learned interests and abilities could be developed and expressed as freely as possible. If these determinants and signifiers of adult class membership as we know it were eliminated, would then (as Herrnstein claims) "assortative mating for intelligence" come to play the determinative role in defining class membership that is now played by these nongenetic determinants? (According to Jencks's data the role of assortative mating in the creation of social classes is now rather negligible.[13]) That is to say, if we eliminated the effects of class, would genes then determine class membership? Merely to ask that self-contradictory question is to highlight the outlandishness of Herrnstein's reasoning, although that did not deter commentators such as Bell from reporting it with a straight face.

The simplest and most obvious answer is, under those circumstances, Who could care? If "class" doesn't mean anything in a different kind of society, what do we care what determines it? But since Herrnstein, like Jensen, has been taken seriously by people who should know better, we must be more analytical than that.

In the first place, the reason assortative mating by intelligence takes place at all in our society (and it surely does to some extent) is because people tend to think (or at least some people tend to think) that a person with the same kind of intelligence as their own is more likely than not to be "their kind" of person. This variant of "assortative mating" is simply one of several ways people have of dealing with their social relationships in a social formation that is at the same time as informally class-bound and class-conscious as it is formally free of class boundaries. That is to say, assortative mating by intelligence makes sense in a capitalist society, just as it would make no sense (nor even be possible) in a rigidly stratified feudal society in which people were permitted to marry only within their own estate. But the kind of society that egalitarians are trying to create would not be a capitalist society either, that is, a society in which liberty is combined with privilege. If intergenerational social class were done away with, and thus the various class cultures we are familiar with today no longer existed, then "intelligence" (however defined) would not be much of a guide to anything in particular. Today in capitalist societies there is some correlation between IQ scores, the way in which one expresses one's "intelligence" verbally, and class culture, but it is the importance of the latter that is the causal element socially. Eliminate the importance of class culture, and the reason for the correlation vanishes; people would be more free to relate to each other however they chose. In a more egalitarian society, that is, assortative mating for intelligence should not increase; it should diminish.

That is a minor criticism of Herrnstein's reasoning compared to what we must say about his typically hereditarian logic. "Equal opportunity" carried to its consistent egalitarian extreme—to the point where so much equalization has taken place that no one has a real advantage over anyone else by virtue of birth—means in effect (for us) that everyone would be provided with roughly as supportive an environment as that in which the average middle-class white American or European child grows up today. (In an egalitarian society the definition of what constitutes "the good life" would presumably be more communitarian and less individualistic than the definitions we are now most familiar with—but we cannot reason ahead of our time.) That would mean that marrying a skilled carpenter need not produce a much different fate for one's children than marrying a skilled physicist. More important, it would also mean that the current pathology-inducing conditions of *social* life—nutritional deficiencies, inadequate health care, alienation from educational and social institutions, discrimination in job markets—would have been eliminated or brought under control.

According to Herrnstein, that would mean that we would have effectively equalized the effects of "environment," leaving only the quality of our genes to determine our individual fates. What is typically hereditarian about that logic is the mindless assumption, lacking either empirical or methodological sense, that "nature" and "nurture" are real and separate *things*, each of which can be isolated by a scientist or policy-maker and its effects observed or manipulated in such a way that we can say that everything not determined by the one is determined by the other. Perhaps only psychologists with no sociological training would fail to notice how patently nonsensical is the assumption that "equal (environmental) opportunity" means the actual equalization (what could that possibly be?) of "environments." "Equal opportunity," in American parlance, or in the minds of the French revolutionaries who created the slogan of careers open to the talents, is nothing more than a legal or (more recently) a sociological norm, not at all a factual description of human lives. Even the most radical policy of equalizing the conditions under which we all begin the "struggle of life" only means equalizing certain *institutionalized* conditions that can be affected by social and economic policy, such as those I have mentioned. It does not mean that we all become the same person with a uniform life-style, and it certainly does not mean that the differential effects of environment are eliminated; on the contrary, they are more likely to be exacerbated than are the mysterious genetic effects that are so difficult to describe. What Herrnstein has done is to confuse our "environment" with certain shorthand descriptions of it that we have invented for ideological or scholarly purposes. "Social class" is only an analytic category at a fairly high level of abstraction, created by human beings in order to help us understand what we do to each other *en masse.* Social or economic positions are not in themselves "environments"; they are merely crude guides to averagely different life experiences that, for some reason or another, we wish to be aware of. But suppose we smooth over the differences between the various averagely different life-styles; suppose we moderate the particular influences, born of relative deprivation, that provide some people with an averagely worse life than others. We will in no way have eliminated the differences in or even the pathologies of social life. We will simply have ensured that the differences and especially the pathologies will occur less often (much less often, we hope), and that sociologically their incidence will have been *randomized,* rather than associated more or less with particular, identifiable groups of people—"classes."

Once the influences of environment are detached from their present association with socioeconomic position (by those egalitarian reforms that Herrnstein so disingenuously fears), aspects of the interaction between individuals and their environments that are now dominated by gross and powerful class or caste differences would come to the fore in their own right. After all, every one of the forms of parent or child behavior that predict a comparatively bleak social future can be found in families of all social classes even now. (Banfield, in his *Unheavenly City,* admits that the various class "life-styles" he describes can be found in all economic social classes: the international playboy leads a "lower-class" life—irresponsibly unheeding of the future—but has enough money not to suffer for it.) Those manifestations of social behavior have nothing whatever to do with genes, and therefore there is little or no danger that any group of people engaging in such behaviors (even making the extremely questionable assumption of assortative mating among them) could ever form a distinctive, self-reproducing gene pool.

Herrnstein does not seem to understand the meaning of the term "class." What identifies a social class is that its members *and their children* obtain a range of benefits by virtue of membership in it that are denied, formally or informally, to members of a "lower" class. Class is thus one of the two major kinds of social grouping (the other being caste) that do indeed distribute benefits or penalties in every area of a person's life. But as I have already argued in staking out an egalitarian position short of the call for "total" equality, class can only have that effect, and indeed can only exist as a useful analytic conception, where benefits and penalties are distributed with a marked inequality. Even occupation, which for Herrnstein and Jensen (as for the functionalists) is the most important distributor of social rewards and penalties, will not operate in that way unless occupational position also is associated, not just with Bell's "income and status inequality," but with strongly marked social-class differentiations.

Since the whole purpose of egalitarian change is precisely to end the irrational and unnecessary association between occupation and the availability of a society's range of goods, services, and opportunities by making those things available to all with an equality as minimal as those necessary inequalities of occupation or income, egalitarians need feel no alarm at all about the possibility that people of different capabilities in such a society might wind up handling different jobs. So what? In an egalitarian society it would not matter that, owing to their differential intelligences, some persons were skilled mechanics and others managed production systems. There would be nothing *crucial* that the production managers could buy with whatever extra money income (if any) was necessary to induce them to perform their "more important" tasks. Thus neither group would be passing on its own life-chances, willy-nilly, to its children. Herrnstein's fear that by eliminating the parameters of class existence we make the effects of "class" worse is an astonishingly obvious contradiction in terms.

How then can Herrnstein and Jensen have asserted that our genes compel the worsening of the effects of class, when the effects of class are exactly what the policies they decry would be aimed at eliminating? How could they insist with such casual self-contradiction that egalitarian reform will mean an even greater likelihood of passing "class" on to our children, when, if it means anything, egalitarian reform means the adoption of policies such that there is nothing to pass on (as though we should worry about passing on the disposition to caries after fluoridation has been instituted)? The answer is that they do not really believe in either the possibility or the desirability of the egalitarian program in the first place, so the pursuit of it is merely self-delusion in their view. What they are really saying is that since egalitarian reformers can't accomplish their goals anyhow, all they'll be doing is worsening the genetic component of class differentiation without really changing the social institutions that signify and incarnate class division. It is as though they had said that fluoridation will only work for the people who have already inherited good teeth, so it is only going to magnify the division between the well-toothed and the ill-toothed classes.

But why should they believe that egalitarian reform is impossible? It cannot be that our genes make it so, for the mere existence of genetic determination only ensures that no one can surpass his or her genetic limitations. Why must we believe that those genetic limitations are so inherently unequal among individuals and groups as to make even the gentlest approach toward social equality impossible of fulfillment? The effects of impingement of a mechanism upon a system cannot be given only by what we know about the mechanism; we must also know something about the *system*. Nothing we know about genes (and, to repeat, we don't in fact know anything about the alleged genes for "intelligence") can tell us what effect their distribution will have on "society" without our having a complete picture in mind of what we mean by "society." (For example, genes would have no effect on a society in which all action was determined by the roll of dice.) What those who initially were so impressed by the façade of "hard" biological science that Jensen and Herrnstein presented to the public failed to realize, in other words, is that the "science" had no implications at all except in the context of a complex social theory which the two psychologists have hardly articulated.

In fact, like all hereditarians from Galton onward, Herrnstein and Jensen in the end simply resort to a banal social theory
in a vain attempt to rescue both their hereditarianism and their
inegalitarianism. They don't really know that the poor—and the
rich—will always be with us because of the influence our genes
have on us. Rather, they conclude that our genes must have a
major influence on us because they are convinced that the poor
and the rich will always be with us despite anything we do. Their
argument makes a kind of sense only when we understand them
to be saying, not that the nature of our genetic constitutions will
cause egalitarian reform to fail, but rather that because
egalitarian reform must fail anyhow, the "laws" of genetic behavior will rule in its place. Having perverted the classic sociological approach, which requires us to acknowledge the necessity only of task-specific elites, not of institutionalized classes,
the psychologists set themselves up as experts not on "intelligence" or on biology but on . . . social stratification. And the
"biological" theory of social structure, unlike that of the functionalists, is indeed nothing more than an apologia for contemporary capitalism and a weapon in the war against social change.

IV. Assuming the necessity of class, as they have done, why
mention genes at all? The answer, according to Herrnstein, is
that in a rational society, those who can be expected to add more
or less worth to materials by their labor can be and should be
differentiated according to their *intellectual* capacities; that is
because he thinks (following Daniel Bell) that the division of
labor in modern industrial societies is properly centered around
the distinction between types of mental and types of physical
labor. To function successfully, the division of labor and its
rewards structure must reflect those differences faithfully. But
those differences are *immense* and *innate.* It is that dual claim
which gives the argument of the biological inegalitarians its
patina of "science." The innate aspect of human intelligence is
seen—that is, Herrnstein and Jensen see it—in the data about
heritability. But beyond that, their crucial assertion is that the
extent of each person's innate or inherent capability is given by
IQ results, which more or less precisely mirror the extent of real
individual differences. Since IQ scores are decidedly unequal, we

are therefore to conclude that people are decidedly unequal and that the extent of their inequality is inherent.

It is because these things are (allegedly) true that it is supposedly useless for egalitarians to try to eliminate or attenuate the impact of class stratification: useless because they cannot eliminate or attenuate the natural reality (represented for us by IQ scores) on which it is based. There will always be a large class of the intellectually inferior, because that is the way some people are, and such people must receive inferior rewards from any "rational" society. Moreover, we have learned of their existence, not from any impressionistic and suspect observations of human behavior, but "scientifically"—from IQ tests themselves.

Clearly, this vision of a society necessarily and eternally restratifying itself requires some empirical grounding that is not given by the mere supposition that some limitations on human intelligence are inherited, or by the mere existence of a wide range of IQ scores. We could acknowledge both those realities and yet also believe that the inherited differential limitations are not likely to be *innately* very great—not likely to condemn any large group of normal people as intellectually "inferior" forever. Why should we believe otherwise? What evidence is there for this new version of inegalitarianism, this updated Calvinism in which the sign of the Elect or the Damned is not worldly success but IQ-test scores?

Herrnstein's (and Jensen's) answer to this question shows that these inegalitarians have one more string to their hereditarian bow.* As though recognizing that their defenses of IQ measurements and heritability studies are inadequate, and that IQ tests otherwise have never been validated, they both give what Herrnstein calls "a pragmatic answer" to their critics. This "pragmatic answer," upon which their whole argument about the necessity of inequality ultimately stands or falls, goes as follows: Whatever IQ scores do or do not "really" measure, and whatever "heritability" really is or is not, the "fact" is that IQ scores correlate closely with other aspects of social behavior

---

*Both Herrnstein and Jensen make much of the alleged fact that IQ measurements can be graphed on a "bell-shaped" curve. The assertion is not quite correct factually; it is also quite meaningless. For a more detailed discussion of this point, see Appendix B.

that are presumably of great practical importance to us. Indices of educational attainment, "success" in life as indicated by income, and place in the occupational hierarchy supposedly offer such correlations to a greater or lesser extent. That being the case, moreover, there is once again an alleged rationale of the capitalist structure of rewards—like the existence of a "normal curve" for IQ results, their fit with occupation and income supposedly shows the naturalness of the particular and extreme way in which we (the IQ-test subjects) discriminate between the "more intelligent" and the "less intelligent."

The correlation between IQ level and occupational attainment is the one they fasten upon most tenaciously. Herrnstein and Jensen (the former at greater length) both make much of the "prestige ratings" of various occupations in a few public-opinion studies, and of an alleged correlation between IQ and occupational prestige; Jensen even mentions the ranking of occupations by their "intellectual demands," as rated by one psychologist writing in the 1920s. Their claim is that IQ is *in any event* a valid predictor of our social achievements. Conversely—and this link in the chain of reasoning is decisive once we have begun to doubt the relevance of their largely spurious heritability data—if our achievements are unequal in the same way as our IQs, then that coincidence may be taken as a vindication of the "reality" of whatever IQ measures and the validity of the way IQ measures it. That "reality"—the reality of the normal distribution of intelligence and its associated widely dispersed units of deviation— is attested to by the *usefulness* of IQ tests, if by nothing else about them. IQ distributes occupation (allegedly), and the occupational distribution manifestly works to society's advantage. Thus it might be said on behalf of Jensen and Herrnstein that, since critics like myself (with our quibbles about the validity of the heritability data) cannot prove IQ is *not* heritable, we should submit our criticisms to the judgment of the ultimate intellectual tribunal: IQ tests being socially valuable, we should agree that the social report they give us must be "true."

In a way, the least interesting aspect of this facet of biological inegalitarianism is that the studies referred to are trivial and silly and the conclusion drawn from them simply false.[14] To the extent that attempts to show correlations in these matters are at all believable (is it really possible to decipher cause and effect from mere census data?), investigators as diverse as Otis Dudley Duncan, Christopher Jencks, and Samuel Bowles and Herbert Gintis, using different methodological frameworks, have found that the best predictor of income level is not IQ score but either the occupational status of one's father ("birth" rather than "utility") or educational attainment measured merely as years of formal schooling undergone. To the extent, in other words, that we do uncover correlations between IQ scores and occupational choices or income attainments from census data and more narrowly focused studies, it is owing to these other intervening variables that influence both IQ *and* economic success and account for what superficially appears to be a correspondence between them. Ignoring intervening variables, however—that is, ignoring the facts of *social* life—is what hereditarians do best.[15]

Moreover, lest we think that educational attainment predicts income because the educated also have high IQs, Jencks notes that the strength of the correlation lies rather in the tendency of employers (and personnel directors looking for a cheap way to distinguish between otherwise indistinguishable job candidates) to require formal educational credentials of very doubtful applicability to on-the-job performance. Although meeting those requirements is hard for people with low test scores, inasmuch as most schools deliberately track low scorers away from a college-oriented curriculum, IQ itself appears to mean little once one actually has a job.

> The modest relationship between test scores and wages in most occupations seems to reflect the fact that test scores have only a modest effect on actual competence in most lines of work. . . .
>
> Even in . . . highly technical fields, the difference between good and bad work seems to be more a matter of habits, values, attitudes, and outlook than of knowing the right answers to written or oral questions.
>
> All the evidence we have reviewed points in the same direction. Most jobs require a wide variety of skills. Standardized tests measure only a very limited number of these skills. If an individual with low scores has the necessary noncognitive skills, and if he can get into an occupation, his

performance on the job will not usually be appreciably below the norm for the occupation.

Jencks therefore concludes, contrary to Herrnstein:

Such findings do not support the theory that if schools and colleges placed less emphasis on academic standards and cognitive skills, employers would fall back on tests to measure these skills. They suggest that if schools and colleges placed less emphasis on cognitive skills, the correlations between tests scores and status might just fall.[16]

It follows directly from Jencks's analysis that schooling and IQ scores correlate as well as they do because they are very similar experiences, at least as practiced in the United States. Both schooling and IQ scores stress the ability and willingness to do well on written tests of academic subject matter; neither bears any visible, immediate relation to the acquisition of job-oriented skills of any kind—and the likelihood of success for both is strongly dependent on the various background circumstances of one's life which Jencks (and Bowles and Gintis) identify.*

Beyond all statistical analysis, however, the most important point is that the project of uncovering the "causes" of inequality is misconceived to begin with (though once again the erroneous assertions of writers like Jensen and Herrnstein require reply from other social scientists). It is of little use to know "why" stratified social positions are filled by particular individuals or groups rather than others, unless we also know "why" the stratification system exists in the first place. As I have already indicated, the functionalist account of stratification on which Herrnstein relies in no way entails the existence of anything like the American stratification system. Simple reflection can clarify that point further. Within that system there is a sharply graded and differentiated hierarchy of earned and unearned incomes, from the billionaire's inheritance to the handicapped person's

---

*As I have pointed out elsewhere, on the only occasion when Herrnstein attempted to respond to Jencks's analysis of this question, he thoroughly misrepresented it.[17]

welfare pittance. Does family background or IQ "explain" the inheritance and "bad luck" or "lack of conceptual ability" the pittance? Of course not. What explains both the difference and the incredible scope of the difference is our version of the social structure and legal system of capitalism. Historical action, not "functional necessity," has produced a system which guarantees, first, that property can be inherited, and second, that people have to do either skilled labor or skilled white-collar work in order to be paid the equivalent of a decent living. Moreover, even that last clause is a considerable oversimplification. For not only is the stratification system hierarchical in principle but the hierarchy takes the form of a steeply graded pyramid—but not because that's the way people are "naturally." On the other hand, it is not merely that the resulting gradations of reward are arbitrary, either. On the contrary, far from being the result of an innate stratification, they exist because those with the power to do so created them. Over the past century great pains have been taken by the owners and managers of capital to ensure that technical expertise is concentrated in a smaller and smaller percentage of the work force, that those who are excluded from the ranks of expert are trained only to be narrow detail workers, and that a "reserve army of the unemployed" remains available to help "discipline" the lower ranks of the employed. (And, as noted earlier, out of motives of self-defense, trade unions have often connived in this last process as well.) The system of rewards, then, perfectly mirrors the managerial class's theories about the appropriate methods for organizing workplaces so as to maintain managerial control and inhibit worker autonomy. As Harry Braverman puts it, this method of dividing labor up into finely specialized tasks, some of which require great amounts of skill while others require none, "gives expression, not to a technical aspect of the division of labor, but to its social aspect."[18] That is, what is being reproduced is not the necessities of production but the social division of classes. All this having been accomplished, people then sort themselves out (or more accurately, are sorted out by the institutions, such as schools, that they encounter in their early years) to fill the pre-existing positions. Various aspects of human psychology, and perhaps even biology, may account for the way they are sorted out relative to each other. That they have to sort themselves out in that particular way at all has nothing to do with either psychology or biology; it is rather the result of efforts by those with economic and political power to structure the social organism in that way. To hunt down correlations between occupation or income and personal characteristics, then, and to present the latter as though they were the cause of the former, is to engage not in social science but in apologetics.

That having been said, it is still worthwhile to look briefly at the actual comments of the new inegalitarians about occupation and IQ simply for what they reveal about the ideological nature, and the intellectual level, of inegalitarianism. For the force of the argument, after all, depends entirely on our subjective agreement that the occupational hierarchy in American society (as they report it) is, first, "rational," and second, not replaceable by any different arrangement. I have acknowledged (though not all egalitarians would agree) that one version of a social ordering by "merit," that is, the provision of extra reward (though not on the scale with which we are familiar) to those who could not otherwise be induced to perform tasks that we all agree are essential is a reasonable conclusion to the search for more equality. Is there *any* fit between such an ordering and what now exists in capitalist societies, as Jensen, Herrnstein, and Daniel Bell imply? Is it really true that at present the people who get paid the most money do the most important work and are also the most "intelligent" people; and that the people now doing "less important" work could not do the more important work equally well?

According to Herrnstein, "the ties among IQ, occupation, and social standing make practical sense," and society is thus wisely "husbanding its intellectual resources" when it informally enforces those ties by holding the more important occupations "in greater esteem and paying them more." We have already observed that occupations cannot be differentiated from each other by income, and more important, that "society" does no such thing. (It is indeed a sure sign that a social theory is fatuous when it requires the personification of "society," as though a collection of disparate and conflicting classes and groups could be characterized as one collective entity.) Just the same, what are some of these intellectual discriminations that help society "husband its intellectual resources" and thus validate IQ testing as an index of human ability?

In the passage just quoted Herrnstein is contrasting the intelligence "we" demand of engineers and ditchdiggers—which seems reasonable enough until we reflect on his casual assumption that there must be a *career* in ditchdigging, just as there is a career in engineering. At the same time, he approvingly presents a tantalizing sample of a table from a World War II study of the civilian occupations and IQs of enlisted men. In its original form, this table—which, though an outdated report on an unrepresentative sample, is the only "hard" evidence he has ever offered—showed at least 10 points of average IQ difference between the following pairs of occupations (higher average IQ listed first): public relations man and foreman (or machinist or musician or airplane mechanic); bartender and truck driver (8 points); accountant and production manager; salesman and auto mechanic; sales manager and cabinetmaker (or electrician or lathe operator).*

Furthermore, the comparisons Herrnstein does give are only for *men*, who turn out to do all the husbanding of society's intellectual resources on their own. When challenged with the obvious argument that many women of high IQ are not being rewarded at all, or not equivalently, for the work *they* do, Herrn-

---

*From Herrnstein's use of these occupation "studies" we also discover, sadly, that there are no depths to which he will not stoop to bolster a shaky case. In an article from which he quotes in his book, there is a graphic figure horizontally divided into segments, each representing a 5-IQ-point spread and each containing a vertically (and neatly) arranged list of all the occupations for which the mean IQ of the people filling them falls within that segment. Thus, if there are more jobs in which people have mean IQs falling within one segment than in another, and the job-title list under each segment begins on the same line, the first list will extend farther down the page than the second. The authors fill in this "chart" for all such segments, and then draw a line from left to right across the page that curves just below the *bottom* title in each vertical column. Lo and behold, Herrnstein then tells us, the job lists are longer in the middle of the page than at its extremes, and the line takes the shape of "the familiar bell-shaped curve"! Art imitates nature again! Unfortunately, it turns out that the original authors broke down job titles very finely in the midrange segments while telescoping titles at the extremes. Of the 21 job descriptions given for the 117.-5–122.1 *(sic)* column, 14 could easily be telescoped into the three categories of "clerical office worker," "draftsman," and "lab technician," leaving only 10 job descriptions in that column. In the high-IQ column we could, conversely, break down "accountant" or "chemist" into several subcategories each, with as much or more reason than the authors had to decompose "clerical office worker" in the middle column. Do that throughout, and we will have 10 job titles to a column and thus a straight line running beneath our vertical job-title lists. So much for the "bell-shaped curve"!—and so much for the integrity of hereditarianism.[19]

stein could add nothing to his earlier comment in summarizing a study of high-IQ persons:

> Women's salaries were substantially lower than the men's and did not correlate with contentment. Notwithstanding their poorer salaries, on the average, the women reported greater satisfaction in their lives than the men. The housewives, who were earning less money than anyone else, expressed about as much satisfaction as any other group in the sample. There is little here to support the feminist argument that a housewife's life is intolerable, especially for educated, intelligent women. It would be hard to pick a brighter group than the women in this study, yet they seemed to be adjusting easily to their lot [*sic*]. To give but one example of the many striking cases, a woman whose I.Q. of 192 places her close to the top of the entire sample, and whose retested intelligence at maturity was, again, virtually at the top, was raising eight children, including three sets of twins. According to the account at the latest report, she had no outside activity at that time other than an interest in the P.T.A., but was apparently content, if not serene. Of course, such tranquillity may be gone now, fifteen years later.[20]

Herrnstein thus offers us two fascinating conclusions. First, in every case mentioned either directly or by implication, he rates more highly the job that pays more and is also (for men) either relatively nonproductive or only involves paperwork that is often irrelevant to any effort at extending the real wealth and consequent economic well-being of society (not to mention its artistic wealth and cultural well-being). He seems to have no historical understanding of why such jobs exist: that it is not (again) technical necessity but rather "the separation of conceptualization from execution—the removal of all possible work from the shop floor, the point of execution, to the office—and the further necessity of maintaining a shadow replica of the entire process of production in paper form," that "brings into being large technical and office staffs."[21] He thus simply describes the existing division of labor without in the slightest degree seriously analyzing it, let alone justifying it.

Second, "men's work" is ranked by him primarily according to the income it generates and by the alleged correlation between occupational income and IQ. Adjustment to their "lot," which is a fundamental assumption in justifying the women's role, is only incidental to his argument about men; it is to be ignored when speaking of bartenders, PR men, and so forth. Again, instead of using the findings of social science to support prejudice, he is actually using prejudice to validate the findings of social science.

Throughout his entire corpus of work Herrnstein has only one other comment on this subject, which is central theoretically to his entire argument. There he claims to have "refuted" Jencks's remarks about "credentialism" by insisting that we must want "a surgeon to know anatomy," "an airplane navigator to know trigonometry," and "a grocer to know how to add or, at least, how to operate his cash register." "If learning the tools of a trade is at all correlated with IQ," he adds, "then the network of correlations is not an accident, not even a bourgeois conspiracy."[22]

It is hard to say which of these two versions of his argument is stranger. Anyone who has ever flown in a plane with one engine out (or an engine pylon mounted incorrectly!), or driven in a car with inexplicably failing brakes, or worried about the dangers of faulty wiring, will be able to make his or her own judgment about whether society is (or was) "wisely husbanding" its intellectual resources in terms of who is entrusted with these tasks. Similarly, we are all capable of making our own judgments as to whether high-IQ women who are past the age of childbearing and child-rearing (entirely leaving aside the question whether that latter task might not be apportioned more equally between the sexes) are contributing the most they can to society when relegated to the boards of powerless voluntary associations or doing ill-paid white-collar work (why not make them suffer the way men do?). The sociology of the remarks about credentials is equally baffling. As we all must, I know several estimable grocery-store owners or employees who operate their cash registers quite nicely—that the only mistakes they ever make are in their own favor I take to be a sign of real intelligence—without showing any other signs of special "cognitive ability," and in fact I should think the job not beyond the "innate" range of any person with an undamaged brain. Surgeons are generally considered among the *less* intellectually oriented members of the medical profession, and their job demands no more "cognitive ability" than that of any skilled craftsman. My family doctor is undoubtedly more intelligent than most surgeons, and the sorts of things he does—such as diagnosis—demand a great deal of conceptual skill; his and his peers' contribution to the national health and thus to productivity is *much* greater than that of an equivalent number of surgeons. But the surgeons get paid more. As for mathematical navigators, Herrnstein has yet to explain why they get paid much less than, say, successful PR men. Yes, I would want my navigator to know his trig, but no, I could not care less if my PR man was illiterate.

There is no point in spending more time on these absurd, even imbecilic, examples of "society's" wisdom or "pragmatic" intelligence. The real point is that only someone remarkably unsophisticated about the workings of an industrial economy would think that theoretical physicists and chess players are or should be its most highly rewarded inhabitants, or that middle- or lower-range white-collar workers, real estate agents, political scientists, television network executives, and so on generate more useful goods and services than skilled or even semiskilled industrial workers. Only ignorance of the world outside research laboratories (and perhaps within them) can have allowed Herrnstein so to overvalue "cognitive ability," when anyone who has ever dealt with a successful manager of any kind of physical or intellectual production knows that the traits that leap to the eye in such a person are decisiveness, drive, instinct, strength, vigor, shrewdness, application, "personality," manipulativeness, the ability to learn from experience, and only secondarily the kind of ability that gets tested by IQ tests. Only ignorance of the world could have us not know that in corporate bureaucracies, public or private, administrative featherbedding is the exception rather than the rule, or that corporate executives get salary raises, not cuts, when productivity or sales drop. Such examples could be multiplied endlessly; the irrelevance of IQ to real productivity, and that of real productivity to pay, are both completely clear. Vague references to "occupational status" cannot change the fact that the number of occupations for which we can actually define what exactly gets done, how well, and by whom, *and* what it is worth to us, is minimal. So far as anyone knows, there is no consistent relationship of any kind between income and social utility. Income is simply a function of marketplace and political power, both of which are generated by a long train of historical circumstances, some accidental and some carefully arranged, but none necessarily having anything to do with "merit" or "usefulness."[23]

Indeed, it seems clear that Herrnstein has simply done what so many intellectual inegalitarians do: he has failed to question the social value of his own most prized possession— "higher mental faculties," as he has called it. Thus he has failed to realize that what he and I do can in the aggregate be displaced by technological advance ("Sunrise Semester") a lot more easily than what spot-welders do; and that when we have machines and systems to do what accountants and controllers do we will still be trying to find human beings willing to work in factories or mine coal. In the end, we will have to make the working conditions of factory workers and miners more like those of accountants and controllers now, and we will find that the average IQ scores of the former (if we are still giving IQ tests) will rise sharply. Even today, we have no grounds at all for believing that if, after a period of mutual and intensive retraining, prestigious and well-paid high-IQ public-relations men, stock analysts, or real estate brokers switched jobs with prestigeless, lower-IQ truck drivers or with any random sample of housewives, the real productivity of society would in the long run be any the less.

V. To this kind of argument, finally, Herrnstein has replied by asserting that on the "evidence," there already exists an irremediable lower class, so that these theoretical considerations are irrelevant. The "evidence" he refers to is the fact that there are millions of poor people in the United States who, he tells us, are "functionally illiterate" and thus hopelessly "disadvantaged" when it comes to keeping up with the pace of modern technology. Thus to the general theoretical argument for the necessity of the existing class division he adds this "practical" argument, claiming in this case, not that certain jobs must be done by poor people, but rather that certain people must always be poor because, as we can plainly see, they are so inadequate.[24]

But the "evidence" of the United States Census is of even less value than the evidence of the IQ/income "correlation." To be sure, situational poverty—that of the elderly, the ill or disabled, the alcoholic—can exist anywhere. As for the poverty that allegedly *must* come to millions by virtue of their productive incapability, its necessity is a complete myth, as we realize if we simply look at the problem of poverty from the perspective of the economic costs of overcoming it. Just from the standpoint of middle-class self-interest, the current cost to Americans of dealing with a large underclass—the bulk of the costs, that is, of crime, crime prevention, and punishment; of welfare and social services taken up primarily by the poor; and of forgone production from those barred from productivity by the various miseries the cycle of poverty imposes on them—probably requires more onerous taxation than would the implementation of "full employment" programs combined with wage supplements. Even from this "incentives" standpoint, modern poverty—the existence of a real lower class—probably imposes more strictly economic costs than it grants "practical" economic benefits. As Herbert Gans has put it, we have so large a lower class because we seem to derive other benefits from its existence and from our refusal to do anything about it—for example, getting the "dirty work" done by people who have no choice, thus enabling the rest of us to feel socially and morally superior.[25] But are those people the kinds of people who must be poor? Every nation within the world capitalist economy has a lower class of some size or other, but it is only those nations in which different racial or ethnic groups commingle that have an indigenous lower class which manifests the "culture of poverty." We could multiply the genetically inferior cultures to a point of absurdity, including, in addition to black Africans, southern Italians, North Africans and Turks, the Irish in England, Indians in Latin America, Hispanics in the United States, the untouchables in India, the Bangladeshi, French Canadians (who would apparently be perfectly adequate if still in France), and so on. Otherwise we are forced to recognize that it is not innately low intelligence but grossly uneven economic development which accounts for what look like indigenous cultures of poverty to the incurious eye of the sociobiologist. The American disease, in other words, is not even a necessary corollary of welfare capitalism, let alone of a more egalitarian "postindustrial" society.[26] A people's "indigenous" culture is no more the cause of their inability to find productive work than their "innate" diurnality is the cause of their setting off to work in factories early every morning.

As for the notion that technological advance outpaces the capabilities of the potential work force, that is as devoid of substance as the notion that poverty is necessary. On the contrary, technological advance, by creating such instruments as adding machines, pocket calculators, key-punch machines, and continuous-flow production systems, makes it easier for the person of average intelligence to do jobs that used to be reserved for those with special mathematical ability—as by reading off from dials the states of a production process that in the past could be supervised only by someone conversant with all the complicated techniques utilized in the process. To the extent that "technological progress" really is progressive, it is because it enhances the powers of the average competent person (even though originally the progressive technique may have been comprehensible only to its inventor). Thus it is that we would rather be operated on by a substandard surgeon of 1980 than by the greatest surgeon of the eighteenth century, simply because of the much more sophisticated equipment, training, and knowledge available to the former. Similarly, today's average backyard tinkerer can do things with an auto engine that would have been beyond the capabilities of the "genius" Watt.

Indeed, the major criticism of technological "progress" is that these techniques can be used by an aggressive management in such a way as to deskill specific tasks and thus centralize workplace power further with management.

> [We] have two central characteristics of the relations of production under capitalism: management/capital owns the means of production and hence has the prerogative and wherewithal to direct the development of production technology; and capital/management is forever striving to minimize its dependence upon those who labor for it, in part by appropriating for itself the "intelligence of production" (the skills of the workshop) and by separating conception and

control from execution, thereby enhancing managerial authority over the process of production.[27]

To repeat, that is an aspect of consciously chosen policy, not technological necessity.* Moreover, the skills and the intelligence of trained workers turn out to be not so easily dispensable as the ideologues or "scientific management" have thought (or hoped).

> Workers show much ingenuity in defeating and outwitting the agents of scientific management before, during, and after the "appropriation of knowledge." . . . In any shop there are "official" or "management-approved" ways of performing tasks, and there is the workers' lore devised and revised in response to any management offensive. Not only does management fail to appropriate these "trade secrets" but . . . it is not necessarily to their advantage to appropriate them. Shop management usually knows this.[28]

Or, as one manager was heard to add on reflection after having first said, "We want absolutely no decisions made on the floor": "We need guys out there who can think." In sum, the deskilling threat of advanced technology in and of itself is greatly overestimated. When that deskilling does occur it is usually because it has been carefully programmed to occur; because management consciously desires to polarize the intelligence of society. Then, to be sure, we confront the situation in which "this destructive tendency feeds on itself . . . the simplification and rationalization of skills in the end destroy these skills, and with the skills becoming ever more scarce, the new processes become ever more inevitable—because of the shortage of skilled labor!"[29] But if we abstract technology (unrealistically, of course) from the patterns of social control that surround it, there

---

*The author of the foregoing quotation recounts an interview he had with shop managers who attempted to convince him that a new technology couldn't be operated by the workers but had to be operated from the office. Item by item he pointed out that the workers were visibly observed to be doing what the managers said they couldn't do, in the course of maintaining the automatic machinery. "Finally, they looked at each other and smiled, and one of them leaned over and confided, 'We don't want them to.'"

is no reason to believe that the intelligently productive life is beyond the reach of any non-brain-damaged person who really desires it—*if* the ways in which we now deploy capital are restructured.

Admittedly, we cannot do more than state this double negative. It again would be compounding Herrnstein's error to claim that the very limited evidence we have about the effects of technological advance on intellectual requirements is anything more than ambiguous. But nowhere except in utopian fantasies can we find a prognostication that highly demanding, abstractly intellectual work is going to become the average work of even "postindustrial society." Moreover, some of the increase in what Daniel Bell has misleadingly called "the knowledge industry" is merely an outgrowth of attempts by management to deepen the social division of labor—consciously to remove all "intellectual" work from the ambit of laborers—so that control of the work process remains firmly outside the grasp of the working class. Some of it is also simply an outgrowth of the centralization and monopolization of capital. As the managers of multinationals, conglomerates, oligopolies, and state monopolies become more and more removed from the actual production process, they are forced to develop more and more complicated and extensive systems of internal bureaucracy in order to coordinate activities that in a more decentralized and community-controlled system would not have to be coordinated in the first place. Furthermore, the competition of centralized capital for markets, investment funds, and above all prestige requires that all units develop white-collar armies that duplicate each other's activities in the fields of selling, public relations and advertising, political lobbying, and financing; gradually all enterprises, great or small, commercial, nonprofit, or governmental, must adopt this form of organization in order to survive. Some of the jobs that are thereby created require a good deal of intellectual ability and some do not, but most of them are unnecessary in the first place except as they maintain the over-all rule of monopoly capital.

Most of all, a physically more productive economy has supported a growing number of workers in service rather than in manufacturing employment, a tendency exacerbated by the fact that, given the nature of industrial labor from the early nineteenth century until fairly recently, "upward mobility" so far has been defined as the ability to escape from it. But these service jobs are usually not intellectually demanding in the sense that IQ supposedly measures intellect (though some of the new service jobs may be extraordinarily demanding of human sympathy, flexibility, and other such qualities). The conventional distinction between "white-collar" and "blue-collar" work obscures the reality that many jobs of the former type are no more oriented toward independent intellectual understanding than traditional factory work: probably less so, if factory workers were allowed to take an interest in the organization of their own productive processes. As Braverman notes,

> the most rapidly growing mass occupations in an era of scientific-technical revolution are those which have least to do with science and technology [which] need not surprise us. The purpose of machinery is not to increase but to decrease the number of workers attached to it.

Thus "the apparent trend to a large nonproletarian 'middle class' has resolved itself into the creation of a large proletariat in a new form."[30] The sectoral growth data he summarizes very strongly suggest, not that there are too many intellectually skilled jobs available, but that there are too few for those—from any social class—who could be trained to fill them. It is the pace of job construction that is inadequate; as is the degree of our willingness (in the United States, at least) to eliminate arbitrary and discriminatory constraints on labor mobility, as well as the extremely negative social conditions which go to create so much of what is called "learning disability."

In sum, if the citizens of a democratic society made the best effort possible to train everyone up to the limits of his or her capabilities and to generate useful tasks up to the limit of everyone's training, then immensely more equality than now exists in any modern society would be eminently "practical." Of course, as the new conservatives argue, "we" cannot "afford" much more equality: current efforts to bring it about through the mechanisms of income redistribution and resource transfer are much too expensive for the increasingly marginal results they produce.[31] That, however, is because we are citizens of a pseudodemocratic, not a democratic, society. Capital, for us, is so structured as to have for its purpose the increase of profit, not the generation of useful tasks. Concomitantly, we do not attempt to train all citizens to the limits of their capabilities, for that would be a pointlessly expensive effort in the absence of tasks to which they all could fruitfully apply themselves. But this behavior is a technological or functional necessity only of corporate capitalism.

Thus when Herrnstein insists that "any society" needs gradients of social reward "no steeper than necessary," he is uttering a truism to which even Mao Zedong would have given eager assent, as will almost any egalitarian. For we have no reason to believe that "no steeper than necessary" implies anything like the kind of inequality we suffer from now. Since the new inegalitarians are so fond of statistical evidence, it is worth reporting here that in Jencks's analysis of the data about mobility, IQ, and income, he concludes that even assuming a high heritability figure, "if all the nongenetic causes of inequality were eliminated, the income gap between the top and bottom fifths of all male workers would fall from around 7 to 1 to around 1.4 to 1": a prospect well within the range of what we could reasonably mean by "economic equality."*[32] Moreover, we are quite capable in principle of separating the distribution of many vital goods—health care, education and training, housing, to name the most obvious—from the jobs-and-income stream: if not totally, at least much more so than is now the case. By rearranging our institutions so that increments of reward to "elite" positions could purchase only goods or services that are essentially luxuries, we could move considerably closer to an egalitarian social order without doing away with the notion of "incentives" at all.[33]

To return, finally, to Daniel Bell's remark about a society being "absurd" if it is not led by its "best men," we can now see that as a gratuitous extension of functionalism, wholly apart from its sexual aspect. (On the question of sexual equality, see Chapter 5 below.) It is obvious that we are all better off if social tasks which are both essential and difficult to accomplish are

---

*That 7 to 1 ratio is very false to our experience of the extremes of economic reward and penalty in the United States, but it must be remembered that by dividing the population into income fifths, as did Jencks, we hide those extremes.

done by people capable of doing them well; that too is a truism. But the difference between democrats and neo-Platonic "meritocrats" (for whom Bell and Herrnstein seem to speak) is that the latter think we can discover *beforehand* who the "best" are, and indeed, like Plato, assume that the purely verbal phrase "best men" has a real corollary in real human societies. Democrats, on the contrary, see no evidence that there is a visible "elite" which can or should be nurtured, trained, and installed in office. Meritocrats from imperial China to contemporary France have asserted that people like themselves must be given a monopoly on office if a social order is to be "best." Democrats, on the other hand, propose that there are probably many more people capable of making intelligently forceful decisions than there are positions from which such decisions will be made; the most "successful" society will therefore be one that cultivates everyone's talents to the fullest and rotates as many people as possible into leadership roles.

We cannot establish, of course, who is right and who is wrong on that question. But we can make two points to sum up this discussion. First, in our own society, who fills those leadership roles seems to be much less important than what sorts of activities the structure of society encourages them to undertake. A good portion of what is done by the "best men" in our major business enterprises—planning sales campaigns, preserving commercial secrecy, restricting output and fixing prices, lobbying for government aid, engaging in international diplomacy, "informing the public" about the effects of products and processes (lying)—not only fails to add to real social wealth but may actually detract from it. If the price of "meritocracy" is the neglect of genuine responsiveness of elites to the people for whom, in the end, they work, that price may be much too high to pay. Or, to put it another way, if we follow Bell and Herrnstein in their definition of what an elite is, we may be defining it in a socially harmful manner.

Second, any implication that, on the evidence, there must be a small number of qualified people who can only be discovered by tests or other "meritocratic" arrangements is unwarranted, as is any implication that such people need be an insulated elite (or class). The distribution of IQ scores and their alleged and partial correlation with occupational rank is no guide at all to the amount of underlying intellectual talent that is potentially available to us. The millions of people who have been labeled "below average" by the IQ testers are "below average" only because every "normal" frequency distribution requires that a large number of observations be below (and above) average, not because they are humanly inferior or incompetent to do socially important work. Given what we know about the various conditions, ranging from the subtle to the manifestly hideous, which block the expression of human potential, and given also what we know about the ability of human beings to express an underlying trait in so many culturally diverse ways (with the appropriate training), we should probably reach a conclusion quite contrary to Herrnstein's. With respect to those inherited capabilities necessary for performing socially useful work, normal people probably vary much less than IQ tests are permitted to suggest, if only all were given a chance to develop their talents to the fullest. Thus the existence of genetic diversity among people should pose no serious obstacle to the attainment of any state of social equality we may desire to reach.

The only pragmatic truth offered by the analysis of IQ scores is the pragmatic truth that many people, including some academics, are well served by the status quo and will use any means, including that of making intellectually shoddy arguments, to help maintain it. But if IQ tests are to be put to the task of maintaining the status quo, there is no point in pretending that their "heritability" has anything to do with their utility for that purpose. IQ tests can be put to such use only because the realities of power and social-class division stand behind them; the assertion that they actually do measure some real aspect of human nature is no more than a meretricious attempt to sugar-coat that power and that class division. We choose for various historical reasons to reward the working and nonworking members of our society with greatly disparate incomes. That choice having been made, the population then sorts itself out into the existing income-generating positions according to various of its characteristics. Among these, IQ and whatever underlying native capacity it may reflect have only a negligible independent effect.

I concluded the previous chapter by suggesting that the existence of genetically different races within a society is not in itself a necessary obstacle to equality. That comment can now be extended. The present genetic condition of social classes suggests no inherent, necessary obstacle to the attainment of greater equality in the future; the pseudotheory of the heritability of IQ suggests no inherent obstacle to the attainment of greater equality in the future. The social policies of the past and the inertia of the present, not the genetic makeup of the population, cause our system of widely dispersed rewards to persist.

CHAPTER

RATIONALIZING
INEQUALITY: SEX

I. To get a complete picture of the prejudice and self-interest at work in the new inegalitarianism, we turn finally from questions of race and class to the question of sex, or gender. Within recent years, the sociobiology of sex has replaced the sociobiology of race as the cutting edge of inegalitarianism—perhaps owing to the fact that even in the United States it is more acceptable to proclaim the inferiority of women than the inferiority of blacks. In any event, male supremacy (like white superiority for Arthur Jensen and his followers) has now become the subject of "scientific" discourse.

The typical method of these efforts, which can be observed in the work of such popular sociobiologists as Lionel Tiger, Robin Fox, and even the more careful Edward O. Wilson, is to appear to establish some kind of sexual inequality in the case of primates and other animals, to "discern" a similar pattern for "primitive" or hunter-gatherer human societies, to note further the facts of male dominance in our own type of society, and then to "speculate" that "genes"—that is, evolutionary adaptation— account for the alleged regularity of this pattern. Quotation can only begin to convey the flavor of this kind of argument:[1]

The dominant male in hominid societies was most likely to possess a mosaic of qualities that reflect the necessities of compromise: "controlled, cunning, cooperative, attractive to the ladies, good with the children, relaxed, tough, eloquent, skillful, knowledgeable and proficient in self-defense and hunting." Since positive feedback occurs between these more sophisticated social traits and breeding success, social evolution can proceed indefinitely without additional selective pressures from the environment.

The list of basic human patterns that emerges from this screening technique [in which hunter-gatherer studies are studied] is intriguing . . . adult males are more aggressive and are dominant over females . . . the societies are to a large extent organized around prolonged maternal care and extended relationships between mothers and children. . . .

In hunter-gatherer societies, men hunt and women stay at home. This strong bias persists in most agricultural societies and, on that ground alone, appears to have a genetic origin. No solid evidence exists as to when the division of labor appeared in man's ancestors or how resistant to change it might be during the continuing revolution for women's rights. My own guess is that the genetic bias is intense enough to cause a substantial division of labor even in the most free and egalitarian of future societies. . . . Thus, even with identical education and equal access to all professions, men are likely to continue to play a disproportionate role in political life, business, and science.

General social traits in human beings, classified according to whether they are unique, belong to a class of behaviors that are variable at the level of the species or genus in the remainder of the primates (labile), or belong to a class of behaviors that are uniform through the remainder of the primates (conservative). . . . Evolutionarily conservative primate traits [include] aggressive dominance systems, with males dominant over females. . . .

Sociobiology relies heavily upon the biology of male-female differences and upon the adaptive behavioral differences that have evolved accordingly. Ironically, mother nature appears to be a sexist . . . at least where nonhuman animals are concerned. . . . Human social behavior is the product of many interacting factors and it is certainly unlikely that sexism is entirely biological. But it also may not be entirely cultural. One way of shedding more light is to make some predictions and try to interpret the realities. . . .

Assuming once again that human behavior has evolved to maximize individual fitness, interactions with others should be patterned with regard to genetic relatedness. . . . This has implications for differential male-female parental strategies. Women have the primary child-care roles in all human societies. Females know that they share 50 percent of their genes with their children, while males must take the female's word for it. It is therefore adaptive for females to invest heavily in the well-being of the children. Males are predicted to be less predisposed in this direction. . . . The woman can be counted upon to take care of the kids. She will lactate; he will not.

What will he do? Like the male hoary marmots inhabiting a highly social colony . . . the human male can maximize his fitness by interacting with other adults. By competing with other males, he can retain access to his female and also possibly attract additional mates. This line of reasoning thus provides further support for the "biology of the double standard" argument presented above, and it also suggests why women have almost universally found themselves relegated to the nursery while men derive their greatest satisfactions from their jobs.*

---

*This quotation is from a popularized presentation of sociobiology by David Barash, with an approving foreword by Wilson. There is something charmingly innocent in the reference to "hoary marmots"—the subject of Barash's own empirical work, actually. His point is that male marmots in colonies socialize only with other adults and pay no attention to "their" children, because they have neither a sexual nor (marmots being vegetarians that lack an opposable thumb and are therefore unable to be food gatherers) an economic function. In "isolated families," on the other hand, male marmots play with their children, "essentially because they have nothing better to do." The former, more typical behavior is said to be "adaptive" when "seen from the viewpoint of an individual male seeking to maximize his fitness." It apparently never occurs to Barash that human males live in "isolated families" at least as much as in "social colonies," and that unlike marmots they very definitely have an economic function even if they can't nurse their offspring. Thus he sails along into sociobiological reason-

Only a single lifetime is needed to generate the familiar pattern of sexual domination in a culture. When societies grow still larger [than a primitive hunter-gatherer society] and more complex, women tend to be reduced in influence outside the home, and to be more constrained by custom, ritual, and formal law. As hypertrophy proceeds further, they can be turned literally into chattel, to be sold and traded, fought over, and ruled under a double morality. History has seen a few striking local reversals, but the great majority of societies have evolved toward sexual domination as though sliding along a ratchet.

The average temperamental differences between the human sexes are also consistent with the generalities of mammalian biology. Women as a group are less assertive and physically aggressive. . . . The physical and temperamental differences between men and women have been amplified by culture into universal male dominance. History records not a single society in which women have controlled the political and economic lives of men. . . .

So at birth the twig is already bent a little bit—what are we to make of that? It suggests that the universal existence of a sexual division of labor is not entirely an accident of cultural evolution. But it also supports the conventional view that the enormous variation among societies in the degree of that division is due to cultural evolution. Demonstrating a slight biological component delineates the options that future societies may consciously select. Here the second dilemma of human nature presents itself. . . .

There is a cost, which no one can yet measure, awaiting

---

ing about human males without even noticing that neither kind of male marmot can in any way be a sociobiological paradigm for humans, although if anything the atypical noncolonial variety comes closer to filling that role. He also seems unaware of how inappropriate it is to describe marmots as though they were utility-maximizing neoclassical economists, or any other kind of human being with human motivations, living in institutions (the "isolated family," the "social colony") that are only metaphorically related to their human analogues (if such they are). This kind of naïve anthropomorphism makes one think that a century of advance in the philosophy and methodology of science has simply passed sociobiologists by.

the society that moves . . . from juridical equality of opportunity between the sexes to a statistical equality of their performance in the professions. . . .

If [a] new Adam and Eve could survive and breed . . . in total isolation from any cultural influences—then eventually they would produce a society which would have laws about property, rules about incest and marriage . . . initiation ceremonies for young men, courtship practices including the adornment of females . . . certain activities and associations set aside for men from which women were excluded. . . .

It would take a separate book to isolate the methodological fallacies and quantum leaps of ideological faith inherent in all of these passages. In general, though, what they possess in common (to use a favorite phrase of the sociobiologists) is the tendency to make an initial biological fact the cause of later social facts or alleged social facts, and to assume that evolutionary adaptation based on genetic selection accounts for the supposed fit between the two. This is assumed to be so even when (as in the third and fifth selections) no evolutionary mechanism can be specified that makes any sense at all of the result, especially given the fact that men and women in modernized societies have much more knowledge of the inputs into and significance of their behaviors than the inhabitants of "early hominid" societies.* They also possess the common characteristic of assuming that the relative invariance of a behavior suggests that there must be a biological foundation to it: a foundation so significant that (as the third, seventh, and eighth passages suggest) we must be very dubious about the prospects of changing the social structures that allegedly have been erected on that foundation. The over-all inference one is clearly meant to draw from this kind of proposition is that, as the phrase "evolutionarily conservative

---

*Are we supposed to believe, for example, that early hominid women knew they shared 50 percent of their genes with their children; or that in, say, modern Germany there is a socially or statistically significant difference between knowledge of paternity and knowledge of maternity? Or that there is a gene which, in a "natural selection" process extending over millions of years, somehow has favored and thus continues to be passed on by men who don't much care about their paternal role?

primate traits" and the last quoted passage make plain, relations of dominance and subordination between the sexes are probably the way they are because they make sense both biologically *and* socially.

These arguments are also virtually dataless, as a perusal of the surrounding materials in the original presentations will demonstrate: in every case there is nothing but an account of one or two animal species or early human societies, followed by a casual assertion of "universality" that goes no further than common prejudice. Thus a further stage in the development of sociobiological inegalitarianism has become the search for "hard" evidence of biologically determined inequality between the sexes from studies of the brain, the hormones, and the glands. A major thrust to produce both ethological and physiological studies of this kind is generated by the Harry Frank Guggenheim Foundation (for which Lionel Tiger and Robin Fox are research directors), which spends well over half a million dollars a year to support research on "the traits of dominance, aggression, and violence." Although the pattern of research support by the foundation in some areas is eclectic, the study of "dominance" and "aggression" has become, in general, a code for the attempt to establish biological male supremacy: an attempt which now generates dozens of studies per year in the United States, Latin America, and Western Europe.

Amidst this burgeoning research effort and literature one book, Steven Goldberg's *The Inevitability of Patriarchy*, unabashedly proclaims what the others only speculate about. The book has gone into two editions, the second incorporating a lengthy response to critics of the first. Goldberg has appeared on British television debating leaders of the women's movement; work by his popularizers appears in such choice publications as the *New York Times Magazine*; and the most famous of all sociobiologists, Edward O. Wilson, quotes him as a source of record on "the prevalence of male domination." (He is one of two sources for the generalization contained in the seventh selection quoted above.) Moreover Goldberg, just like Jensen, has been taken seriously, that is, viewed as a pathbreaking scholar whose work must be dealt with from now on as genuine social science. "A cogent answer to the propagandists of both sexes," a highly reputable sociologist perplexingly remarks (no *male* propagandist could possibly find anything to disagree with in it); "a brilliant new scholarly study," claimed the reviewer in *Harper's;* "the only work I have seen so far that links biology to social and political organization cogently," wrote a distinguished political theorist in a summation echoed by the reviewer for *Commentary*; even a critical (female) reviewer called the first edition of the book "objective." To drive home the meaning of all this critical acclaim, the cover of the second (paperback) edition informs us finally that "no one who wishes to be taken seriously on the subject of sex roles and political authority, or on all the questions of the male-female relationships, can ignore *The Inevitability of Patriarchy.* "[2] The plaudits may be far from the truth, but the last statement hits home, for as an artifact of propagandistic mythmaking Goldberg's work is inspired. He has taken a theme so central to the popular ideology of sex-role differentiation that it becomes crucial in works as far from ordinary patriarchalism as C. A. Tripp's *The Homosexual Matrix,* or Susan Brownmiller's *Against Our Will.* [3] Abandoning all camouflage, Goldberg reveals the real thrust of the sociobiological approach to women.

To be sure, Goldberg has no standing among the leading exponents of sociobiology, and one might well ask, Why not consider instead Wilson, or Tiger, as more indicative of the meaning of sexual hereditarianism? (though Wilson himself disavows Tiger). But to treat Goldberg as some kind of sport would be to misunderstand the sociology of ideas and the nature of attempts to establish a "science" of human behavior. For Goldberg has done nothing more than attempt to find an explanation for the sexual division of labor beyond vague evolutionary mysticism: an explanation that takes off from the propositions about aggression and dominance elaborated by Tiger and Wilson.

Goldberg takes three approaches, separable yet clearly associated, to establish "the inevitability of patriarchy"; together these approaches make up the methodological program of sociobiology in the realm of sex. First, he draws conclusions about human differences on the basis of animal and particularly primate studies. Second, he purports to find regularly observable *psychological* differences between male and female humans (see the seventh quotation above) which, he argues, can only be attributed to underlying physiological processes and structures. Third, he deduces from the alleged invariance of certain cultural or social formations which discriminate between men and women that there must be an underlying physiological root of such discrimination.

The fact is that these are the only approaches a sociobiologist can take to the question of male supremacy, since there is no empirical way to link individual biology with social behavior. All reasoning must thus proceed by deduction. That in itself is not a criticism of the sociobiology of sexual (or any other) relations, since much scientific reasoning proceeds in that very same way. However, the kinds of deductions that sociobiological "science" makes are not testable in the same way as are deductions in the physical sciences, for it is impossible to arrange to test a counterexample (e.g., we cannot arrange to study kinds of societies different from those that already exist, as we could arrange to create and study, in a laboratory, relationships between subatomic particles that do not appear in "nature"). Sociobiologists who want to study gender relations, therefore, will inevitably examine the same material Goldberg has, for there is no other choice—except to remain studiedly neutral on the subject by refusing to study it at all. Once committed to a program of "empirical" investigation of gender inequality, however, we cannot but uncover the same "facts" that Goldberg uncovers, or similar ones—at least, not if we proceed as sociobiologists. That is because, as noted earlier, assuming primarily biological causes of a social phenomenon leaves us unable to discover any but secondary social or historical causes of it. We are thrown back upon the assumption that genes or hormones must lie at the source of gender differentiation in social formations, and thus sociobiology almost inevitably slides over into inegalitarianism.

Alternatively, perhaps, we could argue either that gender differentiation is not very significant, or that it may be one of those social processes which is not implicated in human biological development. But few sociobiologists have made either of these arguments, and indeed, to make either of them would be to cut off one of the most noteworthy institutions of human society from study. The only thing Goldberg has done that is different from what any other sociobiologist would do (in addition to the straightforward ideological aggressiveness with which he presents his case) is to claim *already* to have discovered the causal, biological agent of gender inequality in human society. His biological inegalitarianism, however, inheres in the conventional procedures of any sociobiology that is prepared to view human social inequality as a biological phenomenon.

Put most simply, Goldberg's claim is that by nature women can never be the equals of men in the quest for positions of leadership either in society at large or in the home. He supports this assertion by arguing, first, that there never has been a society where women were the equals of men, and that this suggestive fact must be explained. Second, he offers as the definitive explanation the notion that men on the average, owing to their greater level of secretion of the "male" hormone testosterone, which allegedly produces our capacity for "aggressive" behavior, are much more likely than women to exhibit a *drive to dominance.* Although some women are more aggressive than some men, the overwhelming expectation of male superiority (in this sense) is internalized by most people, he speculates, as a generalized expectation that any particular woman is unlikely to have leadership capabilities. (This reasoning clearly can be applied in all areas where there is both male predominance and yet some overlap in the distribution of whatever traits produce the relevant skill: e.g., mathematics or engineering.) In the end, therefore, Goldberg's thesis seems like an extended commentary on Daniel Bell's remark, quoted earlier, that a society "that does not have its best men at the head of its leading institutions is a sociological and moral absurdity."

Goldberg specifies that in his usage the word "aggression" refers, not to "pugnacity or belligerence," but to a tendency variously to compete, to be enduringly single-minded in non-child-related pursuits, to sacrifice pleasure for control, to need to assert one's ego, to impose one's will on the environment, to resist doing what one has been told, to dominate in relationships with the other sex, and, he adds puzzlingly, "all the tendencies, emotions, and actions that represent these factors." He then says that these "tendencies, emotions, and actions" are "the connecting link between sexual hormonal differentiation and differentiated social institutions. . . . The voices of our hormones are *emotions,*" which themselves are the source of "virtually every important nonreflexive action taken by a human being." These hormonally generated emotions, he adds, should be thought of as "needs" or "feelings" which will be cued "in any conceivable social environment." For this reason, any environmental argument that posits the possibility of social change leading to sexual equality rather than patriarchy is inadequate, for the needful male behavior "is not primarily a function of values or economic factors, but of the psychology that males bring to any environmental setting, the 'needs' that any environmental situation will cue in individuals with this physiology, and the behavior that males manifest as they satisfy these 'needs.' The behavior is the behavior that I subsume under the term aggression."[4]

This is a remarkable passage. The problem with his argument is not that the tendencies he identifies (competitiveness, etc.) do not exist, for of course they do, nor that male dominance of hierarchical public life is not the way of the world, for of course it is. The problem rather inheres in the attempt, typical of all sociobiological inegalitarianism, to explain male dominance by "innate" tendencies which, as related specifically to maleness, exist chiefly in Goldberg's own imagination, or more broadly in our cultural imagination and its arsenal of ready-made stereotypes.

When we look more closely at these "tendencies" we see, first, that several of them are not tendencies leading to dominance behavior at all, but are simply descriptions of it. Of course dominant people are more competitive; dominance consists in entering and winning competitions. Of course dominant people have a greater tendency to impose their will, since dominance consists in the imposition of will (just as professional baseball players have a "tendency" to hit baseballs hard). And of course people who dominate the other sex have a tendency to dominate in relationships with the other sex. The question is, What has any of this got to do with being male? Some of the other aspects of the "aggression" construct that Goldberg lists might perhaps be described as emotional states or ego needs that are independent of, but can lead to, dominance behavior, but why are we supposed to believe that men actually have these emotions and needs in greater strength than do women? And though he may have identified some "ego needs" that can lead to dominance behavior, what reason have we to believe that dominance behavior is usually, let alone necessarily, based on these particular needs and emotions at all?

What Goldberg actually does is to "establish" the existence of men's ego needs by arguing that otherwise we could not explain the existence of dominance behavior. In the midst of all this verbal ingenuity, it is easy to forget that we have never actually made a controlled (or even an impressionistic) observation of any of these so-called ego needs and the emotions they generate in operation; we have been given no instruction in how to recognize them other than to assume that they must be present whenever we observe male dominant behavior; and nothing has been said to justify the assumption that male dominant behavior has anything to do with the presence (or absence) of these emotions. The whole argument, in fact, really has nothing to do with these "emotions" or "ego needs," which are an afterthought designed to answer criticisms of the simple physiological proposition that "hormonal differentiation" generates dominant behavior on the one hand and submissive behavior on the other. Faced with the argument that mere physical difference does not necessarily have any important effects in the realm of structured social behavior, Goldberg responds by turning the physical difference into a difference in comparative sexual psychology. But the chain of reasoning that enables him to make that leap has no content beyond simple, man-in-the-street prejudice.

Looking for a justification of the physiological proposition that is supposedly the foundation of the psychological theory and thus of the theory of patriarchy, we naturally turn to Goldberg's discussion of the "male" hormone, testosterone, and its effects. The first such reference begins with the promising remark that "only human biology is relevant to aggression: vague reference to other species is fraught with potential for abuse." But the next two sentences tell us that the promise will be broken: "However, there is one area of inquiry that falls between ethological data and the direct study of human biology; this is the experimental study of animals that resemble humans in the physiology of the system being studied. Those who categorically dismiss the possibility of the relevance to humans of such research should ignore this section."[5]

If this sounds very much as though Goldberg is now doing exactly what he has warned us against doing, that is indeed the case. It is not even that the "experimental study of animals" gives suggestive material to add to what we know about humans themselves. On the contrary, Goldberg apparently could not find a single study which demonstrates, or even implies, a direct relationship between "male" hormones and some relevant human behavior. (We can be sure that if such a study existed, Goldberg would have found it.) The best he can do is assert that "only the most fanatic purist or the behaviorist for whom such a conclusion would be intolerable would deny us the right to suspect strongly that the same central nervous system differences found in experimental animals will be found in the brains of men and women within ten years."[6] Most of that time is up as of this writing, and we have not yet heard from Goldberg or any other sociobiologist, but no matter. What is truly astonishing is that a biological mechanism so powerful and so invariant that it is held to cause an immense range of complexly differentiated political, social, and economic behaviors in humans should suddenly become nothing more than the object of a strong but apparently baseless suspicion. Such reasoning is typical of those biological inegalitarians who are often reduced to exploiting the animal kingdom in their otherwise fruitless search for "biological" causes of human social behavior, which they can never manage to observe among humans.

Their problem is that, as most of the "behaviorists" whom Goldberg slurs know well, there is good reason to doubt that anything definite about conscious states of mind in humans can be deduced from the work behaviorists have done with experimental animals. The nature of the central nervous system in experimental animals and in humans is irrelevant to any argument about human *social* behavior because human impulses and "emotions" are mediated by language and culture in a way that animal impulses are not. Thus, nothing about cultureless, languageless animals tells us how humans, with their much more complex and self-conscious perception of themselves and their environment, will or will not respond (except in the very simplest and most directly "animal-like" situations) to what in animals would be a clear-cut signal for a predictable act of "aggression."

Actually, even here I have overstated what we can learn from animal studies. Those studies, as several critics have recently demonstrated, are highly ideological even within their own discursive framework. That is, the experimenters or observers in some of the classic studies tended to impose not merely a "human" interpretation but a particular, ideological viewpoint in assessing what the animals had actually done in response to a stimulus: for example, ritualistic fighting behavior was interpreted as "aggression," and the interpretation was then overlaid with the emotions and ideology that sophisticated humans attach to that word. No one, however, has the slightest idea whether or not the animals were engaging in what we would consider acts of aggression.[7]

Like Arthur Jensen's "discovery" of the influence of genes on "intelligence," Goldberg's discovery of the influence of testosterone on structured dominance patterns among humans is thus nothing more than a hoax. No doubt men and women do have different amounts of both testosterone and estrogen in their makeup, and no doubt those hormones have some differential impact on certain behaviors. But as for evidence that these simple physiological "triggers" might have a determinative impact on our collective selection from among the many possibilities of complex social and political institutions available to us, there is none. The physiological component of the "aggression construct" is as meretricious as its psychological component is empty. We are implicitly told that there is empirical data—which does not really exist; that there have been observations—which have never in fact been made. That is the typical strategy of the biological inegalitarians: to postulate as the cause of unequal behavior an unobserved, untested agent and to pass over the truth that this agent has never been observed or tested with respect to that behavior. For a century or more they have been engaged in this kind of falsification: from Patrick Geddes' theory that "sperm and ovum exhibit the qualities of male *katabolism* to female *anabolism*," thus generating a "dichotomy between the temperaments of the sexes," to Goldberg's invention of the political effects of testosterone, nothing has changed except the sophistication with which popular stereotypes of female domesticity and male aggression are rationalized as eternal and natural.[8] If one theory doesn't work, the biological inegalitarians go on to the next, but all have the same pseudoscientific structure.*

II. Just as has always been the case with the inegalitarian-isms of race and class, we see that sexual inegalitarianism proc-eeds with a massive disregard of the ordinary canons of empiri-cal reasoning. That is only a part of the difficulty with it, how-ever. The argument for the inevitability of patriarchy, like a coin, has two sides, the first revealing a theory of the human organism and its nature, the second revealing a set of inferences (which cannot be dignified by the word "theory") about the na-ture of political and social behavior and institutions. The sociobi-ologists are typically innocent of any knowledge in this area; we might say they do not even have enough information to misuse it. Here Goldberg too proceeds via a series of conceptual mud-dles that, like his contempt for careful empirical argument, sug-gest the willful single-mindedness of an ideologue.

The particular kind of conceptual muddling by means of which he masks a child's-eye view of political life is *reification:* "the mistake of treating a notational device as though it were a substantive term"; of treating as one concrete entity what is actually only a word or a label attached to a variety of quite distinct concrete entities.[10] The labels here are "aggression" and "male dominance." (Note that the much more careful Wilson also uses these labels in the same manner.) The fallacy consists of lumping together an indiscriminately broad range of human behaviors or institutions under those two rubrics, and then treat-ing the rubrics as though they defined a *single* type of behavior and a *single* type of institution. It is an argumentative device peculiarly helpful to those who are trying to fit our various social orders and their possibilities into the straitjacket of monolithic

---

*According to one biologist who has done a thorough summary of the work on biological differences between males and females, we are next due to be inun-dated with a crash program of studies in the lateralization of the brain and the alleged effects of differences in brain laterality on the social behavior of males and females. Here too, it will only be possible to generalize such studies into a theory of male "superiority" in this or that endeavor by ignoring most of what else goes on in the world—i.e., cultural and environmental pressures that lead in the same direction as the alleged brain differences.[9]

biological causation and thus of "inevitability"—helpful, that is, if no one notices what is going on.

Thus, in the methodological essay from which I quoted earlier, Goldberg makes the following crucial comments:

> When we say that the environmental presence of a hierarchy (any hierarchy) or member of the other sex cues dominance behavior in the male we mean merely that the male feels, more strongly than does the female in the same environmental setting, the need to attain hierarchical and dyadic dominance (just as the female feels more strongly the need to cater to the crying infant). . . . So whenever a hierarchical situation arises it will be the males who have the greater need (who feel the greater pressure, whose feelings first motivate them to act in the appropriate way) to attain hierarchical dominance. . . . The "appropriate behavior" is that which we subsume under our construct. Now a hierarchical situation is, by its nature and definition, a competition for positions far more limited in number than the individuals who would like to attain those positions. The positions will be attained by those whose tendencies and action most nearly mirror that which is necessary for attainment, and these will be males.

As though to make the point even more strongly, he adds:

> There is no conflict between our discussing male-female differences in the behavior that is a precondition for hierarchical dominance in hormonal terms and the differences among males in non-physiological terms. Women (in general) are precluded from manifesting the necessary behavior by their lesser need for hierarchical attainment (and by the socialization that conforms to the reality of the males' greater need), so we need not present any other reasons why it is *always* males who attain.[11]

In an earlier discussion Goldberg somewhat tempered these comments, acknowledging that "an exceptional configuration of factors will someday result in a woman's being elected president." He insists, however, that authority will continue to be primarily associated with men, as much among women as among men; and over all, he again concludes:

> Male energies are directed toward attainment of desired positions and toward succeeding in whatever areas a particular society considers important. The fact that women lose out in these competitions . . . is an inevitable byproduct of the reality of the male's aggression advantage . . . [in that] because so few women succeed in these competitions . . . the society will attach different expectations to men and women (making it more difficult for the exceptional aggressive woman to attain such positions even when her aggression is equal to that of the average man).[12]

All in all, the argument is quite clear: whenever men and women compete for the same scarce good in "hierarchical" or "dyadic" situations, women (with rare exceptions that prove nothing) must lose. This proposition is stated even more explicitly by one of Goldberg's popularizers, George Gilder, writing in the *New York Times Magazine:*

> The hard evidence is overwhelming that men are more aggressive, competitive, risk-taking, indeed more combative, than women. In fact, even feminist scholars Carol Jacklin and Eleanor Maccoby, chairman of Stanford University's department of psychology, acknowledge decisive* biological differences between the sexes . . . [in] their scrupulously objective and voluminous text on the subject.[13]

Gilder then goes on to explain this phenomenon, following Goldberg, as "partly a result of greater aggressiveness and larger physical stature, partly an expression of the need to dominate." Again, we are left in no doubt as to the causal relationship between male aggressiveness and male dominance over women.

However, this assertion of the inevitability of male supremacy in direct male/female confrontations is quite false (except of course in sports, and anyone who thinks that athletic triumph is

---

*"Decisive" is a pure invention by Gilder.

what social life is all about can believe in male supremacy with a good conscience). Its falsity, moreover, has to do with the great diversity in the kinds of "hierarchies" and "dyads" we actually encounter, a diversity which Goldberg (and Gilder) ignore. We can see this in looking both at experimental evidence about male-female encounters (which Maccoby and Jacklin summarize at length in their "objective and voluminous text"), and at male-female confrontations in our own political universe.[14]

On the basis of the many experimental studies that have been undertaken, Maccoby and Jacklin conclude (quite contrary to what Gilder says they conclude) that aggression, which males do seem to have somewhat more of in certain forms, does not necessarily lead to domination. The reason for this discrepancy is that *successful aggression* in social life is quite a different affair from mere aggressiveness. We cannot assume that aggression will lead to dominance, but must discover for ourselves whether it really does so. Moreover, if Goldberg's thesis is borne out and it is superior male aggression that leads to male dominance, then that dominance must be based on compliance and submission by women, since we know that at least in our own society men do not rule women in the public political realm by direct force or the direct threat of force. (In any event, only a male dominance which is based on female compliance fulfills the hypothesis that knowledge of the male's greater aggressiveness is internalized in a decisive manner by all humans.)

Do we then find male dominance and female compliance in experimental or observational situations? There are indeed studies, Maccoby and Jacklin remark, which "have shown a remarkable degree of consistency between the dominance relations found among certain primates and those found among young human beings," but only, they add, "when dominance is defined as toughness." On the other hand, they point out, it is possible "that perhaps being tougher does not imply a generalized dominance among human children. If dominance is thought of as successful efforts by one person to control or manipulate the behavior of another, it is clear that there are many ways to do this other than through physical force or the threat of it." They then go on, logically, to investigate studies of compliance: for as Hotspur replied to Owen Glendower's boast that he could call spirits from the vasty deep, "Why, so can I, or so can any man;

but will they come when you do call for them?" Is the expectation of male dominance a generally internalized expectation, as
Goldberg asserts?

Again, according to Maccoby and Jacklin's summation of
the available experimental evidence for our society, the answer
seems to be that although men do direct more dominance-ori-
ented behavior toward women than vice versa, "girls are not
generally more compliant, conforming, or suggestible than boys
across all subject matters and sources of influence"; they will
not come when called. (This finding would not have surprised
Freud, who once said ruefully that "the aggressive impulses of
little girls leave nothing to be desired in the way of abundance
and violence.") The one exception to this generalization which
shows up in the studies they summarize is that girls are more
likely to be compliant toward adult authority figures of either
sex (parents and teachers) than boys, although, as they add, "It
is possible that girls form a coalition with the more dominant
adults as a means of coping with the greater aggressiveness of
boys, whose dominance they do not accept." But in adulthood
itself, the most that can be said is that "neither sex shows an
overall tendency to be more susceptible to social influence from
peers."[15]

These various experimental findings, inconclusive as all experimental studies of human subjects must be, at least help us
assess more clearly what actually does go on, as opposed to
Goldberg's and Gilder's *assertions* about what goes on, in the
real worlds of dyadic and hierarchical leadership. As the Jacklin
and Maccoby remarks about "toughness" indicate, and as ought
to be perfectly obvious, the types of "competition" that do take
place in the social world, and the types of "dominance" that
result, are strikingly different from each other. Let us look first,
for example, at direct competition between men and women over
scarce goods, so that a man's gain is a woman's loss and vice
versa. Offhand we can think of three types of this direct competition between men and women in our own society: competition
about the making of laws or the assertions of claims to rights
that will affect men and women differentially, and are known to
have that effect and intention; competition for office; and competition for authority within the nuclear family.

The first two types of competition are conventionally political; and although we have few hard data about them as such, what we have casts a different light on the hypothesis of the *inevitability* of patriarchy. In no case (Switzerland being perhaps an exception) has a mass movement of women for the vote —the basic equal right that women originally were denied in parliamentary societies—been long resisted by men. Of all the instances of male-female competition outside the family, this has certainly been the most clear-cut, and the results are unequivocal. It will not do for Goldberg to claim that the suffrage was granted to women by the altruism of men, for the theory of patriarchy makes no room for "altruism" in men's combat with women (altruism, according to Goldberg, is one of the virtues of women): men want only to be dominant when in direct confrontation with women. In any event, women in most societies endured a good deal of violence from men, and it did not deter them for long. Nor could it be claimed that the men who supported women's suffrage were merely following out the dictates of their own political beliefs, or hoping to gain some kind of political advantage, for that would be to say that the hormonal drive is so weak that it can be overcome by mere ideas about political values and short-run political expediency. Nor, finally, can it be claimed that universal suffrage is a mere façade behind which patriarchy still holds secret sway, for if male dominance is inevitable why did men not simply do the obviously "patriarchal" thing and continue to deny women the vote? It is quite true, of course, that women did not gain full citizenship in any real sense when they gained the vote; they remain massively discriminated against, on precisely the grounds Goldberg advances, in all societies that have universal adult suffrage. But though an outside observer would indeed have to argue (as I shall later; see Chapter 6 below) that the meaning and thus the power of mere suffrage in itself were greatly overestimated by both the suffragists and their opponents, that argument is mostly hindsight; the energy and passion that went into that fight was as much as either side could muster at the time—and women won the battle.

In most modern states, similarly, anyone who directly opposes equal rights for women is immediately put on the defensive. The fate (at this writing) of the Equal Rights Amendment in the United States should not be allowed to obscure the issue, for in fact that amendment easily passed every test it would have had to pass in a strictly majoritarian setting. As it happens, the American constitutional system heavily loads the dice against all social change, and women are only incidentally the victims of this arrangement (slaves and the propertyless being its original targets). But the history of politics in the advanced industrial societies is a history of, among other things, one advance after another in this area, as old rules about property, authority over children, the right to sue, and restrictions on work fall by the wayside. Only in the realm of what are today called "reproductive rights" has resistance been steadfast, and then only in some societies. The biological theorist will have to explain what it is about the biology of Swedish men or Japanese men (the latter not especially noted as champions of sexual equality) that made those nations pioneers in the legalizing of abortion on demand; or why the fight over birth control in the United States divided not men from women but Protestants from Catholics; or why the most elite body of men in the United States tortured the Bill of Rights virtually out of shape in order to declare the unconstitutionality of laws prohibiting abortion on demand. Again, it will not do to adduce policy considerations, such as demographic or economic problems, or ideological antagonisms; these may in fact explain why women have won most of the battles they have won, but the inevitability of patriarchy dwindles to nothing more than a strong likelihood if its laws and institutions can be overthrown by merely contingent material changes. Of course, since many women accept the cultural stereotypes of themselves as morally superior but politically and materially inferior to men, these advances have been brought about only by alliances between female and male reformers; but on Goldberg's reasoning it is inexplicable that men supporting gender equality should overcome men opposing it. Indeed, that outcome is only comprehensible if we emphasize the determination and strength—that is, the "aggressiveness"—of the female input.

As for competition for elective office, we would think, surely, that no application of the theory of patriarchy could be more clear-cut: "the positions will be attained by . . . males." But that is not always so, even if James Callaghan might like to believe it. Women lose elections against men, and women win elections against men. Given the historical exclusion of women

from electoral politics, and given the fact that a substantial
minority of every electorate still thinks of them as second-class
citizens, they still lose more often than they win.* To see just
how deeply erroneous is Goldberg's claim, we need only consider
the fate of women in electoral competitions as compared with the
fate of blacks (in the United States). In the last quarter of the
twentieth century we can often predict the outcome of a black/
white competition for electoral office in most states and cities of
the Union knowing virtually nothing but the racial makeup of
the electorate. Where whites predominate, the white candidate
will win except in rare instances; the black candidate cannot win
if the white even subliminally succeeds in polarizing the electorate. But male candidates make few if any attempts to polarize
the electorate by gender, a tactic they would surely adopt, and
successfully adopt, if Goldberg were correct about the expectations of men *and women*. In short, even in the United States
(where female causes and female candidates have a harder time
than in strictly parliamentary regimes in which parties adopt
issues and candidates are elected as representatives of their
parties), Goldberg's assertion that men *must* defeat women in
competition is simply and demonstrably false. Of course, women
lose out dramatically (and in fact fare worse even than blacks in
the United States) in the process of *recruitment* for positions
of authority, including candidacy for political office. But it is the
behavior of men, already monopolizing those positions and desir-
ing for whatever reasons to maintain their monopoly, which
explains recruitment patterns. (The chief of those reasons is
undoubtedly the propensity of people to feel more comfortable

---

*However, the fact of women's second-class citizenship, and the compelling need
for "affirmative action" to abolish it in many social arenas (see Chapter 6 below)
should not mislead us into romantically pessimistic conclusions about the political status of women in the United States or elsewhere. Given the conditions of
competitive party politics, it only takes a committed minority against change to
paralyze movement on any issue which sharply divides the polity. Thus in the
United States, where an antifeminist backlash has perhaps been more aggressive than in any other liberal society, all the evidence is that the sexual
inegalitarians of both sexes are in a decided minority. They are, however, in a
position to make their single-minded dedication count politically, and that is
particularly so because, owing to centuries of exclusion, the pool of potential
female leaders, spokeswomen, and "role models" for *egalitarian* commitment
is comparatively so limited.

with those they describe as being "like" themselves; a propensity strengthened in this case by the heavily "masculine" cast which men have given to the language, humor, and behind-the-scenes behavior of political life, women in many cases being the derided object of all three.) No evidence exists that women exclude themselves from recruitment by virtue of their own diffidence—a negative proof which, though no more than suggestive, will hardly surprise anyone who has observed the great number of dynamic and forceful women whose apparent energy is not being put to use in our society's decision-making institutions.[16]

Of course, all of this has now been made perfectly obvious by the rise of a highly politicized feminism all over the world (a trend to which Goldberg appears completely oblivious). Has there been some quantum jump in the amounts of testosterone secreted by women? Or especially by educated women, who have spearheaded the movement everywhere? Women are now much readier than they ever were to engage in direct political combat with men, and biological data cannot account for political events such as the occurrence of "patriarchy," its apotheosis, or its subsidence. What explains political movement is what has always explained it: a change, however brought about, in the real interests of a large number of people combined with the perception by some of them that the change has occurred; and with the conceptualization of a means for responding to it on the part of people who know how to persuade others. As a concrete example, we can think of Margaret Thatcher's belief in old-fashioned bourgeois liberalism, combined with a class-conscious resentment of social democracy, an ability to present that ideological position more compellingly than others, a dedication to make the world conform to her ideas of right and wrong, and a social position from which it was feasible to launch a career based on that dedication. None of that either requires or is compatible with an explanation based on hormones or expectations derived from them.

It is even more striking to see what we discover when we look at the kind of direct sexual confrontation that occurs within the family. In linking "dyadic" and "hierarchical" structures with each other, Goldberg quite clearly implies the conclusion—necessitated by his notion of the inevitability of patriarchy—that

men monopolize authority in nuclear families. But again the
fairly substantial literature on this subject fails to bear out his
hypothesis (except, as we will see, in one limited sense that
actually weakens rather than strengthens that hypothesis).[17]
We will only miss this point if we confuse the traditional legal
and institutional subordination of and constraints on women in
the family with the actual interpersonal dynamics of familial
behavior. As to the latter, who holds the reins of authority in the
nuclear family appears to be an open question, depending much
more on the situation and the personalities of the people concerned than on anything about their genders. Where men in
modern societies clearly have had the upper hand—as in the
distribution of property rights or decisions about where to locate
the family—it has been due to factors entirely external to the
individual male/female relationship, namely, the state of the
laws and the identity of the main breadwinner in the average
family. (The first of these, moreover, can be and, as noted above,
has been changed.) On the other hand, we might think that the
decision whether to have children, and how many, is at least as
central to family life as these; many men will certainly be aston-
ished to find out that they are always dominant in that realm.
Once property rights are equalized and the economic factor inop-
erative for whatever reason, a real fight for control over the
family will usually come down to a struggle marked by various
kinds of attempted emotional blackmail. The husband's threat to
use physical force may well be a part of that struggle—but
nothing we know about marriage can lead us to think that the
"winner" can ever be predicted.

No doubt men often can and will resort to force to settle the
question of dominance in the family (though surely much wife-
beating has nothing to do with decision-making strategy but is
rather a simple outburst of generalized frustration or anger, and
comes about because hitting his wife is often the only thing a
man can be successful at). But at this point Goldberg's reification of the term "male dominance" finally betrays him completely. For real physical abuse, or the threat of it, most often
represents the husband's acknowledgment that he has lost control over the family, that he cannot obtain "dyadic" dominance
and is thus reduced to substituting naked force for legitimate
authority. It is true that wife-beating is and possibly always has

been epidemic (if not endemic), but to say that is quite different from saying that *therefore* women expect men to dominate them and accept the institutionalization of that domination. On the contrary, women are afraid that domination might occur—that is, that men might use superior force to punish or compel them —and they often work to prevent that, either singly or in concert. There is no evidence that most women think such brute domination is either natural or necessary. To put the case in Goldberg's own terms, men resort to force, not because there is an expectation that they must rightfully dominate, but because no such expectation exists.

III. Thus we see that Goldberg commits two major conceptual errors in his use of the notion of "aggression." He first confuses direct physical aggression of men against women, which occurs in "dyadic" relationships (or is otherwise considered criminal in most societies), with the quite different kind of "aggression" inherent in a fight over comparative social status. The two types of "dominance" that may result are also entirely different from each other, and Goldberg naturally confuses them also. It is possible for superior physical force to tell in a dyadic relationship, but at least in modern societies it is no longer decisive (at any rate between the sexes) in "hierarchical" relationships.

In its most obvious application Goldberg's biological argument is simply wrong. In tacit admission of this failure, Goldberg offers an alternative version of the "aggression" construct in which it is not men's will to dominate over women that leads to male monopoly over public authority, but rather a universal deference tacitly paid men by virtue of a recognition that if they are not paid that particular kind of homage—if their special ego needs are not met—their pent-up physical aggression will explode. As he puts it at one point, women will not be appointed to head bureaucracies because we all know that men in their tremendous emotional need will not be able to stand being under female authority (we must assume that this is a true account of Goldberg's own feelings): orderly governance will be wrecked by men's sexual rebellion, and chaos and old night will rule.[18] We might call this aspect of gender war indirect competition between men and women.

If we are to believe that fear of pent-up aggression is the fundamental factor in the social selection of leaders, then surely it must follow that in all social formations those whose dedication to pacific behavior is most suspect, whose aggressiveness is most ready to be unleashed at the slightest provocation, will be the ones selected. But is that actually the case?

Surely not. To begin with, Goldberg's application of terms like "leadership" and "competition" to both primitive and advanced industrial societies (and all other kinds of social formation) is another glaring example of the fallacy of reification. The expectation of force and the appreciation of its uses may very well be more central in certain primitive societies, but that does not mean that the choice of leaders is necessarily based on their reputation for being forceful and aggressive. On the contrary, though Goldberg entitles his work "the inevitability of *patriarchy,*" he seems not to realize that in many such societies patriarchal competition for leadership hardly takes place in our sense, for (as far as we can tell) there is no concept of a "career" leading, if one follows its charted paths "aggressively," to leadership. On the contrary, in "classical" patriarchies legitimate authority passes to what we would call eldest sons (though the actual kinship relation might not be the same in every society) regardless of how they behave; and leadership in the larger social group—the village, the tribe, the commune—falls on some among those eldest sons who have reached a certain age. The selection of leaders, in other words, is rule-bound and hardly at all subject to deliberate manipulation by people choosing to behave in one way or another, forcefully or otherwise. Leadership is also, in all "primitive" societies, task-specific, devolving upon those with appropriate skills in particular situations. And of course we can see this lack of attention to ambition and aggression even more clearly by reversing the coin of our observation, so to speak: in our society a woman who is skillful and ambitious enough can attain to leadership—but that is impossible in a true patriarchy, where ambition and skill, let alone sublimated frustration, are not rewarded.

The theory that "universally" leaders are chosen out of a concealed psychic process that makes a fearful expectation of the use of force the root of all public behavior is thus false. Even more important, it is also systematically false in our own experience of life. For despite the prevalence of international or civil warfare around the globe at any given moment, there are many societies in which most political offices are far removed from the expectation of overt or even sublimated violence.

What Goldberg has done (perhaps unwittingly, since like most biological reductionists he knows nothing of politics) is first to have confused aggressiveness with the ability to issue authoritative commands, and then compounded his error by confusing the ability to issue commands with the capacity to hold political office or exercise informal political powers. Perhaps, having encountered various definitions of "power" as the ability to get others to obey one's commands, he has failed to understand their operational significance. Most political life in legalistic societies is most definitely *not* carried on by the giving of commands, except in the formal and limited sense that by virtue of the position one fills one is able to pass on commands issuing elsewhere—the "elsewhere" very often being the pages of a statute or rule book, as interpreted by a quite unaggressive functionary. By and large, in this process negotiating and bargaining and other manipulative abilities are much more likely to be called into play than is any tendency to "dominate." By the same token, one is much more likely to fill positions of less-than-ultimate political authority by having taken exams, gone to certain schools where useful contacts were made, picked up certain kinds of useful knowledge, or been a willing dogsbody for a local or regional political machine or economic bureaucracy than by having developed and expressed a striving for dominance.*

We advance through hierarchies at least as often, and probably a great deal more often, by doing what we've been told to do than by exhibiting what Goldberg calls the male's "relatively great resistance to doing what one has been told to do." We do not seize power; we wheedle our way into it. The flow of excess testosterone in experimental animals causes biting and scratching behavior—but we know what will happen to the ambitious man who bites or scratches (or kicks or punches) just one competitor for power in a complex organization. To use the single

*Robert Dahl's classic study of New Haven politics, *Who Governs?*, notes one commentator, reveals that "contrary to the public image of political leaders as uniformly scheming 'politicos,' a large proportion of our leaders enter politics in a way that may be more accurately described as drifting than as climbing."[19]

word "aggression" to refer to these extraordinarily differentiated types of behavior is completely to lose our intellectual moorings—and those who think the behaviors are not different should ask themselves if they have ever seen an ambitious rat, a charismatic hamster, or a corrupt baboon.

The difference between animals and humans, in other words, is that whereas in animals the direct effect of testosterone secretion always leads to "success" of a kind, its direct effect on human behavior—that is, the general aggressiveness and readiness for physical encounter of the "oversexed," bumptious teen-age boy—would, if it persisted into maturity, disqualify a man for a wide range of leadership positions in any technologically complex society.

This general discrepancy between merely physical behavior and political behavior shows up most clearly in one study which Goldberg manages not to mention in his pursuit of alleged empirical data, though it must have been available to him.[20]* Testosterone levels were measured for a group of twenty-one young men in prison. The men with higher testosterone levels in their blood sample had committed more violent crimes during adolescence—that is, more crimes of "aggression." If Goldberg's animal data mean anything at all, then perhaps testosterone really had induced, or made possible, a higher level of adolescent aggression. (There are many "ifs" in the interpretation of these data, of course.) But as "dominators" these men are total failures, their environment totally out of control, no positions of

---

*Goldberg does discuss at length, as does Wilson, the famous Money-Ehrhardt study of girls whose genitalia had been masculinized *in utero* when their mothers were given artificial progestin, a male hormone. But the use to which the sociobiologists put this study is more comical than anything else. They emphasize, for example, the fact that the masculinized girls tended to be tomboys who preferred wearing slacks to dresses, without explaining how that preference could be "biological" when in some cultures males wear the equivalent of dresses and females the equivalent of slacks. They both also emphasize the athletic ability and interest of the tomboys, but there is not the faintest evidence, or reason to believe, that that kind of ability in either children or adults bears any relationship to the kinds of aggression, or ambition, or whatever, that produce leadership among adults. Money and Ehrhardt themselves have been careful not to claim that the study proves anything about the relationship, if any, between biological masculinity and sociological "maleness," an obviously sensible precaution on their part, since it is impossible to disentangle cause from effect in the behavior of the affected girls.[21]

leadership or decision-making available to them. When out of prison they can probably find women to beat, but if that is what Goldberg means by dominance in a "dyadic" situation his argument is, again, hopeless. Rather than being a related version of hierarchical dominance, as he has it, this kind of "dominance" is available to and practiced chiefly by men who are incapable of achieving hierarchical dominance. The study strengthens our view that the two kinds of behavior are, if not opposed, at least distinct; on the only evidence so far available to us, testosterone explains how men attain the status of convicts a good deal more easily than it explains how they attain the status of leaders.

In the end, Goldberg's understanding of leadership is limited almost entirely to the kinds exercised by the chief executive and military leaders in a society which uses competitive elections of one kind or another to fill the former post, and expects to have to engage in war at some point or other. He is unable to speak to the kinds of authoritative behavior expected from political or organizational subordinates (which is to say, most decision-makers in an organizational world). His proposition is irrelevant to the choice of members of a primarily deliberative body; of an administrative bureaucracy, a judicial system, or any other set of positions filled according to real or alleged merit; of ideologically defined delegates to an assembly or tribunal; or of officeholders in any system marked by the institution of regular rotation in office. Needless to say, his "theory" is also irrelevant to an explanation of how power is attained in hereditary monarchies, of which there have probably been more in human history than any other kind of political system, and which place absolutely no stress upon any "will to dominance" in either males or females—many of them having gone so far as to allow the succession to pass to females (see below, pages 155–56). In sum, if we put the very best (and undeserved) face on the biological theory, the most it has "proved" is the unequal likelihood of male success in the quest for one particular and very untypical kind of political office in one particular kind of political society.

Thus we see the sociobiology case requires, in addition to the massive exercise in reification that insists on treating labels like "aggression" and "dominance" as concrete, uniform things rather than loose guides to a very diverse reality, the further reductionist argument that what is *real* about human society is not what we actually observe. We are to ignore the prevalence of nonviolent, bargaining behavior in various collectivities, and notice only those aspects of existence we share with animal species: the dominance of instinct, the irrelevance of reason and language, the resort to force. All human institutions in which reason rules, instinct is subordinated, and the resort to force is infrequent are to be ruled out as epiphenomenal: mere appearance rather than reality.

This continual redefinition of the alleged source of "patriarchy" has for the ideologue the special attraction (as such saving redefinitions always do) of making the supposed causal agent of "male dominance" something that can never be observed—a subconscious expectation inhabiting the same murky realm as those clever and unobserved genes that, according to Jensen, after millions of years have managed to differentiate human beings according to their chess-playing abilities. The descent into mystification serves both political and intellectual purposes. Politically, we clearly can't do anything about that which can't even be seen. Intellectually, Goldberg is relieved of the obligation of having to present real evidence for "the inevitability of patriarchy"; and, like Senator Joseph McCarthy asserting that the abstention of an ex-Communist from subversive activity was a sure sign that he was still secretly engaged in it, is able to argue that the absence of visible "aggression" in leadership behavior is a sure sign that underneath everything it really exists. But it is not coincidental that the biological inegalitarians race from one fallacy in empirical reasoning to the next: that is what the ideologue must do who is trying to create an eternal, unbreachable "ought" out of an ever-shifting "is" that even now is changing before his, and our, very eyes.

IV. To be sure, in our civilization women always have manifested, and still do manifest, a good deal less "aggression" in and "ambition" for public life than do men. There are so many perfectly obvious reasons why this should be so—ranging from institutionalized patterns of socialization to the apparent demands of family life to harassment by men—that the search for a biological explanation seems nothing less than willful. The ideologues of inequality search for a timeless cause of that condition precisely because the social universe with which we are most familiar has changed drastically and is still undergoing change. The reality of our situation, furthermore, is that women have been major participants in and on occasion major beneficiaries of the process of change—so much so that, gradually, the force behind all those causes of the persistence of "patriarchy" is becoming attenuated.

To take only the most obvious instance, the kind of authority men now exercise with respect to women is entirely different from that which existed in, say, fourteenth-century Europe. In fact, the kind of direct authority men had over women in previous civilizations, both politically and in the home, does not even exist any more. Men do not have property in women or legal authority over them; they have only, first, the support of a tradition of sexual inequality, and second, as long as they can keep it, an unrepresentative chance to fill impersonal positions of authority. Moreover, in the world of production (and reproduction) the change even during the past century from a low-technology to a high-technology social system is so awesome that familiar clichés about all the rest of humanity living more like each other than any lived like those of us who inhabit modern industrial societies are hardly off the mark at all. To say, therefore, that men dominated women then and still dominate them now is to deny that anything has happened while almost everything has been happening. And to say that because men dominated women in the past they must do so in the future is to be guilty of an astonishing *non sequitur.*

Furthermore, even within the last generation, in the United States and elsewhere, the political position of women has been undergoing a major transformation. The American literature of this transformation is by now quite extensive, and we need not rely on merely impressionistic observations of it.[22] Among the striking developments pointed up by that literature are the increased readiness of Americans of both sexes to support a female presidential candidate (the British, of course, have far surpassed Americans in this regard); the massive influx of women into local and state electoral politics and public administration; the extent to which voter mobilization in statewide and national elections is a task that has fallen on professional women and housewives; the proliferation of interest-group and community political activities by and for women; first signs of the mobilization of working-class women into political activity, including the affairs of trade unions; and most decisive of all, the creation of a plethora of self-help organizations aimed explicitly at teaching women how to do politics: how to campaign for office, appeal to voters, define issues, and so forth.

Moreover, the legal status and accomplishment of women is not the only aspect of political life that has changed drastically over the centuries. In the age of democracy the nature of political authority in general has changed as well in every important respect. Equality is the norm of modern societies, and never more so than in the political realm itself. To this development Goldberg seems to be quite blind. As noted earlier, from his Hobbesian standpoint decision-making and productive relationships seem to occur only in centralized, executive-determined bureaucracies. We might all as well be living in the age of Louis XIV as in an era of constant and notorious struggle over the very definition and disposition of legitimate authority.

A typical assessment of the era, appearing in the *New York Times* toward the end of the 1970s, generalizes my remark about the proliferation of women's interest groups in saying that "a strong new political force—forged from the proliferating local activist organizations formed to stabilize and renew neighborhoods—has grown to maturity in America." The *Times* goes on to add that "this lobby is replacing traditional institutions that have lost their vigor and credibility"; that it is "now generally considered to add an important new dimension to participatory democracy"; and that the new activists—despite being perceived as "radicals"—"have been winning legislative and policy battles against both city and Federal officials."[23]

Certain institutions which we have taken for granted until very recently are quite clearly being called into question, so much so as to generate defensive reactions from some antiegalitarian political theorists who now worry about "the ungovernability of democracies."[24] Those institutions include not only the hierarchical centralization of decision-making in both political and economic institutions, but of even more importance for Goldberg's thesis, in authorized representation as well—or at least our traditional view of it. In that (Hobbesian) view, we empower persons to exercise authority over us in our name but not under our control; not just presidents, governors, and mayors but even members of a parliament, a congress, or a city council are to some significant degree thought of in that light. But that kind of empowerment is exactly what has been challenged here and abroad during the past two decades, and as a notion of representation it is now clearly on the defensive. Instead, on issue after issue, in jurisdiction after jurisdiction, the notion of representation as direct delegation, and of leadership as strictly responsive, is on the rise.

The personal delegation of restricted authority, quite obviously, makes the representative's leadership role a much more limited one than does his or her empowerment. And what is significant about the "proliferation" to which the *Times* refers is that the organizations of which it speaks are tending to cast aside the old style of leadership, or even to see that itself as the enemy. Instead of leadership being asserted by the ambitious individual, in the new model it is created by constituencies who choose representatives (that is, spokespersons) on the basis of declared interest, expertise, skill in bargaining, verbal ability, and trustworthiness. "Aggression" and "hierarchy" are only secondary values in this model; the primary values become emotional bonds of community and consensus. In this new democratic perspective the characterological disadvantage of women, if there is one, tends to disappear, and the underrepresentation of women among the new activists becomes a function of nothing more than their current underrepresentation in the pool of experts and other trained people from whom spokespersons are likely to be drawn. Above all, the new grassroots politics with its norm of responsive representation demands that like represent like; it therefore becomes less acceptable for men to represent women on issues about which they (or some among them) tend to differ as groups, and the pool of female leaders must *ipso facto* be extended. By the same token, as the exclusion of women from positions of responsibility in productive organizations gradually becomes more and more unacceptable, and if policies are adopted that successfully overcome that exclusion, there will be further increments to the number of women trained to engage in one kind or another of leadership role in technologically advanced societies. Concentration on glamorous positions of national leadership tends to hide all these developments from our view, but it is what happens today in grassroots and in educational and productive and service institutions, where effective leadership behavior is learned, rather than at the visible top, that will determine the shape of our future.

V. We have seen, then, that Goldberg's positive case for the necessity of male dominance is worthless. There is still, of course, what might be called his negative case, his argument that no other theory of the universality of male dominance is imaginable: that is the second of his two simple propositions about the inevitability of patriarchy. But as it happens, this proposition turns out to be as tendentious as the other.

To be sure, gender differentiation is both universal and self-evidently biological in its origins, but to think that the symbols of that differentiation are also biological is to confuse the basic phenomenon with its contingent side-effects and symbolic elaborations. To explain the recurrence of any particular symbol system in diverse cultures, we need ask only if the system serves some reasonable purpose. Differentiation itself often serves cultural or political purposes, but the most obvious factor in the perpetuation of a particular symbol in one or many cultures is that those who benefit from it have the power to perpetuate it; and those (if there are any) who do not benefit from it, or benefit from it less, or are aware that they benefit from it less, lack the power to change it. Seen in this light, the recurrence and perpetuation of male supremacy in politics is not difficult to understand.

Of course, no historical explanation purporting to deal with the entire range of human cultural phenomena can really be anything more than a useful guess. Sociobiologists seem to be in a rage to believe that we can construct a "scientific" explanation of the murky, really invisible human past—for most of which we have at best third-hand evidence inextricably marked by our own biases and prejudices. Theirs is a mental state less in need of a natural scientist to point out the hopelessness of the desire than of a psychiatric therapist to uncover its origins. The crucial difference between explanations of social phenomena is not in their "scientific validity" but in the purposes they serve. Goldberg's explanation, like that of other sociobiologists, is designed primarily to create a sense of resignation in the minds of people, especially dissatisfied people, and thus inhibit the resort to collective social action. Nonbiological explanations, by contrast, are often designed to demonstrate that collective social action aimed at social change may yet prove fruitful. Since there is not the slightest hope that anyone will ever "know" for sure why the past was as it was, our choice among competing plausible explanations really tells much more about what we hope to accomplish in the present and future than it does about our scientific method.

Essentially, Goldberg's canvass of the history of male domination limits itself to hunter-gatherer societies and modern industrial societies; we can add to it as well a consideration of the great agrarian/trading civilizations, from ancient Egypt to feudal Europe. The question he asks is, How can there be other than a biological explanation for the appearance of institutions of male supremacy in these various historical cultures? The only puzzle, though, is not the one implied by the question, but rather why he thinks the question so daunting in the first place.

The emphasis on hunter-gatherer societies takes up a good part of *The Inevitability of Patriarchy*, as well as of Lionel Tiger's *Men in Groups* and similar documents of male supremacism. That is not surprising. It is a long tradition in political and social thought to justify theories of "human nature" by reference to human groups designated as "primitive," who are presumed to be closer to "nature" and thus to being "natural man" (or woman) than the more sophisticated people who are observing them. For more than two centuries each new claim by a traveler or other outside observer to have discovered the "real" nature of primitive life and thus putatively of human life in "the state of nature" has become the subject of intense debate. Goldberg's approach to this debate, unfortunately (and in this also he is a typical sociobiologist), is to treat the ambiguously perceived subject matter of dispute and arcanely differentiated interpretation as a set of self-evident "facts."*

*Cultural anthropology is inherently a study in ambiguity, since our knowledge of the meaning to the participants in them of cultural institutions different from our own must always be different from, if not less than, their own knowledge. Anthropology is therefore a discipline in a constant state of self-criticism—of most of which Goldberg (like Tiger) seems unaware.

It is not simply that what seems like "male dominance" to the outsider with his or her own cultural expectations may feel like no such thing to the subjects of the observation; or vice versa. More to the point, even in those societies discussed by Goldberg, where it seems clear enough that the sexual division of labor favors men over women, the political institutionalization of leadership may not be as closely related to that division of labor as it is in our own. Since leadership in most hunter-gatherer societies is neither specialized nor centralized but instead is task-specific and diffuse (as far as we can tell), any notion of a biological necessity that produces, as Goldberg has it, a distinctive and universal psychology of male leadership must be sheer invention. Hobbes was closer to a description of his own society than of the "state of nature"; Goldberg may have perceived the sexual reality of hunter-gatherer societies, but he has completely missed their diverse political reality.

That male *political* dominance is truly "universal" is, then, a meaningless or tendentious assertion.* However, that point is made only to demonstrate the nature of the inegalitarian argument. On the whole, probably everyone would be satisfied with the observation that in most hunter-gatherer societies what passes for political decision-making (in our terms) seems to fall to male hands on a systematic basis. But it is not at all difficult to offer an account of this tendency with no reference to biology at all. Generalized institutions of male dominance would surely have come about in the first instance simply because men are on the average stronger, and the less complicated are cultural institutions, the more likely is the question of dominance to be decided by simple physical superiority. As to why the question of dominance should have arisen at all, a sexual division of labor must have been perceived as the obvious prototype for any fundamental division of labor: the easiest to arrange and, again, to enforce. In some cases, women may have seemed to be the most available form of property; in others, the resort to force against outsiders may have seemed necessary for group survival.

Thus in any hunter-gatherer society the sexual division of

---

*For an interesting critique of the universality claim, see the note by Eleanor Leacock in the March 1975 *American Anthropologist.* As of this writing, there has been no response to her critique as far as one can tell.[25]

labor must originally have made at least a kind of crude sense, given the facts of human reproduction and the kinds of nontechnological interactions such peoples have had with their environments; and thereafter men were surely able to hand down whatever institutionalized expectations did arise from one generation to another—to create a tradition. They would have been able to do that because the means of dominance in such societies were simple and transparent and men more easily controlled them. Perhaps even more important, though the organizational abilities of women have always rivaled those of men (Lionel Tiger's notorious assertions to the contrary notwithstanding), the comparative closeness of women to all phases of the reproductive cycle does exercise a potential limitation upon them. Women can organize themselves for all tasks, but they are still different from men. When men realize there is a potential benefit for themselves to be gained from a division of labor that restricts the activities of women, it is much easier for them to implement it than it would be for women to compel an egalitarian division of labor. Contrarily, for women to be victims of their immersion in the reproductive cycle, once men have perceived that as their primary role, nothing at all has to be done; it is enough that no one, male or female, makes an effort to change what then appears the most obvious ("natural") relationship. Men do not get pregnant, bear children, or nurse them afterwards. Thus the nature of the woman-child relationship indicates women as being better adapted to give continuous care in the "home" (that is, any child-centered environment), unless they want to make an issue of it. Moreover, when such a society faces external crises that must be dealt with over great distances, the particular form of organization and skill that men have attained as hunters will usually be more relevant.

None of this bespeaks a biological *necessity* in Goldberg's sense. There are hunter-gatherer societies in which the so-called natural relationship once did not appear so inevitable to either the women or the men. Moreover, the participation of women in foraging and gathering expeditions was apparently much more extensive than sociobiologists oriented toward male supremacy have been willing to admit: more extensive, and also more crucial to the survival of such societies than hunting. However, given the considerations mentioned above, the development to a state of affairs in which women's participation outside the immediate domestic setting has to be negotiated seems thoroughly expectable. The gradual substitution of agriculture for foraging would also tend to lead to the restriction of women.[26]

In that sense and that sense only can an ultimate exclusion of women from, or limitation of their input into, the "body politic" be said to have a partially biological origin. But note that this explanation of the "universality" of male dominance in hunter-gatherer societies does not postulate any mysterious and inalterable cycle of hormonal release—male aggressiveness—female deference to male aggressiveness, passed on from generation to generation because it is genetically adaptive. It merely recognizes the potential functional implications of greater male physical power combined with the comparatively greater "drag" of maternity as contrasted with paternity. But that potential is not automatically converted into an institutionalized reality. For that to happen men must desire to dominate; there must be some available rationalization for that domination; and women must find the pains of resistance greater than the pains of compliance and the interests served by compliance greater than those served by resistance. Only then can a gender-defined dominance/subordination relationship be long maintained. As I have already suggested, though, such conditions do not obtain in advanced industrial societies. Thus the "example" of hunter-gatherer societies, whatever the proper interpretation of the "facts" about them, proves nothing at all.

As for more immediately premodern civilizations, again a pattern of institutionalized male dominance seems general, but here the nature of the pattern is quite clearly ambiguous. The evidence we have suggests, for instance, that in several cases religious leadership—one of the most basic forms of political leadership in such civilizations—was at least shared by women if not dominated by them, but was then *expropriated* from them by men. In many of these civilizations, moreover, both land and rulership were allowed to pass to women, without any of those male rebellions that Goldberg suggests would have been "inevitable." As one writer has observed about the "underside of history":

It must be clear that class structures have always included women, and that women have had differential power in each society based on class position just as men have. The fact that at each level in the class system they have less power than the males at the same level should not obscure the basic fact that women of the elite in all historical eras have wielded substantial amounts of public power. While the immediate political and cultural settings are different, Indira Gandhi, Mrs. Bandaranaike, and Golda Meir all came to power out of ancient traditions of women rulers in Eastern cultures, including the Judaic tradition of women judges and an Indian tradition of ruling queens. Industrialization generally acted to limit the power of women, partly because of the associated dismantling of the large landed estates that had been the source of much of women's power from Sumerian times on. It happened that western historians interpreted the position of women in industrial societies as the human norm. Their anti-woman bias has produced a rewriting of world history that substantially obliterates the contributions of upper class women.[27]

The only forms of domination that appear to have been reserved exclusively to men in all these civilizations were the control of overseas trade and the supervision (below the level of the ruling king or queen) of bureaucratic and military apparatuses. But again, surely no hormonal explanation is needed to account for (or possibly could account for) those facts. Once men could establish a tradition of male dominance, then their monopolization of public roles would be furthered by their superiority in (nontechnological) fighting, their comparative independence from the requirements of the reproductive cycle, and the need to find roles other than landownership for elite men in a society of large landed estates. Lacking the only available means of rebellion—that is, sheer physical force and weapons—how could women be expected to have done otherwise than accede to and sometimes even internalize as "natural" the established sexual division of labor and of land? The prevalence in all such civilizations of elite women who either ruled or played the role of "power behind the throne" testifies to men's recognition that women were not really deficient in any of the qualities (other than physical strength) necessary for leadership. The difference between such social formations and our own is primarily that where legitimate authority was defined very rigidly, hierarchically, and theologically, it would have been difficult if not impossible to find nondisruptive ways of formalizing that role on an egalitarian basis. In the absence of a public ideology of egalitarianism, male strength and weapons monopoly and the comparative subordination of women to reproduction would always tell against efforts to reverse old traditions and create a new tradition of sexual equality.

All these conditions, however, which held true even in the early years of industrialization, are now becoming outmoded. Indeed, a quite opposite perception has begun to obtain in the industrialized West, so much so that in some of the world's richer societies the problem may well become one of getting women (and men) to have more children rather than fewer. With the coming of advanced technology, including the development of various licit methods to control, stabilize, and limit the effects on women of the reproductive cycle from conception through infancy, the exclusion of women from public life begins to seem obsolescent. To be sure, available birth-control methods, prenatal and maternity care technologies, and infant-care systems are still far from ideal and far from fully implemented anywhere. But the *perception* of what is possible in the contemporary context has to be wholly different from that perception in pretechnological social formations. Moreover, the gradual replacement of physical power by technologically aided skill as the *sine qua non* of almost all socially desirable careers makes the only distinguishing feature of maleness no longer a clear-cut social desideratum, just as advanced technology generally renders primitive versions of the division of labor anachronistic. Like the existence of poverty, the sexual division of labor now serves purposes of social control rather than any "necessary" function. In every way, then, "woman's lot" is no longer perfectly obvious. It is no longer unambiguously true, if it ever was, that "women are to nature as men are to culture";[28] and women with new lives to lead are becoming, not hidden exceptions, but rather (to the applause of some and the censure of others, including the biological inegalitarians) heralds of a possible future.

The historical context in which the technological "liberation" of many women seems at last possible is also sharply
different from what it was previously. As I have noted, the moral
norms around which modern industrial societies are ordered are
strikingly different from those we encounter in the human past.
Impersonal democratic norms gradually have the effect of pre-
cluding, or at least rendering suspect, the erection of formal,
legal barriers between different kinds of people within a single
legal jurisdiction. The resort to sheer force to defend privilege
in the face of assertions that it is illegal is even more indefensible.* The determination of men, therefore, to hand down whatever gender privileges they have to their male children is not
easily realized when land is no longer the key to social status and
social survival; and when the most common public ideology is not
the idealization of a sacral, hierarchical, and "natural" order but
is instead a generalized rule of formal equality. It is also probably very important that whereas the fathers of daughters would
in an earlier era have found the eventual social subordination of
their daughters "natural" and unproblematic, they are now confronted with a very problematic choice, in that there are available ideologies that justify either subordination *or* equality.
Many will choose the latter once that choice is realistically available, and thus the pressures for sexual equality mount still
more.

In this new context, the fact that there is an abundance of
women in places like the United States or Sweden who either
have no children at all or are forced to sustain only slight inter-

*Recently in my home city, two men's baseball teams usurped the use of a field
which had been scheduled for the playoff finals of a women's league. When the
women protested, the men refused to leave. The women sat down on the field
and obstructed play, and though the men harassed them verbally (and viciously) they did not use force. Officials, on being consulted, said that the
women were in the right. When the men still refused to leave, and it became
clear that only force would move them, the officials of the men's league (who
are men, of course) canceled the game; neither game in the end was played,
but the men's defeat was worse in that their game had already been under
way and was wiped out. I cannot imagine how Goldberg would explain the
actions of the officials, nor the clear sympathy of the town's daily newspaper
with the women. As though he had imbibed during his childhood an outdated
Marxist cynicism, he refuses to acknowledge that social norms have a force of
their own. His materialism, as Marx said of the Hobbesian variety, is vulgar
and simple rather than historical.

ruptions in their search for viable careers becomes more than a mere fact: it becomes an available norm. That there are, in such societies, more than enough talented women available to fill leadership positions on an egalitarian basis becomes an invitation to have them do just that, and sets in motion an ineluctable trend (unless equality is to be openly forsworn). Thus where men once ruled by what seemed right and necessity to almost everyone, they now seem to many women and men to rule arbitrarily and without necessity: the tradition at last loses its rationale.

Indeed, beyond mere tradition, and beyond the determination of men with power to maintain a monopoly of power by people "like themselves" (a determination visible in all human groups that perceive of themselves as distinctive), what sustains male dominance of the public realm today is not any age-old aspect of our "natural" humanity but that very modern invention, the double day for women. Absent the institutionalization of the double day, all defenses of male monopolization of public life would instantly be revealed as rationalizations. Hardly anyone today dares publicly to defend the natural right of men to rule; what is asserted instead is the need to maintain traditional family life, and the continued relegation of women to a domestic role allegedly is the means of accomplishing that. But that is to replace a real (or at least apparently real) necessity of a more primitive existence with a transparently contingent one. The double day for women, after all, is a creation of capitalist development: of the institutionalization of unrestrained, forced-draft economic growth; the confinement of women to the domestic sphere and the privatization of child care in the context of a complete separation between workplace and home; the subordination of workers to the tyranny of industrial processes and the suppression by violence of all protest against that subordination in any of its aspects; and (as Marx pointed out) an increase in the length of the average working day—all of these factors being combined always with the specifically female subordination to the reproductive cycle.

Now, however, not just reproductive anarchy but those other aspects of industrial civilization as well are capable of being reworked—and indeed the length and nature of the average working day, as well as the direction of economic growth in general, will probably require very drastic change if technological civilization is to survive. The double day may and probably will linger on for generations after it has stopped being a functional necessity, for it is what people have become used to: the best explanation of the persistence of any social phenomenon, after all, is the likelihood that tomorrow will always be much like today unless a large number of people make a dedicated and painful effort to the contrary. But the more the obsolescence of our existing arrangements between the sexes becomes recognized by members of both sexes, the more likely it is that change will eventually take place.* In that sense the campaign for sexual equality in general, and for an end to the double day and even better means of controlling the reproductive cycle in particular, is fully rational and worthy of engaging people's energies. It is a campaign for an attainable end that is supported rather than contradicted by the social norms by which we purport to live, and it is based on a reasonable reading of the unknown past and a plausible assessment of the open future.

In contrast, the campaign for patriarchy is a campaign to deny democratic norms, based on a mystification of the past and a dogmatic view of the future. Nowhere does this come out more clearly than in the one serious effort the sexual inegalitarians have made to apply their ideology to public policy: George Gilder's polemic against the proposal of some of America's military leaders to give women a combat role in the military. That proposal is based precisely on a recognition that advanced technological society is qualitatively different from earlier societies. In general, military planners now question whether young men any longer make the best soldiers, and propose to replace them with older, more experienced and technically skilled personnel (three out of five soldiers, it has been said in one Department of Defense report, are essentially unproductive). Moreover, military service has now become a low-prestige as well as low-paying job for young men; the armed services are therefore dissatisfied with the young men who volunteer for service, and hope to

---

*In Sweden, the most advanced industrial welfare state, there is already a host of rules and regulations designed to make possible the equalization of the working day between husbands and wives—though, to be sure, implementation is slow and encounters resistance.[29]

replace or augment them with female volunteers, or even with a conscript army that includes women.[30]

These plans, of course, are not based on any egalitarian ideology but on a professional assessment of the situation by those charged with making that kind of assessment. It is against those military professionals that Gilder turns his inegalitarian scorn and anger. But here we must ask, how is it that he finds it necessary to excoriate Pentagon leadership for proposing that women be trained for combat if the superiority of men in this realm is biologically given—as it must be in this realm if it is in any at all? Surely if women cannot compete with men on the battlefield, as according to Goldberg and Gilder they cannot, we will find that out as soon as maneuvers start. Why is Gilder so concerned to prevent the test from even being made?

The true content of these arguments, ultimately, becomes apparent when we discover, in the midst of this polemic, Gilder's eulogy for "the warrior mystique, the chivalric tradition, the aggressive glory of the martial style." But the fact is that the "evolutionary symbolism" (as he terms it) of these institutions is a thing of the past. Gilder and Goldberg have written not social science but a romantic poem of force. But it is a bad poem, constructed out of inappropriate and secondhand imagery borrowed from the privileged world of genuine science, instead of their own honest account—which might have been interesting— of their deepest desires. Like all romantics, they are glorifying not nature but nostalgia, nostalgia for what used to be (perhaps) "nature" but is now only an anachronism. They are exhorting us to recapture "nature" because the dynamics of historical evolution are leading us in a different direction entirely—away from presumed male supremacy based on our physical capabilities and toward sexual equality based on the subordination of physical prowess to the demands and possibilities of organized technology.

"Patriarchy" turns out to be, not a natural inevitability, but the hope of ideologues who are afraid of change and who want to persuade the rest of us that the privileges they enjoy are "necessary." But the absurd society is not that in which the best men do not lead (or represent, or administer) but that in which they do: in which half of the available talent, and importantly different kinds of value articulation, remain unexpressed.

Amidst all the talk of stagnation and even decay in advanced capitalist societies, not least of them the United States, one of the most obvious causes of all is hardly ever spoken of: that barriers of race, class, and sex repress the productive skills of a major portion of the human race.

PART TWO

―――――――――――

―――――――――

――――――

THE
PREVENTION
OF
EQUALITY

CHAPTER

THE NEW INDIVIDUALISM:
KEEPING THEM
IN THEIR PLACE

"One Law for the Lion and the Ox is Oppression."
—WILLIAM BLAKE

The corrupt use of "science" is one tactic in the pursuit of inequality; that tactic has probably received the most contemporary attention. It is also possible to pursue inequality by the propagation, not of corrupt principles, but of self-serving principles that, like Jensen's theories as to what accounts for the shortfall in average black IQ, depend for their force on our willingness to close our eyes to social reality. Anatole France gave us the classic critique of this kind of principle: the law in its majestic equality, he wrote, forbids rich and poor alike to sleep under bridges, to beg in the streets, and to steal bread. A contemporary connoisseur of inequality might add that it also forbids blacks and whites alike to establish civilian control over police forces, to violate seniority rules, and to receive any special preference in seeking job training, or admission to a profession, or representation in the decision-making organs of business and government. Needless to say, that same kind of law makes similarly "equal" demands on men and women. What France intended as satire, though, has become a means by which the inegalitarian can promote the institutionalization of injustice while proclaiming himself to be the only true upholder of the just. The purpose of this chapter is thus to contrast two conceptions of justice with respect to their implications for the real implementation of our notions of equal citizenship. In so doing we move from what I earlier called the weak version of inegalitarianism to its strong version: but as we shall see, the strength of this version is based more on the social acceptability of its arguments than on the cogency of its principles.

Nowadays, arguments about the meaning of equal citizenship usually proceed by way of a debate about "affirmative action," or, as it is called by its critics *in extremis*, "quotas" or "reverse discrimination." It is a topic that has caused a furor far out of proportion to its actual impact on American society; in no other policy arena recently has there been such bitterness between the contestants on either side, and old alliances (as between American Jews and American blacks) have decisively fractured as a result. The feverishness of the discussion suggests that profound and painful issues are at stake: that suggestion is correct. For the idea of "affirmative action," properly conceived, is part of a much broader and in some respects novel conception of "representation." As Daniel Bell perceptively observes (speaking of John Stuart Mill's argument in favor of proportional representation), "the logic of minority representation is the quota"; or, as another critic puts it, "quotas by any other name" are still quotas.[1] We should forbear, therefore, from prolix discussion, à la Justice Powell in the *Bakke* case, of how we could implement "numerical goals" or "affirmative action guidelines," or whatever, that are somehow not "quotas." There is an immense literature that attempts to make such distinctions, and that literature may well be very useful for policymakers. But it will probably not change the mind of anyone who is already convinced that "affirmative action" can only be meaningful if it takes the form of "reverse discrimination."[2] Rather than engage in public-relations exercises designed to pacify such critics, then, we should confront the matter of principle head-on. They are correct: it is useless to conceive of "affirmative action" as merely open-recruitment procedures designed to give all applicants for positions an "equal chance." "Affirmative action" can only have the effect that is hoped for—the effect that, as we shall see, would justify it—if employers and boards of admissions are compelled (or compel themselves) to accept a significant proportion of applicants from minority groups, even if to accomplish that end they must accept many whom they would otherwise have passed over after giving due consideration to what would traditionally be thought of as their credentials. Thus, as France might put it were he a contemporary sociologist, the law in its majesty forbids advantaged and disadvantaged alike to benefit from discrimination, from quotas; how in good conscience can we possibly propose to undermine that fundamental rule of formal civic equality?

That general rule, as its proponents understand it, applies to the worlds of education, training, and employment as follows: in liberal societies people generally get what they deserve, or if they don't they should, and that's all they should get; and what they deserve is purely and simply a consequence of their own individual character and actions, nothing else. A government or any public agency (or even private agency imbued with a "public interest") that violates that rule takes sides among social groups and thereby loses its properly neutral character, thus becoming a mere part of the group conflict of society. Hegel put it more profoundly than anyone since: a public agency behaving in that way can no longer claim to be behaving as part of a legitimate state, but is reduced to being merely another actor in contentious civil society: rather than helping us transcend the prepolitical rule of might makes right, the state merely reproduces it. Only generalized unfairness, or civil disorder, or both, can be the result.[3]

But why, in an obviously unequal society, is it a violation of the rules of legitimacy for a public authority thus to "take sides," to represent the weak in preference to the strong, the poor in preference to the rich, blacks in preference to whites, or females in preference to males? As we look at the specific arguments in favor of the rule I have informally summed up above, we can see the apparent force of the individualist argument. But we can also see the ways in which, consciously or not, its proponents turn their principle into a defense of the status quo, that is, of unequal privileges already won in the past.[4]

II.

According to the individualist principle as I have described it, to say that people deserve or "merit" some reward (at least some reward that is in short supply) is to say that to deprive them of it would be to deprive them of something to which they have a "right." To do this, to take from them what is rightfully theirs and give it to someone else, is to "discriminate" against them. That is the claim made by critics of those opinions in the *Bakke* and *Weber* cases that defended the principle of "reverse discrimination" without qualification (on grounds of race, that is). According to the critics, Alan Bakke had a *right* to enter medical school, a right which some black applicant with lesser test scores and thus less "merit" did not have; Brian Weber had a *right* to enter a job-training program which some black person with less seniority did not have. Because Weber did not get what he merited he was discriminated against unfairly; as would Bakke have been had the Supreme Court's decision in his case gone the other way.[5] But what is this "merit"?*

---

*In the *Bakke* case, the medical school of the University of California at Davis set aside places for black applicants (and applicants from other minority groups) who had combined MCAT scores (the MCAT being the required aptitude exam for all premed students) and college grades lower than those of white applicants who, other things being equal, would have been admitted. Bakke was, or claimed to be, one of the latter. The Supreme Court's decision in the case was, at the time, highly ambiguous. Four justices agreed that racial quotas were constitutional if they favored blacks, and that Congress had not intended to bar them by the Civil Rights Act of 1964 (which forbids discrimination on the ground of race). Four justices interpreted the will of Congress differently, without reaching the constitutional question; they argued that Title VI of that act expressly forbids discrimination based on race by institutions receiving federal assistance (as did the medical school). The ninth judge, Justice Powell, in what in effect became the opinion of the Court, argued that the "equal protection of the laws" clause of the Fourteenth Amendment to the Constitution, not the will of Congress, made racial quotas unacceptable, but he also said that race could be used as one of several factors in assessing applicants for admission to professional schools. Critics of "affirmative action" thought that this resolution of the case was unsatisfactory, especially as the ruling in favor of Bakke only applied, in the minds of four of the justices, because of the congressional language regarding federally assisted institutions. From their point of view they turned out to be right. In *Weber*, a 6–3 majority of the Court upheld a voluntary affirmative-action plan established by the Kaiser Aluminum and Chemical Corporation offering black applicants places in a training program ahead of whites with greater seniority, even though the company denied ever having itself discriminated against blacks. (The denial, of course, was almost certainly false.) Here the question was

It is, in fact, exceedingly difficult to understand, from these critics, of what Alan Bakke's "merit" (or anyone else's) is supposed to consist. Presumably, by obtaining good grades and test scores he is thought to have earned credentials of some kind, but why are these credentials especially deserving of reward? It could be argued, of course, that society will be better off if we reward people like Bakke rather than people like the black person with lesser grades and scores who was accepted into medical school ahead of him. This argument, the argument from social utility, is a serious one, and we shall consider it at length later (pages 188–96). But that is precisely the argument that the critics of "affirmative action" and "reverse discrimination" eschew, for they are concerned rather to assert that a moral or constitutional wrong has been committed, not that some index of social productivity is under threat. Why then, we must ask, are credentials of these kinds alleged to be meritorious?

The answer, always implicit in arguments about "merit" and sometimes made explicit, is that the good worker has done something, has accomplished something, and accomplishment ought to be rewarded; the beneficiary of a quota has done nothing, has merely been somebody, and the mere accidents of birth are not deserving of reward. This will not do, though; it is pure sophistry.

The obvious difficulty is in deciding what we mean by "accomplishment," and what the "accomplishment" actually consists of. "Objective" measures of "intelligence," for example, measure something that we are at least partially born with. As I have pointed out earlier, though we must presume they exist

---

whether Congress had intended to prohibit such actions by private agencies; the majority's finding that it had not flew in the face of the clear intentions of those who spoke for the Civil Rights Act during the congressional debate over it, and was based on a readiness by the majority to find "reverse discrimination" not constitutionally suspect. The majority read its view of the reasonableness of "reverse discrimination" into the minds of Congress, and the vote-switching from *Bakke* was apparently based on the absence of a specific prohibition such as that in Title VI in that part of the statute being interpreted in *Weber*. Most recently in *Fullilove* v. *Klutznick*, the Court went even further and by the same majority upheld an act of Congress establishing a racial quota favoring blacks in a program of government loans to small business. In retrospect, therefore, the present Court (as of 1980) seems to have endorsed the constitutionality of racial quotas in general, though Congress can forbid them in particular.[6]

we have no idea what the parameters of "intelligence" are for a given individual. The "A" student may be a person who is very adept at the kinds of tasks our tests create and has thus never worked very hard at doing them—has actually "accomplished" very little. A "C" student, on the other hand, may have worked with immense effort to overcome either innate or environmental handicaps (just as a woman showing great diffidence in a job interview compared to a more "aggressive" male may actually have devoted immense effort to overcoming the effects of the social prejudice against the manifestation of such "aggression" by females). Unless we know the applicants in question quite intimately we can do nothing but guess that there is any relationship at all between their "credentials" and their efforts. From the standpoint of ethical obligation, therefore, the safest presumption—the only safe presumption—is that any student who has got to the point of even being within the pool of applicants that a serious professional school is willing to consider has worked very hard to get there—has "accomplished" something "meritorious." But from the standpoint of any imaginable moral philosophy, greater accomplishment from the same amount of effort does not deserve greater reward. Moreover, we must add to this that people whose parents, and other role models, have been discriminated against in the past will often, through no "fault" of their own, find it impossible to believe that putting forth effort will do them any good. Even the incentive to put forth comparatively greater or lesser amounts of effort, that is, may be an outcome of the circumstances of one's birth as much as an index of one's comparative "personal" will to "accomplish." All in all, then, to make a linkage between grades or scores and moral desert is to be wholly arbitrary.

If we are really interested in moral desert, the only unarbitrary policy we can adopt is that anyone who strives to any extent to master an area of competence deserves a chance to do so, and thus that no particular accomplishment in the realm of accruing credentials is any worthier than any other. That is an argument for "open admissions," or admissions by lot, of course. In the absence of such an egalitarian system, some people are going to be excluded from the institution or career of their choice, and no reason for excluding them is morally better than another (again, social utility aside). To be so excluded or set back or dropped down in some set of rankings that is crucial to one's future, merely as an outcome of a comparatively low score on some kind of rating system, is to be discriminated against for no reason that has any moral standing. This is the kind of discrimination that Alan Bakke and his supporters were fighting for; the issue of "merit" that they supposedly raise is thus completely spurious.*

Worse yet, not only is the application of "objective" standards in the moral realm thoroughly arbitrary, it is equally arbitrary to suggest that such standards can be, should be, or ever have been the sole or even the most important criteria for "getting ahead" in American society. For just as at some times our ideas about credentialing are pointlessly rigid, at other times for other people they are very flexible, and very helpfully flexible indeed. In the United States as in every other society (as the sociobiologists might say), many and various forms of preference are recognized as legitimate on one occasion or another. To take an obvious example, applicants to institutions of higher education are privileged (i.e., have a better chance of gaining admission) not only if they get good grades and high college-board scores but also if they are children of alumni of the institution to which they are applying, or if they are gifted athletes or artists, or if they are recommended by important donors to the institution, or if their admission would provide regional "balance." At our undergraduate institutions, in other words, a socially and intellectually diverse student body is generally thought to be more of a desideratum than is a student body of highly qualified scholars and intellectuals. Even at the level of preprofessional graduate school training, the emphasis on quantitative factors is not nearly as strong as most people think it is: college professors who fill out reference forms for their stu-

---

*A great deal of complex and sometimes unedifying philosophical discussion has taken place recently around this topic of "merit," most of it concerned with the question of deciding what a person has to *do* to "deserve" a given reward. Ethical philosophers can get very exercised about whether an "intelligent" person, for example, has actually "done" anything (inherited favorable genes?) and thus merits anything. I have only begun to convey a sense of the difficulties one encounters in pursuing this train of thought. All in all, these discussions leave the lay person convinced that social utility is the only comprehensible principle of "merit."[7]

dents, at least, are well aware that a good many of the specific questions they are asked in making a recommendation have to do much more with "personality" and "character" than with pure intellect. Both of those, of course, are variables that are notoriously slippery in application.

In the world of work and careers the situation is no different. Obviously, again, veterans are privileged when they apply for civil service jobs, whether they volunteered or were conscripted, saw combat or not; those who are not veterans are discriminated against in job competition very directly. Union members with seniority are privileged in applying for various training programs or for advancement, and those with less seniority are discriminated against. Indeed, in the *Weber* case Brian Weber's entire argument (rejected by the Supreme Court majority though supported by the opponents of affirmative action) was that he had more seniority at Kaiser Aluminum than some black workers who were selected for its training program ahead of him; no critic of the Court's decision has ever been able to explain why "seniority" should take on any particular moral or constitutional significance. But then they would also have to explain what "merit" has been possessed by those professionals who have enjoyed the rewards of restrictive rules of entry to their professions (e.g., lawyers and doctors); by businessmen, bankers, and brokers who were privileged by virtue of coming from an acceptable social background; by public employees who belonged to the right ethnic group in the right place at the right time; by craftsmen whose acceptance by a trade union has been contingent on their recommendation by members of their own family; and by academics who through most of their careers have engaged in neither productive scholarship nor innovative teaching but have rather been "good old boys," expertly mimicking the values of their superiors.

This contrast between the two types of "credentials" that have been crucial in the achievement of various kinds of social "success" makes clear that the meritocratic model of how social recruitment actually works is totally unrealistic. This meritocratic model is of an ordinal ranking process, in which the "best" person (according to some single, quantifiable scale) is fitted to the "highest" position, the next best to the next highest, and so on, individual "merit" being matched with career demands at every step of the way. It is not surprising that this model has come to be accepted, by people who ought to know better, as a realistic model of what goes on in the worlds of admissions, hiring, and promotion, for it is the model apparently employed (and only employed) in the academic world. Since academics do most of the writing about philosophical matters such as "affirmative action," their own presuppositions come to infect the discussion of types of social behavior quite remote from their own.

Even with respect to the academic world itself, however, the ordinal ranking model is, as I have just suggested, quite delusive. Academics certainly pretend to follow it when they are choosing among applicants for job vacancies or granting tenure, but the pretense is not even thin to anyone who has actually taken part in the process. Chance, bias, personal connections, the state of the market, and inertia figure far more importantly in it than measurable considerations of ranking do. As for the world outside the academy, the ordinal ranking model has an almost total lack of congruity with what people actually do in their admissions and employment practices. The reality of most personnel decisions in this (probably in any) society is rather what has been called the "skill pool" model.[8] That is, those persons possessing the requisite qualifications for a given position to at least the minimal degree necessary to do an adequate job in it are viable candidates for that position—they form the skill pool for it. Historically, performance on "objective" tests has sometimes been important evidence of those qualifications in certain fields, but so too, beyond all allegedly technical or intrinsic criteria, have been the various factors I have referred to above: ancestry, membership in an appropriate "old boy" network, ambition, "personality," appearance, the ability to manipulate others, "character," and so forth. In the prestigious occupations of business, politics, the law, and even medicine, wielders of authority—whose own performances have never been explicitly judged against any "objective" standard—mostly recruit as their potential successors the people who seem to be most like themselves; who satisfy vague criteria such as "leadership capability," *"real* intelligence," or "all-around ability," which often are little more than euphemisms for the personality characteristics the person making the judgment is comfortable with. For certain career lines, of course, the skill pool is drawn more narrowly and defined more rigorously than for others—for Harvard more than for teachers' colleges (though perhaps that is an inversion of rational priorities), for nuclear engineering more than for civil engineering. But only in the most technologically advanced and abstruse careers are factors extrinsic to any truly ordinal ranking of skills totally discarded. Most of the time, the question is not whether other factors than pure "technical" skill are going to be taken into account by us, but which ones. Nor is it necessarily unreasonable that these seemingly extrinsic considerations play such an important part, since, as we have seen, there is no greater moral desert in high test scores than in a likable personality.

In sum, there are no "objective" criteria of merit such that it is wrong to "discriminate" in favor of people who fulfill them, or right to "discriminate" against those who do not. Whatever our rules are, of course, they should be consistent and defensible in the light of reason. If Alan Bakke had any moral case at all, it was that the university which rejected him had itself first (and foolishly) adopted a quantitative scale (grades plus MCAT scores), had led him and others to believe that this was the scale on which their performance would be measured, and had then arranged exceptions to its own scale via racial quotas. It could be argued that for a public agency to make numerical scores determinative in the first instance was to give them some kind of official stamp of approval; that a public agency should never fail to fulfill reasonable expectations established by itself; and that to legitimate and then renounce a particular standard in the same breath was to do just that. On the other hand, this analysis also makes us realize that if the Davis Medical School board of admissions had never publicly adopted a quantitative standard at all, but had rather announced that many qualifications for admission had been taken into account and that their relative importance could not be stated precisely—in other words, had done what any reasonable board of admissions ought to do— then the situation to which Bakke objected would never have arisen. The explicit racial quota would still have been open to constitutional attack on other grounds (see below, pages 176–79), but neither Bakke nor anyone else would have been able to argue that he personally had been wrongfully deprived of a position that he deserved.

In short, we do not "deserve" anything more than what we have been led to expect we deserve, and even that expectation may always justifiably be frustrated if overriding considerations of social betterment demand fundamental policy changes (otherwise there could never be policy changes!). With the exception of those fundamental rights without which a democratic political system cannot even begin to exist—the rights to vote, to speak freely, to assemble peacefully, to hold office—we do not know whether an individual has a "right" until *after* someone has made an authoritative decision about the kinds of values the social order should be trying to maximize. None of us has a right not to be discriminated against; what we have is the right not to be discriminated against on grounds that the legitimate decision-making organs of our society do not accept as valid. It may be a voting majority, a collective consensus, or a supreme court or some other board of review interpreting a constitution or statutory law that makes such validations; but whatever the case, they must be made *before* we know what our "rights" are. No one has a right to earn the rewards that accrue from calling oneself a professional until the standards for belonging to a particular profession have been established; no one has a right to the privileges of seniority or to guarantees of employment unless recognized union contracts or public legislation have established that right; no one has a right to a civil service position until the rules for maintaining a civil service (in place of, say, a "spoils system") have been promulgated.

In all these cases, the rules and standards must—unless there is to be complete "rotation in office" or "open admissions" in every walk of life—be drafted so as to include some kinds of people and exclude others. Then the only serious question left is not whether we are going to discriminate, but how; not whether someone is going to be deprived of a potential benefit, but who. For then we have acknowledged that no one has an absolute right of selection, and that many are going to be excluded from the careers they desire to pursue. These exclusions cannot be made to seem "fair" unless there is a consensus on some reasonable ground for making them. In our society there has never been such a consensus about tests and scores in actual practice; their validation exists only in the ideology and propaganda of the anti-egalitarians. In reality "merit" has been assessed every which way, depending on who had the power at a given moment to enforce their particular definition of it. The "merit system" is a fable—a mutually agreeable fable told to each other by the beneficiaries of past definitions of "merit," who pretend that those definitions were much more precise than they ever really were, and who thus try to persuade each other, and the rest of us, that they have never received anything but their own "just," "individual" deserts.

III. Thus "merit" and "discrimination" are both, in themselves, pseudo-issues. The critics of "affirmative action" do not really mean that discrimination is unfair. They mean, rather, that discrimination for or against *groups* is unfair. More specifically, they assert that what they call reverse *racial* (or ethnic) discrimination is unfair—that it is no more acceptable than ordinary, straightforward racial discrimination. This rejection of membership in one or another human group as a valid ground of representation is at the heart of the new individualism; the allegedly fundamental principle behind it is expressed sharply by Carl Cohen and Nathan Glazer, and by Justice Stewart (dissenting) in *Fullilove* v. *Klutznick:*

> Title VII of the Civil Rights Act forbids all deliberate discrimination by race, save only in cases where racial classification is absolutely essential to give redress to *identifiable persons* injured by racial discrimination and *where the injury done them was done by the same party upon whom the numerical program is imposed.* One purpose only may justify numerical schemes using racial categories: the *making whole* of those to whom redress for racial injury is specifically owed, by those who owe it. . . .
> Injuries are suffered in fact, claims made and burdens carried, by individual persons. Civil society is constituted to protect the rights of individuals; the sacrifice of fundamental individual rights cannot be justified by the desire to advance the well-being of any ethnic group. . . .[9]

We are indeed a nation of minorities; to enshrine some minorities as deserving of special benefits means not to defend minority rights against a discriminating majority but to favor some of these minorities over others.

Compensation for the past is a dangerous principle. It can be extended indefinitely and make for endless trouble. Who is to determine what is proper compensation for the American Indian, the black, the Mexican American, the Chinese or Japanese American? When it is established that the full status of equality is extended to every individual, regardless of race, color, or national origin, and that special opportunity is also available to any individual on the basis of individual need, again regardless of race, color, or national origin, one has done all that justice and equity call for and that is consistent with a harmonious multigroup society.[10]

Under our Constitution, any official action that treats a person differently on account of his race or ethnic origin is inherently suspect and presumptively invalid. Under our Constitution, the Government may never act to the detriment of a person solely because of the person's race. The color of a person's skin and the country of his origin are immutable facts that bear no relation to ability, disadvantage, moral culpability, or any other characteristics of constitutionally permissible interest to government.[11]

What ground other than mere repetition can be offered to justify this one exception to the general rule that discrimination in pursuit of a valid social goal is permissible? (The critics never deny, that is, that it is a valid social goal to attempt to find ways to better the lot of previously excluded or oppressed or enslaved peoples; they merely insist that this one, quite obvious method for doing just that is unacceptable.) It can be no answer to say that the Fourteenth Amendment to the United States Constitution is thereby violated. Declarations of unconstitutionality are the first step in an argument, not the last. Otherwise, one is thrown totally on the mercy of Supreme Court justices: Justice Stewart's remarks, with which Cohen and Glazer are in complete agreement, are from a dissent. Indeed, a typical irony of the formal constitutionalist position is that Cohen's article from which I have quoted purported to establish conclusively that

Brian Weber's case against "reverse discrimination" was unassailable except by the morally and constitutionally ignorant. But these turned out to be a majority of the Court, and Cohen's article appeared in *Commentary* barely in time to be hopelessly and permanently outmoded by the Court's decision to the contrary.[12] Neither "equal protection of the laws" nor any other constitutional provision has a transparent meaning; it is necessary to give *reasons* to justify the assertion that one's own interpretation is correct.

Moreover, the general Fourteenth Amendment principle that all citizens are owed "equal protection of the laws" is one that defenders of "individualist" ideals would do well to shy away from. Necessarily, interpretation of that elusive phrase demands a prior determination as to who is deserving of "equal protection," under what circumstances, and what would make that protection really "equal." The first thing law students learn, after all, is that "circumstances alter cases," a rule of thumb which is hardly less relevant in the discussion of constitutional doctrine than in any other legal context. To take the idea of "equal protection" most literally, does the state owe equal police protection—that is, must it make the same number of police officers available—to any two jurisdictions of the same size? Or of the same population? Is as much "protection" owed to some inner-city slum as to the Rockefellers' Pocantico Hills estate? More, because crime is more likely to be committed in the slum than on the estate? Less, because the object of any putative crime is likely to be much more valuable on the estate than in the slum? The same, because the same number of people live in both? Nothing in the notion of "equal protection" gives us the slightest clue as to the most appropriate answer; it may even be that there is no "most appropriate" answer, that any answer is as defensible as any other. To invoke "equal protection" when someone has asked that it not be invoked is always to assert that they have asked us to make a distinction which is not "reasonable"; that only means that, just as with the general distinction between "discriminatory" choice and "fair" choice, we will have to decide what it is that makes a "reasonable" distinction reasonable.

Thus, prior to 1976, when the majority opinion in *Craig* v. *Boren* suggested that henceforward government-enforced classifications by gender would be as suspect as classifications by race, the Supreme Court had interpreted the Fourteenth Amendment so as to permit a great variety of discriminations by gender on the grounds that they were "reasonable." In recent decades these permissible discriminations had included laws that discriminate against female bartenders if they are not the wives or daughters of male owners; exclude women from juries unless they request to be registered for jury rolls (on the grounds that women are "still regarded as the center of home and family life"); deny widowers a property-tax exemption available to widows, on the grounds that the burden on the latter as a group is heavier; compel married women to use their husbands' surnames in seeking drivers' licenses; and so on. Even in the same term that saw *Craig* v. *Boren*, only a bare majority of the Court, in *Califano* v. *Goldfarb*, invalidated a provision of the Social Security Act treating the old-age benefits of widows and widowers differently.[13] A court still so sharply divided on the question of gender-based discrimination, and which not so long ago contained a majority that would endorse the Goldberg/Gilder view of sexual equality, hardly encourages us to think that the Fourteenth Amendment is a trustworthy guide to the comparative rationality of different types of discrimination, especially as the same Justice Stewart who is quoted above in dissent from *Fullilove* v. *Klutznick* issued a majority opinion two days earlier, in the Hyde Amendment case of *Harris* v. *McRae* (upholding the denial by the government of Medicaid payments for abortion), in which he asserted that "indigency," unlike race and (now, perhaps) sex, is not a "constitutionally suspect" category.[14] In plain layman's language, that technical terminology tells us that it is permissible to make legislation which has the effect of discriminating against the poor, as opposed to legislation which discriminates against, say, blacks or women. What these quite puzzling distinctions between race, gender, and class suggest is that we can read whatever principles we will into the Constitution so long as we can give persuasive reasons for them. But it is the reasons that must be persuasive, not mere invocation of the wholly ambiguous phrases of that document. To repeat over and over again that racial or even reverse racial discrimination is uniquely impermissible, without explaining why, is not to give reasons.

However, when we look at the reasons actually given on occasion for making race a totally unacceptable category of discrimination even when the intention is to reverse past injustices, it is difficult to find them persuasive. Perhaps the most plausible is one that is not always expressed overtly, though it probably lies behind all the statements quoted above: that on the historical evidence "race" is simply too dangerous a category to be given any kind of official sanction. That way, it is sometimes said, lie the Nuremberg Laws. (Justice Stevens makes this reference directly in his dissent from *Fullilove* v. *Klutznick.*) But the cogency of this warning disappears on reflection. In the first place, most affirmative action in fact has to do with gender, not race, and no one has ever perceived any such danger lying down that road. In the second place, the danger of group representation is not in the principle itself—it has been a major principle of American life, from the "balanced tickets" of New York city and state elections to the control of different areas of public employment in urban areas by different ethnic groups—but in the fear that some groups will be excluded, or worse, as were Jews in Nazi Germany. But we must remind ourselves that in the United States this alarm is indeed raised mostly by Jews (sometimes writing as though the United States were but months away from becoming Nazi Germany) and hardly ever by blacks. This is a very noteworthy fact, since if compulsory ghettos are ever re-created in the United States they will likely be for blacks, not for Jews or Slavs or any other white ethnic group. Blacks are well aware of that, and yet they flock to take advantage of affirmative-action programs, demand representation and sometimes even resegregation in all walks of life, and form caucuses in every profession in which they have any membership to speak of.* They understand, that is, that although the principle of

---

*It is sometimes asserted that in the United States black people themselves oppose affirmative action, since when Gallup polls ask people whether they think jobs and admissions to higher education should be allocated on the basis of "individual merit" *or* "membership in a minority group," most blacks, like most women, choose the former answer. However, these poll results tell us nothing about "public opinion," though they certainly provide validation of Justice Frankfurter's proposition that "on the questions you ask depend the answers you get." It is hard not to believe that the pollsters are as disingenuous as those who interpret their "results." The appropriate question, of course, would be something like: "Should we rely on institutions that have previously dis-

pluralist group representation may pose all sorts of dangers for the efficient cooperation of diverse elements in maintaining social order, it certainly poses no danger of the institutionalization of genocide. Hitler was not a pluralist, nor did he believe in the "representation," à la John Stuart Mill or any later pluralist, of any social groups whatsoever. His principle, indeed, was the very negation of pluralism, in that he insisted on the "representation" (through himself) only of the *Germanness* in everyone, that is, of their *likeness,* and the exclusion and ultimate extermination of those who were not truly "German." The principle of representation through affirmative action allied with the principle of compensation to disadvantaged groups certainly entails the imposition of marginal costs on members of comparatively advantaged groups; but to treat compensation to previously excluded minorities as though it were equivalent to the violent exclusion of minorities is perverse. The perverseness of the argument reveals that whatever those who put it forward intend, they are not concerned with fundamental principles of justice.

As for the other reasons given for the wrongness of "reverse discrimination," they are hardly more persuasive. "Injuries are suffered in fact, claims made, and burdens carried by individual persons," writes Cohen. We know, however, that we constantly use gross categories in allocating cost and benefit, on the presumption that we are more likely in that way to turn up a useful number of the kind of individual case we are looking for than we would be if we searched for specific individuals. There are programs that grant tax incentives to employers who employ ex-convicts, or the physically handicapped, or participants in vocational education programs, but provide no method for establishing the need of individual participants; so too, under the Comprehensive Employment Training Act, the physically handi-

---

criminated to reward individual merit, or should we make sure that they do so through affirmative-action requirements?" What people mean by "merit" when they are asked about it is itself a very tricky question; undoubtedly most people who would benefit from numerical quotas also think that they as individuals deserve the benefit on one ground or another; for a further discussion of this point see pages 185–86 below. In any event, with public opinion the proof of the pudding is always in the eating (never in the polls), and the *behavior* of women and racial or ethnic minorities with respect to compensatory programs tells its own irrefutable tale.[15]

capped are automatically eligible for job training regardless of individual need. All recipients of old-age retirement benefits are (in the United States) eligible for hospitalization under Medicare, although unlike Social Security itself Medicare is not paid for solely by the contributions of the insurees. Indeed, any means-tested program of welfare benefits which defines need (or "disadvantage") as substandard income is subject to Cohen's objection, but since it would be prohibitively costly to ask every individual to establish need on a personal basis, we usually forgo that effort and use the categorical definition instead. And as we have already noted, veterans establish claims to various veterans' benefits without ever having suffered in any particular way. In all these cases, of course, we can argue that all individuals in the category as grossly defined have done something, or been deprived of the chance to do something, to such an extent as to merit some slight additional recompense from the rest of us. But surely *all* veterans have suffered on behalf of their nation no more than have *all* blacks or women been discriminated against by it, and therefore deserve neither more nor less by way of compensation.

Moreover, not only do we often allow claims to be made in general rather than by specific individuals who have been clearly designated as "injured," but we also invariably do unavoidable harm to "innocent" persons. That is not an accident, it is a necessity from which there is no escape. Every regulation is perforce a taking; every program, public or private, imposes a burden on someone while distributing benefits to someone else. Cohen's suggestion that we can avoid injuring the "innocent" is palpable nonsense. "Society," as Norman Mailer once remarked, "consists of people hurting other people"; at the very least, that is certainly true of competitive capitalist societies.

Thus, when private businesses lay off workers because demand has slacked off, they do not dispense only with those who are themselves guilty of slacking off; when they close down perfectly productive plants in order to relocate where they can exploit cheaper labor and earn greater profits, it is not because the workers they disemploy *en masse* (or the community they denude of capital) have been guilty of malfeasance. Kaiser Aluminum did not give Brian Weber a place in its training program, despite his seniority, because he was a white male, and that did injury to an "innocent" person. But for Kaiser Aluminum to take away a black man's job in a period of contraction, by laying off or firing workers on the "last in, first out" principle, is to do a much more serious injury to an equally "innocent" person—and it is an injury that is done constantly. More fundamentally, when a national government engages in a countercyclical, anti-inflationary policy—raising interest rates, tightening the supply of money, cutting expenditures—it is in the full knowledge that (in the United States) skilled auto and steel workers will be thrown out of work by the thousands and people on "welfare" may be left below the level of mere subsistence. Indeed, whenever political leaders or businessmen call for "belt-tightening," or say that "sacrifices must be made," they mean that other people must tighten belts and make sacrifices; it is not recorded that any politician or businessman has ever reduced himself to penury in order to help combat inflation. Do Cohen, Glazer *et al.* find the standard operating procedure of capitalism itself to be unconstitutional, or morally unacceptable? If they do, they have certainly never said so.

Similarly, many of the same people who oppose affirmative action do not hesitate to argue that productive efficiency requires the dismantling of occupational health and safety controls, which is to say that social utility requires the imposition of costs on "innocent" workers in the most dangerous industries. Zoning regulations impose costs, and so does the granting of exceptions to them. Progressive taxation imposes an exceptional burden on those who have "innocently" earned more than the average, and flat taxation imposes a proportionately excessive burden on those whose earning power is, through no fault of their own, relatively limited.

The argument that public policies must do no harm except to people who deserve to have harm done to them is, again, an argument that there must be no public policies, that all public regulation and control should be abolished. But that is merely a way of ensuring that harm will be done to "innocent" people by a different group of policy-makers (such as the management of Kaiser Aluminum), who call themselves "private" but bestow rewards and impose costs on us all as they wish (see Chapter 7 below). Discrimination—that is, biased or weighted selection— is at the very core of all our social-choice procedures, which indeed do injure many people who have done nothing to "deserve" the injury and reward many people who have done nothing to "deserve" the reward. As we have seen, to claim a reward as of "right" for "merit" is to claim the right to injure someone else. That the opponents of "reverse discrimination" cheerfully contemplate the injury done those excluded from professional training schools by their test scores, but not that done to Bakke and Weber, suggests that they have no real concern for the proper allocation of "injury" to "individuals."

Nor can we be any more satisfied with Glazer's principle of extending "the full status of equality . . . to every individual." What is exactly at issue is not whether but how best to do that. Presumably Glazer and other inegalitarians would agree that women, blacks, and members of several other minorities have in the past been deprived (and in many cases are still being deprived) of jobs in areas ranging from law enforcement and fire protection to banking and high public service, for reasons unrelated to actual performance criteria; and that they have been deprived of entry to professional and other training programs for spurious causes, or for superficially genuine causes which originate, however, in conditions of oppression or exclusion from which white males have been comparatively free. To return to my earlier discussion, they have been subject to the burdens of caste, which were often added to or were causes of the more generalized burdens of class and are, in any event, a heavier weight to bear in a generally open society. The intellectual and moral irresponsibility of any statement which pretends ignorance of this irrefutably established historical condition reveals itself even more decisively in Justice Stewart's remark that "the color of a person's skin and the country of his origin . . . bear no relation to . . . disadvantage," as though they were not in actual fact among the major determinants of "disadvantage."*

People discriminate on the basis of race, and place of na-

---

*The average American, I think, is more ready to accept the visible truth of racial oppression than the more subtle notion of sexual oppression. Nowadays, however, any casual sampling of magazines published by and for women (*Ms.* is a good place to start) will turn up uncountable cases of the conscious slighting of women and their place in the world of affairs, ranging from the lightly contemptuous to the viciously hostile, all utterly without shame—and all demonstrating the strongest possible evidence of an unyielding intention to discriminate.[16]

tional origin, and gender; that is, either overtly or covertly they will take those characteristics into account when dealing with others over whom they have power: they will stereotype. Knowing that this is likely to happen, how better can we stop ourselves from discriminating than by recognizing the truth of our actions and making ourselves consciously and deliberately counteract our learned predispositions: by using the suspect categories openly and positively rather than covertly and negatively? From the standpoint of social utility there are very strong reasons for extending the principles of affirmative action as far as possible in every social realm (see pages 192–96 below); but from the standpoint of doing justice to individuals the necessity for affirmative-action programs, quotas, and the like is simply that the motivations and judgments of those dispensing the rewards of position and prestige are totally untrustworthy. They have never done anything but discriminate against women and various racial and ethnic minorities, and that continues to be so. In the past decade alone dozens of major class-action suits alleging discrimination in the employment, promotion, or compensation of blacks and women have been settled or lost on the complainants' terms by prominent corporations and universities and by state and local governments; hundreds more are wending their way through various state and federal courts. It makes no more sense to rely on the men who have committed those acts of discrimination to behave themselves voluntarily than it does to rely on a plausible, friendly lion not to eat the ox.[17]

The reality of discrimination also casts a different light on the contention of some opponents of affirmative action—a contention put forward as usual without any regard to actual evidence—that people who benefit from compensatory programs are thereby demeaned in their own eyes. That argument, of course, assumes that the beneficiaries of affirmative action know that they are really "inferior" and have *only* received their position because of "who they are"; it rejects the assumption actually made by most minority job applicants, that they are capable persons but that some kind of affirmative-action guidelines are necessary to force their prospective employers to recognize and reward their capabilities. In other words, this argument, like Jensen's, assumes either that there has been no discrimination to begin with or that its victims are unaware of it. A principle which we rationalize only by adopting the posture of an ostrich is hardly compelling.*

As for the alleged practical problem that Glazer points to, does he really believe that it is *more* difficult to decide whether Native Americans, say, have been discriminated against as a group than it is to turn up every single Native American who has ever been the object of any discrimination, or whose parents or grandparents have been the object of the kind of exclusion that is passed on to new generations? Similarly, does Cohen really believe that it would be a more onerous imposition to adopt a general principle of compensation for the injuries of massive discrimination than it would be to have investigative teams hunt down the actual culprits in every single case of discrimination against minorities? Are the white males who will suffer marginally owing to the settlements of those class-action suits really more culpable (of what?) as individuals than those who would suffer marginally if a generalized principle of compensation throughout the business or education sector were adopted? In fact, the essence of Cohen's proposal is absurd: the people who are "guilty" in his sense never have suffered and never will suffer, since they are either dead or are themselves the authorities; in the latter case it costs them nothing to be told to compensate, since they merely pass the cost on to their underlings, or to the next generation.

Finally, Glazer, Bell, and others also make much of the

*There is yet another reason why we must wonder about the confidence with which it is sometimes asserted that if people obtain a position on grounds in addition to their "objectively" tested capabilities ("merit") they must feel demeaned. I have already noted that extrinsic factors often play a crucial role in recruitment to prestigious and remunerative careers. Do all those corporate directors, bankers, etc., who got their jobs, first, because they were somebody's son, second, because they were male, third, because they were Protestant, and fourth because they were white feel demeaned thereby? It would be interesting to ask them—and to ask the same question of the doctors who managed to get into good medical schools because there were quotas keeping out Jews, the skilled tradesmen who were admitted to the union because two members of their family recommended them, and so on. Implicit in this critique of affirmative action, clearly, is a notion that whereas it's never painful to be rewarded because you are in the majority or the established elite, it's always painful to be rewarded because you're in the minority or a marginal group. Thus the argument reveals itself as another strategy for "blaming the victims" and thus keeping them in their place.[18]

difficulty of deciding exactly which groups ought to be the subject of affirmative-action programs. But this is a debater's point, not a considered argument. The answer is the same as the answer to all such queries, especially those involving the distribution of benefits by government: people put their case before the court of public opinion or its representatives. In an ideal world they would win their inclusion in compensatory programs (but an ideal world would have no need of compensatory programs) merely if their reasons were persuasive. In the real world they must also have at least some kind of "clout," if only the ability to be a social nuisance; but they still will not win their case if they cannot make the kind of persuasive appeal that it is all too easy for blacks, Hispanics, Native Americans, Orientals, and women to make with respect to the charge of massive discrimination against them. There are indeed groups, such as Americans of Slavic descent, who feel discriminated against in American life and are also excluded from the scope of compensatory affirmative-action programs.[19] In and of itself, however, that is an argument only for extending those programs, not for abolishing them.

All these objections, in other words, have the same characteristic; though they are presented as matters of deep principle, their actual impact is simply to encourage the doing of nothing. The people who offer these arguments never explain how victims, in a situation of merely formal equality, are ever to compete on truly equal terms with those who have victimized them for generations, or who have benefitted from their past victimization. To say, as Glazer does, that "compensation for the past is a dangerous principle" is to do away with compensation, since few people ever publicly admit their culpability in matters of discrimination (except, as I have noted, occasionally with respect to women), and we can usually infer that it has occurred only by analyzing data from "the past." "Justice" which requires nothing more than clearing obstacles out of the way is not justice but its counterfeit. In Glazer's terms, we might say of two families who have been competing in an endless marathon that "justice" merely requires taking off the shackles that the members of one of them have had to wear for the first hundred miles and letting their children run thenceforward on "equal terms." His commitment is against, not for, "the full status of equality" for every individual.

IV. The argument in principle against establishing a rule of representation for excluded minorities as one more extrinsic factor to be considered in addition to the narrow definition of "individual merit" when parceling out social rewards, is thus devoid of substance. However, in actuality most defenses of the rule of rewarding "merit" are only disguised versions of a much different argument: the argument from social utility. That is apparent in Bell's remark that it is an absurd society which doesn't have its "best men" at its head—a remark clearly based on utilitarian reasoning rather than on any notions of doing justice to individuals. It is also apparent in Justice Stewart's peroration in the veterans' preference case, *Massachusetts* v. *Feeney*. Speaking for a majority which upheld the Massachusetts veterans' preference statute, Justice Stewart made it perfectly clear that the Court upheld that "right" against the contrary "right" of women who claimed that the law discriminates against them, on grounds apart from mere personal desert:

> The veterans' hiring preference in Massachusetts, as in other jurisdictions has traditionally been justified as a measure designed to reward veterans for the sacrifice of military service, to ease the transition from military to civilian life, to encourage patriotic service, and to attract loyal and well-disciplined people to Civil Service occupations.[20]

To encourage . . . to attract . . . that is the language not of "merit" but of maximizing social utility. The same thing is true of our reliance on scores in the world of higher education, for the defense of tests, grades, and scores has always been on the grounds that they not only indicate personal merit but also correlate with future job performance, thus indicating an expected contribution to the betterment of society. As Herrnstein and Jensen make clear (see pages 99–100 above), it is the test of social utility, and nothing more, which leads us so to subject people's fates to statistical predictions (sometimes valid, sometimes woefully invalid) that doing well on tests presages satisfactory on-the-job performance. It is accommodation to social forces, and nothing more, which leads us to make seniority the key to job retention and promotion in the skilled crafts and in the civil service; it is the reproduction of existing power relationships, and nothing more, which validates a system of representation that rewards minorities having disproportional resources at their command but not minorities possessed only of disproportional stigma. The reasons behind the failure of millions of American citizens to gain the rewards that others have gained have no more nor less to do with their individual merit or lack of it than the Davis Medical School's decision to exclude Bakke had to do with his merit or lack of it.

What of the relationship between social utility and our peculiar way of making competitive decisions about people and their fates, then? There are two aspects to this question: first, can we really measure social utility, and thus know that one person is contributing more to it than another; and second, what, ultimately, do we think social utility consists of?

In answer to the first question, we must begin by clearing up the strange confusion between "merit" and "meritocracy" that has crept into the discussion of social policy—a confusion epitomized by the inclination of many writers (Herrnstein and Jensen are examples) to treat Michael Young's famous satire on the latter concept as though it had been offered as a serious proposal.[21]

Young described a (somewhat) futuristic British society (of the year 2034) in which all jobs were filled on the basis of IQ testing and a sharply stratified oligarchy developed. He was, of course, parodying a dream that has been explored by writers ranging from Plato to George Bernard Shaw. All such explorations have had in common the assumption that the primary system for allocating individual positions in a society is best built not around on-the-job performance but around "credentials," that is, passage through some kind of educational or training system thought to lead appropriately to one kind of career rather than another. We might call this a system which rewards promise. Unfortunately, no one has ever been able to offer a convincing response to the obvious criticism that (as I indicated at the end of Chapter 4) we waste much more talent and skill than we develop to the extent we actually follow such a model. (Plato's *Republic* can be read as an exposition of just how staggeringly difficult it would be to put "meritocracy" really into effect even in a small-scale, pretechnological society; modern meritocrats who think of Plato as their spiritual ancestor clearly have not read him.) The people who finish, say, at the top of their class in law school please themselves and their parents and their teachers, but we have no knowledge that as a group they have ever contributed more to the practice of law (whatever we might mean by that) than any random sample of law school graduates; indeed, we have no reason to believe that the actual practice of law or any other profession, nationwide, would be any different if there were no class ranks or even no grades at all. The same holds true for all gradations based on tests that purport to predict the competence of policemen, clerks, etc.: only tests that actually mimic the performance situation in a realistic way—that is, only genuine apprenticeships or internships—can begin to be taken seriously as "credentials" of prospective social utility.

Otherwise, it must be reiterated here that credentials of any kind are very poor predictors of eventual performance, so far as we can tell.[22] (It is interesting to note that Davis and Moore, the authors of the functionalist theory of social stratification discussed earlier, explicitly denied the intent to suggest that any known method of recruitment to important social positions is better than any other.) We have no meaningful measures of performance or social productivity; no way of decomposing GNP, or marginal growth in GNP, into individual contributions; no way of quantifying whether one person's social performance has been more helpful to the rest of us than another's. As for "objective" indicators of performance such as test scores and grades, there is still no evidence that they actually indicate any performance in which "society" might take an interest, though they may on occasion predict individual earning power. At any rate, even to the extent such indicators might be valid, it will only be in a very gross fashion. The person who scores 700 on a test undoubtedly has, as of the moment, greater aptitude at whatever is being tested than does the person who scores 350, but as comparisons become much finer than that they also become pointless. We can observe that, inferentially, in the shabby attempts of Jensen and Herrnstein to produce the only "evidence" for the relevance of "objective" tests that they can find —which turns out to be no evidence at all. Moreover, the record of the past suggests that when labor is scarce the qualifications of people previously thought "unqualified" are seen to rise drastically (e.g., American women during World War II). It is our unwillingness to allocate the resources either to open up more positions in institutions of higher education and professional training, or to provide remedial training that will bring people up to the capacity necessary for carrying out useful, well-rewarded tasks, that relegates millions to the technological scrap heap. In effect, we refuse to tamper with the pyramidal, hierarchical division of labor; that, to repeat, is a failure of social policy, not of available human resources.

The second question, though, is the truly crucial one: What do we mean by "social utility"? We have already seen that many extrinsic factors, as well as technically defined or intrinsic skill, play a major role in the decisions we make about the employment of manpower (or womanpower). It is central to the discussion of "affirmative action" or "quotas," then, to inquire whether social utility will suffer if "representativeness" comes to play a role such as has always been played by those extrinsic factors. Affirmative action, properly understood, is much more than an attempt to rectify injustice to groups by bestowing rewards on some of their members; it is fundamentally an attempt to get interests, needs, skills, and ideas that have previously been ignored spoken for throughout the social order. As I remarked at the beginning of this chapter, the principle of affirmative action is subsidiary to a more general principle of group representation. In that sense the entire question of individual "merit" that the *Bakke* case raised is purely diversionary; the response to the critics of quotas is not merely that quotas are as reasonable a way to select from the pool of all qualified candidates as any other (see the argument at page 174 above), but that there *is* social relevance, even potentially "merit," to being a competent member of some social group, in and of itself.

However, looking at the best-known contemporary merito-cratic arguments, we find no comprehension of the issues that are really at stake. When, for example, Daniel Bell opposes "merit" to "representation," we have no idea what he means by "merit." Specifically, we need to remind ourselves that the credentials we require of aspirants to important social positions do not (except in the formal political world, and then usually spuriously) include any evidence of commitment to the betterment of anyone or anything but oneself. Despite the superimposition of welfarist institutions and government regulations of various kinds on the structures of primitive capitalism, Adam Smith's "invisible hand" still rules, for better or worse, in the world of individual performance. But is the question of "individual merit" really that simple to resolve? Exactly what is it that the "best men" do to demonstrate their bestness? Presumably they make wise decisions of one kind or another, but to what end and on whose behalf? It will not do to answer "Society's," as does Bell; we are talking, not about some cultural or geographical entity that is usefully conceived of as a whole for administrative purposes, but rather about our material well-being, and in that realm the truth of the adage about one man's meat being another man's (or woman's) poison is inescapable. It is now widely recognized that in accomplishing every good we also produce some concomitant ill; even purely economic growth in constant dollars does not necessarily provide an unalloyed increment in the sum total of social welfare.[23] Whether an "individual" is deciding what kind of medical specialist to be and where, or what kind of new industrial plant to build and where, social costs as well as benefits will result from the individual decision. Any society, and certainly American society more than most, is made up of a great number of communities defining themselves not only geographically but also emotionally, and either fully or partially conscious of having some interests different from or opposed to the interests of other communities. We cannot avoid confronting the question, which Bell and other opponents of the representational principle avoid, whether that very principle might therefore not also have the *merit* of furthering, if not the over-all social welfare, at least the over-all welfare of some distinct group of people, some definable community, within the larger society.

We have only to think about that issue for a moment to see that the antinomy "merit" versus "representation" is false. Just as a truly meritorious performance in any endeavor represents a fulfillment of the desires of someone other than the performer (otherwise we would not even deign to notice its merit), so a truly representative performance confers merit upon the individual who has engaged in it by providing some additional well-being for those who have been well represented. Mill did not propose proportional representation in elections simply because he thought that method was fair; he also thought it would be beneficial to "society" as a whole to ensure that certain people, such as the highly educated on the one hand and the working class on the other, should have a proportionate say in determining social policy. It is not proposed that we establish racial quotas in hiring policemen because those offering the proposal prefer racial justice to "efficiency" or "order." Rather they question, among other things, whether it is really "efficient" or "orderly" to encourage (by continuing to hire them and thus implicitly condoning their behavior) the well-known predilection of inner-city white policemen for shooting unarmed black males at a strikingly higher rate than they shoot similarly unarmed white males; or, more broadly, whether a police force that resembles an occupying army is really more effective, all things considered, than one that could accurately be perceived as a neighborhood peacekeeping force that would prosecute offenses which harmed the neighborhood and ignore those which did not. Similarly we might suggest that, the bulk of police work being what it is, any society in which half of the police force is not female is an "absurd" society that is multiplying violence and disorder rather than controlling it (assuming police forces to be necessary at all).

To take another but related problem, for quite specific reasons of social efficiency we need many more physicians not only willing to serve in areas inhabited largely by minorities but likely to be trusted and thus properly utilized by the residents. In the same way we need many more women as gynecologists, psychotherapists, surgeons, and general practitioners, for women are often very poorly served by men filling those roles. So too "society" (that is, a particular part of it) badly needs more black and female lawyers "aggressively" to represent interests that the white male legal establishment historically has shown little concern and sometimes even much scorn for.[24]

The same type of comment can be made about ownership and management of the mass media, of small and big business, not to mention the staffing of political institutions themselves (Mill's principle of proportional representation). What is important in all these institutions is that the mere presence of "minorities" at the centers of decision makes it very difficult for leaders to propose traditional exclusionary policies out loud, since the reasons behind those policies cannot be uttered in sexually or racially mixed company; eventually, what cannot be uttered will not even be thought and will no longer find its way into policy. It is inconceivable that a television station owned and managed by black people will accept the relegation of news about blacks to a secondary status, or their continued stereotyping in drama and comedy—practices which are normal and even necessary for white-owned and white-managed outlets catering to a mass (and thus mostly white) audience. It is inconceivable that a newspaper managed and written by women, of whatever ideological persuasion, would relegate news of vital interest to working women to a "women's" or "family" page.

To sum up this point, we can take a single case as a paradigm for all these justifications of representation. In 1964, as the Civil Rights Act was being debated in the House of Representatives, Representative Howard Smith of Virginia, chairman of the Rules Committee, introduced an amendment to add the word "sex" to the list of forbidden discriminations contained in Title VII of the act. His expressed purpose was to defeat the entire act by making a mockery of it; the liberal male congressmen who sponsored the bill perceived this and vociferously opposed the amendment. The amendment, however, survived because and only because Representative Martha Griffiths of Michigan rallied all the female representatives present, Democratic and Republican alike, to speak on its behalf. That strange coalition of anti–civil rights conservatives and women prevailed; the amendment was passed and so too the act, as amended, by the House. In the Senate a similar situation arose. At one point during the long debate on the act Senator Dirksen, who thought that outlawing discrimination based on *race* was "an idea whose time has come," attempted to get the Republican Steering Committee to commit itself to removing the offensive word "sex" from Title VII—a move which failed, again, only because Senator Margaret Chase Smith of Maine also sat on that committee, and it was impossible to muster support for Dirksen's initiative in her presence. Thus "sex" remained in Title VII—and sex discrimination has over the years become the single most litigated area under the 1964 Civil Rights Act.[25] None of that could have happened without the presence of women as representatives (in this instance) of women: just as white policemen will be considerably less likely to brutalize black teen-agers when they are in the presence of black colleagues; just as supervisors will be a good deal less likely to engage in the sexual harassment of women on the job if their own supervisors are women; just as female station managers will be unlikely to arrange an all-male panel to discuss the subject of wife abuse (as recently happened in my own viewing area); just as review boards for military promotions will be less likely to find that black candidates lack "leadership qualities" if black officers are on the boards, or corporate personnel committees to find that females lack what Goldberg calls "aggressiveness" if there are women on the committees.[26]

None of these outcomes is guaranteed, of course. In theory there are more direct ways to achieve the representation of interests that tend to be slighted. In an ideally democratic society, all professional work would genuinely be thought of as public service: lawyers would expect to put in a good part of their time serving those most in need of help, as would doctors, engineers, and teachers.[27] All moves in that direction in our own partially democratic society, such as requirements by medical schools that students receiving certain kinds of financial aid commit themselves to a term of practice in medically deprived areas, should obviously be encouraged. But those kinds of programs are still not satisfactory substitutes for the implementation of more representation in a plural but unequal society, in which you may have to have been born into a certain group in order to be fully and sympathetically cognizant of the problems that others of your kind may face. In any event, we do not demand ironclad guarantees even when, as in what we call "politics," we deliberately seek out representativeness as a characteristic of those we elect or appoint. What is certain, at any rate, is that it is straining our credulity beyond acceptance to ask us to believe that whites are as likely as blacks to serve the interests of blacks, or men as likely as women to serve the interests of women (or, for that matter, millionaires as likely as workers to serve the interests of workers). And since these interests are real interests (at least as real as any others), and they are the interests of a part of that "society" whose utility is supposedly maximized by the recognition of "merit," it is plain that (contrary to the arguments we have been considering) representativeness, mere membership in a caste or class, is not irrelevant in determinations of qualification. Among all those who legitimately belong in a given skill pool, what it is they may be expected to represent rightly becomes one aspect of their "credentials," and of their "merit" if they actually perform appropriately. Community service is not a side-effect of the "utility" we offer, as individuals, to "society," but rather its very core.

To be sure, community representation is not the only aspect of social utility. Obviously we desire that socially important work, however defined, be done by people competent to do it: that is the significance of the concept of the "skill pool." But what reason have we, other than bigotry, to believe the ideological propaganda which assures us that affirmative action, or representation in general, means the over-all devaluation of competence? Once again, aside from the tales told to each other by academics (who are hardly disinterested observers), no evidence for that proposition has ever been adduced. We know that in many cases the kinds of performance that new people bring to old tasks are different: that will often be one of the reasons we want new people doing those tasks. But we have no reason to believe those performances will be not only different but inferior unless we already believe that blacks and women are innately inferior. Otherwise, it cannot be said too often that even taking evidence about IQ or "aggressiveness" at its worst face value, there are still more than enough potentially talented blacks, women, and members of other minority groups to go around; and that not only in the past but in the present as well their talents and skills have been wasted by discrimination. Affirmative action, to repeat the crucial point, is essentially a method for forcing the rest of us not only to allow unrepresented communities of interest to be represented but also to utilize capabilities we would otherwise ignore. To admit that the races, ethnic nationalities, and sexes are roughly equal in capability, but then to suggest that policies deliberately designed to take advantage of that capability will degrade the social order, is to contradict oneself. Only the meretricious arguments of Jensen, Herrnstein, and Goldberg stand behind the fear that our collective material well-being will suffer from the implementation of more equality.

V. To say what we have said so far still does not wholly answer the question whether we increase over-all social utility by adopting policies for greater representation in so many diverse walks of life. The utility to some minority members of implementing the principle of representation is obvious. But that kind of utility is not what we really mean by social utility, which refers rather to "the greatest good for the greatest number." In no immediately obvious way can we argue that *that* "good" would necessarily be served by the widespread adoption of affirmative-action policies. Of course, the people who compose the categories recognized by federal government guidelines as deserving affirmative action are potentially a quite decisive majority of the citizenry, if for no other reason than that all women are included in their number. But for several reasons they are very, very far from forming a conscious majority. First, rather than replacing white males in those instances where affirmative action is practiced, its beneficiaries have mostly been competing with each other for the leavings of "white" society. Second, fundamental differences of social class and group interest divide all these groups both internally and from each other; most notably, white women often conceive of themselves as having more interests in common with white men of their social class than they do with the members of other minorities, male or female. Most crucially, the principle of affirmative action has so far only been articulated as a boon for the educated middle classes rather than (as should be the case) as a subsidiary aspect of the general demand for more egalitarian representation in all areas of the polity and the economy.

I shall return to this point later; suffice it here to say that because the majority has not been persuaded that the extension of representative principles in the guise of affirmative action is in its immediate interest, it must initially be appealed to on other grounds: on the grounds that, as Mill argued in his essay on utilitarianism, the general interest in a larger sense is attached to a particular conception of justice and is therefore realized only when that conception of justice is also realized. That is, we must try to demonstrate that through achieving the greater representation of minorities in all social spheres we accomplish more than merely the efficient servicing of social interests; we also approach more nearly a political goal we have always actually been pursuing. In other words, to demonstrate that it is (metaphorically and literally) rightful for the poor to beg in the streets or steal bread or sleep under bridges even while others are forbidden, we must go beyond arguments about utility to a deeper understanding of the fundamental principles of liberal democracy itself.

What has to be understood above all else is that the demand of previously excluded groups for the suspension, so to speak, of the traditional rules in order to further their inclusion on equal terms into the polity is a demand that society undergo a moral revolution.[28] The revolution that these groups are trying to make, however, is not the kind that attempts to turn the world upside down at a blow, as did the Chinese and Russian revolutions. Rather, and in sharp contrast, it would be a continuation of those liberal democratic revolutions of the eighteenth and nineteenth centuries that brought the notion of "representation," which is now central to all our ideas of legitimacy (including those of "the real majority"), to the forefront. It is a continuation, but with one profound difference.

What makes the liberal democratic revolution different from more encompassing social revolutions is the limitation of its demands to those of formal civic equality. Despite the scorn radicals have had for formal democracy, its formalism is also its great strength: among citizens—not just the rich or the armed—formal democracy does convey a range of potential powers and protections in a roughly equal distribution. However, we must emphasize the phrase *among citizens*. For it is also important to note what the liberal democratic revolutions did not at first call for: namely, a new conception of the political community as necessarily including every adult human being. Rather, the institutionalization of liberal democracy follows a prior determination as to who constitutes the citizenry, who is fully worthy of mutual respect, who ought to be fully represented. Once that determination has been made, those who deem themselves worthy can exclude those whom they deem unworthy from full-scale participation with a relatively clear conscience.

If we pursue this insight, then, we come upon an important difference in the relationship that certain groups have to the original liberal revolution. Put simply, white males, even those of working-class origin, *naturally* belong to the class of those enfranchised by the original liberal revolution; women, black and white, and (in the United States at least) black males do not. (That is also true of Native Americans, and perhaps Hispanics and Orientals.) It is relatively easy, furthermore, to state what it is that is different about white males. Every citizen in the new civil society of liberal capitalism possessed one very fundamental form of "property": the ability freely to sell *his* labor as a commodity on the "free labor" market. This was a form of equality in property never before conceived of or realized in any human society; its practical implication was that the franchise ultimately had to be extended to all men, because capitalism could only entrench itself politically if all men were perceived, and came to perceive themselves, as real or potential "capitalists."

Historically, that is, though the notion of majority rule was developed by philosophers of the rising bourgeoisie, it could be implemented only by extension of the franchise to the working class (at least, the "respectable" working class): to all free laborers. Without a system of suffrage related to the institution of free labor, liberal capitalism was radically incomplete; it had not yet fully realized itself. The suffrage was a structurally necessary aspect of liberal capitalism in that the rationalizing concept of equal opportunity for free men ultimately made no sense without it.

Contrarily, white women and black men (and also black women) did share or had shared a crucially different fate. Most black men in the United States had literally never been free. Despite the Emancipation Proclamation and the passage after the Civil War of those constitutional amendments that confirmed their freedom and bestowed on them full civic equality, including the vote, they remained ex-slaves in the view of most whites. Subsisting mostly as dependent rural laborers, they remained deprived of the effective social status of free labor for a long time thereafter; they remained less than full citizens of the polity. As for white women, even though many of them as individuals were in the nondomestic labor force (more often than men as temporary laborers, of course), it was still possible to argue that women were not free laborers, should not be free laborers, and indeed would be much worse off if they were treated as free laborers (since few people were under any illusions about the real meaning of that condition in the nineteenth century). Through the institutionalization of the double day, most women also maintained their domestic role, a role almost never filled by men. For both historical and practical reasons, therefore, the common image of all women was (and for many people still is) of a class of people who, whatever else they might be doing, remained essentially domestics and essentially (like ex-slaves) dependents; "protective legislation," in fact, was shortly to become the hallmark of that status.[29] Thus the denial of the vote to women was not an exception to the rules of liberal capitalism, for women themselves, as such, were an exception to the liberal notion of citizenship.[30] Despite Victorian rhetoric about how much "better" they were than men and how dangerous it would be to deprive them of their moral superiority (a position that Goldberg and Gilder echo), they, like blacks, were less than what it takes to be a "free person."

Thus white women as well as blacks were a "minority." For we can now see that the real condition of being a "minority" is precisely to be perceived as something less than fully human, above all less than fully independent. That is why the struggle of all minorities (in this sense of the term) for recognition is different from the struggle that incorporated white working-class men into the polity in most capitalist nations. That latter struggle, though it had to be made by workers themselves, required more a political victory than moral invention; the bourgeoisie themselves (their own gravediggers, as Marx said) had earlier defined the version of moral equality that justified the inclusion of white male workers into the polity. (In the United States, for various historical reasons having mostly to do with its foundation in agrarian rather than industrial capitalism, the extension of the franchise to workers actually preceded the great surge of industrialism.)

As I shall argue in the next chapter, the civic rights of "free laborers" are far from being any kind of genuine counterbalance to the more real powers of those who own and control productive capital; the exploitation of labor is as real for white males as for anyone else. On the other hand, in most capitalist societies and certainly in the United States, the time has long since passed when to be born of working-class parents was to be *in principle* debarred from the world of accomplishment and authority. The limits of social mobility in class-stratified capitalist societies are real enough, but they no longer have that oppressive moral dimension. A free laborer within the moral ambit of capitalist political economy is a person who is considered as capable as anyone else of becoming a successful capitalist. The children of workers are not generally felt to be excluded by anything about their human natures from becoming professionals or executives or owners of the means of production. A bit of income redistribution, a touch of institutional (especially educational) reform, and individual hard work are thought, by most people, to make that possible. No Jensen, Goldberg, or Herrnstein has arisen in this century to argue their innate inferiority. Herrnstein's claim, as we have seen, is that "too much" social reform will create a hereditary underclass, not that one already exists (and despite his disclaimers, it is impossible to avoid the impression that when he looks at the potential underclass, he sees mostly blacks).

But expectations are different, and that version of equality does not work in the same way for those who do not look or seem like *citizens.* For blacks and women (to whom this discussion is limited only because in the United States they are paradigmatic, not because they are unique), the position was and is much different. We can see that difference in the extent to which American white male trade unionists have in the past collaborated with their employers—a class with whom they otherwise have usually been on hostile terms—to keep women and blacks out of the work force except on terms that would confirm their inferiority.[31] Even after the extension of the suffrage first to black men and later to all women, white male workers who would fight to the death for the rights of "free labor" would also deny those rights to all blacks and to white women. Rights of citizenship, in effect, had been granted to people who on the whole had not yet "earned" them—had not yet, that is, been perceived as equal, free laborers. Although the reason for the general perception of blacks and women as not being "free men" had been different in each case (and was also uniquely different for Native Americans and Hispanic Americans), the outcome was the same. Broadly speaking, white male workers were finally granted full civic equality because they "deserved" it, blacks and white women in order that they might prove they really did deserve it. But to return to our original theme, to do that they would have to effect a moral revolution. They would have to show that the commonplace expectations about them are false, that "upward mobility" is as possible for them as for white males. But it visibly is not, and thus there is lacking in American society a real belief that members of those groups, once thought incapable of self-government, now really are capable of it and really deserve all the other rights, opportunities, and privileges of citizenship that follow it. Nor will all the invocations of formalistic equality in the world do the trick. It is no accident that decades after receiving the suffrage, both blacks and women in the United States remain trapped in a vicious circle that diminishes in extent only slowly. Since the vote grants citizenship, it seems to most people a reasonable expectation that once having received the vote, "minorities" ought to manifest all the appurtenances of that citizenship thereafter: that is, take on a proportionate share of leadership roles, social responsibilities, and productive roles in the economy. But they do not, and as the years roll on it comes to seem that the fault can only be theirs. Men like Jensen, Banfield, and Goldberg do no more than rush in to fill a vacuum that is begging to be filled. Blacks remain obstinately black, and women remain obstinately female, and both continue to show clear signs of their previous exclusion, of a past which finally comes to be seen by many people (even some among themselves) as ineradicable. Their IQs remain lower; they manifest less "aggression" in the public sphere. It appears that the granting of rights did not accomplish what was promised; the exclusion may well have been justified after all. As that kind of disillusionment sets in, each new right or privilege obtained becomes the enemy of the next one; the people who have already reached the stage of civic (even if not economic or truly political) equality ask, Why aren't you as successful in politics and society as we are? You've had every chance.

Ordinary means of selection and advancement, Glazer and Justice Stewart to the contrary, will never bring about a change in this state of affairs, or at least will not bring it about for an unconscionably long time. In the absence of persuasive evidence to the contrary, too many people will harbor at least a sneaking suspicion that Jensen is right about blacks, or Goldberg about women. Women especially will continue to mobilize themselves as I have described earlier (blacks in the United States have been much less successful on this score, perhaps because of the disproportionately greater burden of social-class exclusion to which they are also subjected), but their victories will remain token victories; their "aggression" will continue to seem unnatural and will not be rewarded, as is men's, by the men who have the power to give and withhold that reward. There will never be so many members of minority groups in positions of importance in a particular community at one time as to justify what must seem like a strikingly novel belief in their real—not merely formal—human equality. Those doubts, of course, will be held even by the objects of discrimination themselves, who as they advance toward adulthood will continue to dissipate their potential skills, or deflect them into the traditional "second-class" avenues. Lacking a proportionate share of role models for leadership-oriented activity, their own ambitions must come to seem, on the average as compared with those of white males, not credible.[32] Moreover, since the primary and secondary training received by minorities and women often encourages that dissipation and deflection (as in the steering of women away from scientific activity), and since their own families often will encourage only the traditional ambitions, they will not be equally prepared to take advantage of any "equal opportunity" that is offered them. As I have suggested earlier in discussing both blacks and women, what is accomplished by the ordinary efforts of capable white males often requires virtual heroism to be accomplished by those who are effectively second-class citizens. Under such circumstances, knowledge that a merely formal rule of "equal opportunity" has replaced the overt inequality of the past is as liable to produce cynicism as hope. Only the creation of leadership classes which forcefully demonstrate the capabilities inherent in the communities of the excluded, while at the same time serving their previously unserved needs, will break into this vicious circle and provide the kind of impact necessary to change such deeply rooted group behavior.

The effects of past and present discrimination can also be described in the reverse way, of course; as the author of one study of racial inequality has put it (in remarks that would apply as well to sexual inequality):

To say that current inequality is the result of discrimination against blacks is to state only half the problem. The other half—the part generally not discussed—is discrimination in favor of whites. It follows that merely eliminating discrimination is insufficient. The very direction of bias must be reversed, at least temporarily. If we wish to eliminate substantive inequality we waste effort when we debate whether some form of special treatment for the disadvantaged group is necessary. What we must debate is how it can be accomplished.[33]

Affirmative action is necessary to combat not only the cynicism or hopelessness of the disadvantaged but the expectations of assured success of the advantaged: in other words, to put everyone on an even footing. Those critics of affirmative action who proceed by ignoring any serious consideration of disadvantage or its obverse, advantage, thereby only demonstrate their lack of interest in eliminating "substantive inequality," or more likely, their desire not to eliminate it. The self-image they try to convey is of wishing only to let the chips fall where they may. But they have read Jensen and Goldberg: they know how the chips will fall. They say they long for a time when only what one was as an "individual" counted, but that time never existed. In the United States, certainly, it was always crucial to one's fate whether one was black or white, male or female, Occidental or Oriental; and never more so than in the "good old days." In the struggle for social advancement large numbers of people remained behind simply because the social definition of people like them—people belonging to "their" group—ensured that they would be given a chance to accomplish nothing; or that their accomplishments, usually achieved by dint of much greater effort than was necessary for those with the right background, would go unnoticed or be denigrated.

All of this, of course, was also true of many people who belonged to no "minority," as I have defined that term, but were simply from an inferior social-class background. A final insight we can derive from this analysis, however, is the revealing light it casts on the frequently encountered assertion that "reverse discrimination" may only be justified, if at all, on grounds of social class rather than race or ethnicity or gender (i.e., special preference for the children of the poor). To be sure, the victims of poverty are certainly a group that can be conceptualized as deserving compensatory benefit in all sorts of ways, especially within our educational institutions. But the argument that poor white males deserve preference before or over middle-class blacks and women is not nearly as compelling as it might have appeared at first glance.

In the first place the latter, as we have seen, bear the burden of a legacy of both formal and informal second-class citizenship that their "middle-class" position very often must fail to overcome. In addition, whereas their importance as models and inspiration for others like themselves is central in justifying "discrimination" on their behalf, that significant role no longer needs to be performed by the children of the white poor. They—or their parents—need money, not inspiration. No one has questioned their innate capacity for a long time, and in the United States at least there are even powerful social myths (the "log cabin," Horatio Alger) based on their alleged potentiality for overcoming deprivation. When they fail to achieve upward social mobility, therefore, it is not because employers or educational institutions discriminate against them on the grounds of their poverty, but because their poverty has denied them a chance to develop their capacities, or an appropriate style for expressing their capacities, even to the extent that they could take advantage of "opportunity" or compensatory treatment were it offered them. When genuinely middle-class women or minority-group members "fail," on the other hand—that is, accomplish less than on superficial indications they might have—it is most often because they have been held back by their (often correct) belief that they will be excluded in any event, or by actual discrimination, or both. That is the internalized belief system that has to be overturned by changing the conditions which seem to validate it.

Thus class and caste as barriers to equality clearly require quite different kinds of attack. The only way to abolish the effects of gross class differentials, as between "poverty" and "affluence," or "worker" and "owner," is to abolish the differentials themselves: to abolish the institutions that allow some to be poorly off or without power through no fault of their own, and others to be well off or powerful through no merit of theirs. Merely increasing the rate of upward social mobility without changing those institutions will only redistribute the impact of class somewhat, while leaving the society as stratified as before within a given generation. Caste differentials, on the other hand, *can* be abolished through (and only through) increased *group* mobility, precisely because their origins are located not only in institutions but also in the historical perceptions about and discriminatory treatment of minority groups. The struggle to throw off the burdens of caste has to be related to the struggle against inequalities of class to be politically effective; but it is a different struggle, and requires a different kind of moral invention.

VI.
This, then, is what I mean by the phrase "moral revolution." Within the context of liberal democracy, a moral revolution is the achievement of "equal rights," or at least effective rights, truly rather than formally. Unfortunately, we hardly expect those who hold a disproportionate share of valued positions to surrender that share simply out of a sense of charity. That is why we must attempt to expand our understanding of what is implied—what is compelled—by the principles of liberal democracy rightly appreciated. Of course liberalism is only an ideology, but it is the ideology of this society and thus it has force. On the other hand, that force is limited: an idea which is perceived by so many people as being against their own or their group's interest, and which furthermore calls forth all sorts of dormant but traditional intergroup hostilities, can hardly spread unchecked. Thus the kind of change that symbolizes and at the same time implements a revolution in our moral perceptions can only be brought about, initially, not by acts of legislation by the majority's representatives (though that is sometimes possible, as in the aid-to-small-business program), but by the decisions of courts in response to lawsuits; or the appointments made and regulations issued by chief executives and public agencies in response to mass protests, "trouble-making" disturbances, or interest-group demands. To rule out these types of "representation" as illegitimate is to say that minority rights have no place in a liberal, pluralist society—a contradiction in terms.

Affirmative action—"reverse discrimination"—is an essential step in the moral revolution that brings minorities into the polity on equal terms; that enables a once-excluded group of people—an "inferior" caste—to achieve the same general level of social esteem and reward as those who were never excluded as such, or have not been for a very long time. For the excluded or slighted, the token—the only plausible token—of success in this revolution is that they come to fill their proportionate share of positions of power, authority, and responsibility within the over-all community; to realize, then, that they can take on new social roles and fill them successfully. Actually, even that is to demand much too little. When one set of interests monopolizes an institution for decades or centuries, the impact on institutional behavior is so great that the effort required to change the course of the institution is correspondingly immense. If, to take just one example, every judge appointed in the United States, at any level, during the next several decades were either a woman or a member of a racial minority, the ways in which our judicial system has ignored or misunderstood the interests of those groups would only begin to be brought under control. Similarly, if all admissions to medical and law school during that same period were of women and "minorities" only, or if for that same period all television stations, public and commercial, were stripped from their present management and turned over to new minority or female management, the arbitrarily imposed inequalities of the past, and the social injustices and pathologies encouraged by those inequalities, would barely begin to be rectified. And that is true for almost every walk of life I have mentioned in this chapter.

These are not practical proposals, of course, but merely a guide to reflection on how deeply we have internalized a specious inequality among groups, both in our institutions and in our psyches, and how intransigent are the barriers to social equality among *individuals* that we have thus created. Recognition of that reality forms the context within which we must judge all concrete proposals for "affirmative action," "reverse discrimination," "benign quotas," and the like. It is pointless to worry that there may be too much representation of excluded and marginal peoples in, as Bell puts it, our "leading institutions": in our lifetimes, there will never be enough.

That is also why the use of the word "tokenism" as a term of abuse misses the point entirely. As a *substitute* for equal citizenship, tokenism is useless to the group that is being fobbed off with tokens, and painful to the individuals who know that their social role is all too much less than it is made to seem. But as a first step on the road to equal citizenship, "tokenism," that is, initial individual accomplishments as a prelude to the drama of collective accomplishment, is absolutely necessary. Of course, such a "moral revolution" will be nothing of the kind if it is simply brought about by fiat, if it is imposed only from the top down. But that is precisely *not* the case with respect to the new principle of representation and its subsidiary aspect, affirmative action, which exist, not because "government bureaucrats" have been attempting to aggrandize their own power, but because for the past two decades so many people have uncompromisingly demanded them; because many second-class citizens have refused any longer to accept their relegation to that status and have agitated for whatever programs are required to end it.

Viewing it in this context, we can see that the idea of group representation is an attempt—perhaps the only viable attempt —to complete the original liberal revolution: to abolish not inequality (*that* would be a new revolution indeed) but the perception that some are *innately* "less equal than others"; to do away with the notion that a "minority" is anything more than a random collection of people who lost the last vote.

What, finally, of majority rule, which together with the notion of "equal protection of the laws" makes up the expression in our society of one law for the lion and the ox?* Put simply, the notion that majority rule is the core of civic equality, and that formal civic equality ought to be the one rule for all, does not work when institutionalized minorities— castes—are locked into a subordinate place in the body politic. There can be no "fairness" between permanent unequals; no fairness between colonizers and colonized; no fairness between the self-governing (in

---

*Interestingly, unalloyed "majority rule" in political decision-making is the equivalent of "ordinal ranking" in the world of job-seeking: those with the most votes dominate all those with lesser numbers of votes just as those with the highest test scores and grades are supposed to dominate all those with lower test scores and grades. Each implements a single standard of choice in a manner that looks perfectly fair on the surface but actually has the effect of consistently excluding disproportionate numbers of identifiable groups of people from equal participation in some realm of social life.

however limited a fashion) and the governed—even if the former are a majority.

In the next chapter I shall argue the legitimacy and necessity of concerted public action (by "the majority"!) to replace the capitalist division of labor with a more egalitarian set of social institutions. Clearly, demands by the previously excluded for representation and compensation will fail if they are not successfully located, as so far they have not been, within this broader strategy for social change. Even more clearly, any such program must include realistic policies not merely for "full employment" but also for the technological upgrading *and* democratization of our productive institutions, for the transformation of a stultifying division of labor. Any majority of those who are generally excluded from the exercise of power and authority under capitalism will only become an effective majority when all its members feel they have something to gain from the implementation of principles favoring minorities; when they feel that what is being sought—specifically, the extension of representative democracy throughout the social order—means not just a new set of privileges for a few at someone else's expense, but rather the creation of an egalitarian structure that is potentially beneficial to all of us.

The proponents of egalitarianism have not as yet succeeded in making that response to our efforts seem reasonable. But the difficulty so obviously inherent in effecting a coalition of all those excluded in one way or another from a reasonable share of power cuts both ways. It is not merely that moral consistency demands recognition of the considerations outlined here, if we are to give more than lip service to the legitimating ideal of equal citizenship for all. Beyond that, and more practically (perhaps), spokesmen for "the real majority" would do well to remember that a "majority" divided into competing minorities is bound to be nonfunctional. No popular movement for more equality, for genuine self-government and equal liberty (or even for mere maintenance of the liberal democratic status quo), will ever attain the status of an effective majority if it is divided at the start by barriers of caste and thus distrust among its would-be supporters. As long as such divisions exist, the aspirations of any majority to moral authority will be mere pretensions, capable of eventuating only in the kind of futile, backward-looking political action that has recently been the hallmark of American political life. A democratic politics without moral power is ultimately a pseudodemocratic politics without any power; it will never replace that class and elite domination which is much less dependent on moral justification simply because it rests on centuries of habituation.

Those barriers of caste will, however, continue to pose an insuperable obstacle to concerted popular political action in the United States as long as public discussion of available alternatives is dominated by those who, having benefitted from the old rules of pluralism, work against the adoption of new rules that might benefit others. Therefore it has to be the function of intellectuals who are part of the movement for more equality—who understand that, in Christian Bay's words, "a society is as free as its underdogs are"—to argue the moral justice of affirmative action, of group representation; to show that the necessary and just price of more equality for all is not only more representation for all but special compensation for some; to support the moral revolution.[34] The precondition for the further abolition of gross social inequality is the abolition of the status of minority: and that can only be accomplished by abolition of the idea that one rule for all is "equality."

CHAPTER

THE NEW INDIVIDUALISM:
THE STATE, THE PUBLIC,
AND LIBERTY

I. It is all too clear that opponents of "reverse discrimination" appeal to "principles" that effectively make it harder for others to attain the social position they themselves now hold. The assertion that nothing further need nor should be done now, though admittedly all sorts of interventions of a different sort were necessary earlier—to help *them*—is transparent. The inegalitarians whom I shall call "anti-statists," or new individualists, or ideologues of the free market, are more subtle: they seem simply to reject government intervention *in toto*. But as we shall see, that appearance is misleading; they too have managed to discover a principle which, even more decisively than "due process" or "equal protection of the law," defends the beneficiaries of past intervention against those who would benefit from it in the present. Whereas the opposition to "reverse discrimination" functions as an obstacle only to upward-mobile blacks, Hispanics, women, and other minorities, the anti-state principle is designed to freeze all class distinctions, all artificial barriers between the lives of people in a society, permanently into place.

Like the images of fairness to which the opponents of special preference appeal, the images that free-market ideology evokes have sunk deep into the common consciousness of many people in all capitalist societies, at least as guiding generalities.

In that sense, anti-state ideology or simple cynicism about the state has come willy-nilly to take on a partially democratic character, not just in the United States but even in some of the more overtly statist European societies as well. Populist anti-statism focuses our attention, not on the popular role of government agencies in "interfering" with the free market, but on their unpopular, bureaucratic role in preventing the free expression, not to mention the realization, of communal and group interests. Thus, free-market ideology has a significance that extends far beyond the influence of its most visible adherents, for it helps set the tone for and define the boundaries of the popular discussion of public policy. Political leaders and political journalists who would not dream of restricting public policy to the steady-state maintenance of a national currency implicitly accept the notion that "government" is primarily a burden and that "government action" usually constitutes an invasion of "rights." Thus professional economists are freed to discuss the "costs" of the public regulation of economic enterprise without ever mentioning, let alone attempting to quantify, its benefits;[1] proposals to redistribute power over immense agglomerations of capital, to redistribute unearned wealth, or to bring industrial workplaces, monopolized mass media, or professions that provide essential public services under democratic public control are assaulted with a kind of libertarian passion one would expect to see directed against a proposal to abolish habeas corpus or freedom of speech.

We must, therefore, confront the argument of these new individualists in order to distinguish between that part of it which simply serves as a mask for privilege and that part which truly does locate obstacles that the pseudodemocratic, uncontrolled state apparatus has placed in the way of genuinely democratic self-government.

II. The analysis of the free-market argument that follows takes off largely from the writings of Milton Friedman and Robert Nozick. In Great Britain we would undoubtedly wish to look instead at Friedrich Hayek; professional economists would be more interested in the works of Ludwig Von Mises and organized American "libertarians" in the writings of Murray Rothbard.

Between them, though, Friedman and Nozick represent the impulses of that approach fully, and furthermore, are more familiar to an American audience (and certainly more influential). Friedman is the most public policy–oriented of all the free-market theorists, and his approach to the discussion of public policy very clearly shows how that discussion instantly becomes ideological and thus alternatively either vacuous or self-serving. Nozick more than anyone else (more even than Hayek or Rothbard) has developed a consistent philosophical justification of free-market theory; the importance of looking at his work as well as Friedman's is to see how quickly even the justifications of a professional philosopher descend into just another version of the ideology that is more readily apparent in less thoughtful theorists.[2]

In what he obviously thinks of as an expression of the viewpoint he publicizes so constantly, Friedman writes that the major functions of government

> must be to protect our freedom both from the enemies outside our gates and from our fellow-citizens; to preserve law and order, to enforce private contracts, to foster competitive markets. Beyond this major function, government may enable us at times to accomplish jointly what we would find it more difficult or expensive to accomplish severally. However, any such use of government is fraught with danger.[3]

There are several striking aspects of this formulation to which we will return later. What is perhaps most indicative about it is the way it typifies the kind of equivocating language in which a casually proffered exception ("may enable us at times") can eat up the alleged rule, sometimes ravenously, leaving us with an accurate feeling for the author's class interests and attitudes but none the wiser about any operational principle he might be pursuing. One finds the same kind of incantation in the writings of all those free-market theorists who refuse to be absolute anarchists. Thus early on in the most reputable contemporary version of free-market theory, Robert Nozick's *Anarchy, State, and Utopia*, we encounter the formulation that the "night-watchman state of classical liberal theory [is] limited to the functions of protecting all its citizens against violence, theft, and fraud, and to the enforcement of contracts, and so on."[4] On page 272, having by then made the minimal state his own, Nozick repeats the formulation in similar terms, ending again with the phrase "and so on." Nowhere in between (or thereafter) do we encounter the slightest clue as to just what actions "and so on" might consist of. When these men do attempt to explain their "principle," we are given no clue as to the limits, if any, on "legitimate" state action.

Why should this be so? What is the real content of the ideology of limited government (but not anarchism) that has to be hidden by equivocation? We can find out the answer to that question if we look, for example, at the alleged distinction between national and internal security and other modes of public collective activity—a distinction which Friedman (and Nozick, too, in a different fashion) treats as fundamental.

This distinction, obviously, makes sense only on the assumption that the state manifests two distinct types of public policy with respect to those two realms of action. Superficially at least, that is a false assumption. As E. H. Carr long ago pointed out, there is no policy describable under the headings "welfare state" or "planned economy" or "public control" that cannot be or has not been undertaken precisely in the name of national defense.[5] Not only that, but in fact the national defense sector of any social order is now and probably always has been perceived as a welfare state by its clientele. Thus when Friedman asserts, in *Capitalism and Freedom*, that the military should be public but long-distance highways should be privately owned and operated, we must charitably assume his ignorance of the fact that the bulk of the interstate highway network in the United States has been constructed in the name of national defense. Indeed, we must wonder if he fails to realize that if the nation had only a national defense sector and no other institutions of planning or welfare at all, we would find our politics taken up entirely (instead of only partially, as now) with squabbles and even serious clashes over the disposition of "defense contracts" (a term which would spread to cover just about everything but the manufacture of pipe cleaners); the location and closure of "defense" plants; the development and distribution of natural resources; the desire to import versus the drive to self-sufficiency (at present in the United States, tariffs on wrist watches, Swiss cheese, and peanuts are justified in the name of national defense); the distribution of income between "defense" and "nondefense" workers; the question of special preferences and rewards for veterans of both military fronts and the industrial home front and their dependents (a conjunction the French have actually made); the amount of money to be spent (and the ways in which it should be spent) on vital services like education and transportation (like the National Defense Highway Act, the National Defense Education Act pays for a much greater proportion of the sector to which it relates than could possibly be explained by any logistics planner); and so on. In wartime, or cold-war time, even redistributive and antibusiness regulatory policies would be justified, as they often have been in the past, on the grounds that the lower social classes will be more vigorously loyal to the *patria* if they get a "fairer share" of the national product and are given reason to believe that everyone is being asked to "make sacrifices." The national defense state would easily become just as bloated as most present states, though it would probably be a good deal less democratic: less subject to those at least partial institutions of public control which tend to disappear whenever the magical phrase "national security" is invoked.

All of this is perfectly obvious; it is hard to believe that even professional economists and philosophers who know virtually nothing of political life could be unaware of it. On reflection, it is clear that what Friedman has in mind by his vague distinction —and Nozick's more elaborate justification of the limited state finally makes this clear—is that it is only policies that redistribute or regulate in the name of a superior goal of social justice that are to be condemned; conversely, to do in the name of social unity what might otherwise be considered an act of class conflict is permissible. Behind these elaborate formulations about what government can and cannot do stands the simple principle of Leviathan.

One expects the well-off and their representatives to oppose efforts at redistribution of any kind: why should people subvert their own interests? In theory, though, intellectuals are the group of people that are supposed to take a detached view of such matters—but how can any intellectual or academic hope to justify such a transparent rationale for self-interest as Friedman's? As a positive economist, Friedman himself is not capable of the kind of abstract theorizing such a justification would require, and that task has been performed instead by the philosopher Nozick. However, on close inspection, even Nozick's sophisticated argument fails to advance a single step beyond Friedman's cruder defense of privilege—perhaps because there is nothing at all where the next step should be.

Nozick's approach is to postulate (as against traditional "left" communitarian anarchists and "pure" libertarians of the right) that the minimal, law-and-order state *is* legitimate but that any more activist state must be illegitimate. How do we manage to come to a conclusion so helpful to the possessors of large amounts of property? The answer, according to Nozick, is that just such an entity as the minimal state (his term for it) would be formed by the purely voluntary activities of freely contracting, stateless propertyholders—if such people existed in a "state of nature."

If, Nozick continues, such people attempted to form a society, their first order of business would be, unanimously (since they would all have *something* to protect, or the hope of getting something if they didn't yet have it), to come together to hire a private protection agency, a sort of giant-sized Pinkerton's or Securicor, to defend them against all foreign or domestic incursions. And since this minimal state *would* be created voluntarily and unanimously by hypothetical rational actors in a hypothetical Nozick world, its minimal activities can be treated *as though* they were voluntarily supported. As conservatives have always known, it is perfectly "legitimate" for a nation to maintain a repressive secret police and an immense and destructive armed force to "protect property," but it is not "legitimate" for it to maintain a handful of factory safety inspectors: *that* use of government is, by contrast, "fraught with danger," and no one ever "agreed" to it.

But why, we reasonably want to know? Why is it that hypothetical rational actors can be imagined as voluntarily creating a monstrous version of Pinkerton's but not a child welfare agency, a safety inspectorate, an environmental protection agency? In attempting to answer that question we discover that Nozick's is a problem of the moral imagination. If we do not accept his morality, then his state-of-nature theory is pointless:

and it is a peculiar, class-bound morality he asks us to accept. Like all previous attempts to rationalize class privilege, it revolves around a very special and tendentious definition of the nature and role of property.

Property, in this tradition, has a moral virtue. It is what is made by *myself* (or earned from the sale of what I have made by myself), out of materials and with tools which I have either provided for myself or recovered from previously undeveloped land, and therefore it is rightfully *mine*. Only I (as Aristotle asserted) can be expected to take proper care of what is mine, and therefore only I have the legitimate expectation of being encouraged and allowed to take care of it. In the modern world, where land has long since ceased to be freely available, that would seem to be a philosophy only for factory owners and great landholders, but no problem. We need only invent the concept of my property in my own body and its powers to universalize the notion of property through personal labor. Perhaps neither the materials nor the tools I use were made by me, but it can be said (very loosely) that I rent them from their owner in return for renting him my labor power. Each earns something in the exchange—the exchange value we call "money"—and each rightfully possesses what is earned, since in each case it is at least a derivative of the supposedly pure "self." Each of us is, as Nozick would say, an "individual" with "rights" of possession, most especially the right not to be interfered with by a more-than-minimal state.

This bit of chicanery, for which we have John Locke to thank, seems almost to solve the problem, almost to lend a plausible reality to what is essentially a Robinson Crusoe fantasy. But it will not survive close inspection of its own premises—even leaving aside Marx's critique of the notion that there can be a fair exchange between him who owns a factory and him or her who owns only personal labor power. For a stable system of exchange does indeed require, as both Locke and Nozick say, a state. This is the state that could come into being, according to Nozick, through the voluntary actions of its inhabitants—hypothetically. But now we see, *pace* Locke, that what people have to protect is *everything produced by their own bodily powers*. Therefore we can also see how nonsensical, if not deliberately invidious, is the distinction between protecting our factories, houses, money, or commodities on the one hand and our children's prospects, our future health and safety, our opportunities for success in life, our desires to cooperate and share with others, and our very access to the protecting state itself on the other. All of these things, for me, are equally conceivable as returns on my investment of my labor power. All are, in Aristotle's sense, "things" which I can be expected to take better care of than anyone else, and of which I have the legitimate expectation of being encouraged and allowed to take care. Therefore, it is an act of moral arbitrariness to suggest that hypothetical rational actors would, to preserve their individualities, create only the minimal state-as-Pinkerton's-Protective Agency: the minimal *police state*. To protect what is "ours" we may just as well be imagined as having created, voluntarily and unanimously, through our separately individual acts, a full-fledged planned economy—not to mention a communal democratic utopia promising the utmost political say to each individual, which we can attain only by achieving a good bit of economic equality as well. Nor do we need the optimistic theories of Marx or Kropotkin about the nature of human cooperativeness to imagine this. We need only take an expansive rather than a contracted view of what people can think of *as their own*—of how far into their future, how broadly across their social space, how intermingled with the lives of others they can extend their vision of "their own"—to see how crippled by sheer self-centered thinking is the notion of the minimal state.

In a revealing passage in *Capitalism and Freedom*, Friedman suggests that if four friends were walking along the street and one of them spotted a twenty-dollar bill, not only should he not be coerced into the "generous" course of action (dividing the spoils) by the other three friends, but "the generous course of action is not clearly itself the 'right' one."[6] In one brief paragraph he thus manages to de-moralize the notions of both friendship and generosity; refuses to confront the kind of life problem that the ethic of redistribution is based on in the real world; and fobs off the amorality of chance in place of a morality of effort. No example of "social" relations could be more revealing.

By way of contrast to Friedman and Nozick, it is instructive to see how an earlier theorist of economic and political liberty,

John Stuart Mill, handled the same problem of defining boundaries between legitimate and illegitimate state action.*In his
Principles of Political Economy, Mill wrote more than nine
hundred pages in defense of free-market political economy. But
throughout that discussion he signally avoided defending the
principle of individual ownership of the means of production,
going so far as to suggest that the healthiest community would
be one in which all workers experienced the educational effects
of ownership and management. He concluded, moreover, by ap-
pending about forty pages in which he discussed possible exceptions to the free-market rule. But rather than avoiding the implications of his exceptions like an ostrich while pursuing the
dangers of intervention like a hawk, he delineated the nature
and extent of those exceptions so carefully that the last part of
his *Principles* can stand as an early exposition of the idea of the
welfare state.[7] Mill himself saw the contradiction in what he had
done, and gradually moved to disentangle himself from it: one
of the last acts of his active political life was to give a subscrip-
tion to the Radical Workingmen's Patriotic League—an organization much more accurately described by the first word in its
title than the third.

For Mill the problem was, on its surface, one of the interplay
between liberty and education. Having described liberty as rational action, he could not avoid recognizing that the exploitive and
stultifying treatment received by the average worker was bound
to make him an enemy of liberty, so conceived; though not a
socialist himself, he supported some socialist organizations simply because they and only they took the education of workers
seriously. He at last saw, one might say, that given the sociology
of capitalism, *On Liberty* was a utopian document; reducing the
relations between people to those of economic exchange and
noninterference could breed civility neither in those who benefitted nor those who suffered from that kind of political economy.

Beyond the question of education and civility, though, Mill
also saw that the problem for liberty was ultimately one of
encouraging rather than discouraging (as did the spirit of his
age and as do the free-market ideologues today) the growth of

---

*Mill is one of several inconvenient liberal philosophers whom Nozick manages
never to mention throughout *Anarchy, State, and Utopia.*

communal moral sentiment. In a rueful summary of Bentham's shortcomings he wrote:

> We have arrived, then, at a sort of estimate of what a philosophy like Bentham's can do. It can teach the means of organizing and regulating the merely *business* part of the social arrangements. Whatever can be understood, or whatever done, without reference to moral influences, his philosophy is equal to: where those influences require to be taken into account, it is at fault. He committed the mistake of supposing that the business part of human affairs was the whole of them; all, at least, that the legislator and the moralist had to do with. Not that he disregarded moral influences when he perceived them; but his want of imagination, small experience of human feelings, and ignorance of the filiation and connection of feelings with one another, made this rarely the case.[8]

So too, all those theories of the minimal state which define the liberty of persons solely as their ability to pursue their own self-interest show the same "small experience of human feelings." The minimal state, according to Nozick, is justifiable because we can imagine people unanimously agreeing to hire a private army to protect their property, out of which arrangement a state doing nothing more than that can legitimately grow. But that is precisely what we *cannot* imagine people unanimously doing. I would not do it; that is, I would not make the armed protection of my real and personal property the first or even second order of organized social "business," for I find that a morally repulsive ordering of what is important in life. That is also true of most of my friends, and I suspect it is true of a good many of Nozick's friends, as well as of millions of people in all walks of life from all nations—including even those in which for decades the controllers of the mass media have propagandized the view that self-interest narrowly conceived is the only real human sentiment. And we do not need eighteenth-century French ideas about the happy lives of South Sea Islanders to support our intuitive rejections of that view either: the Victorian English gentleman's reproof of his godfather, his understanding that our caring for ourselves is inextricably linked to our caring for and duties to others, will do just as well.

Of course, a standard sophomoric exercise in utilitarianism, which Mill himself flirts with in his essay of that title, is the argument that my interest in the interest of others or of society generally can always be reduced to just another aspect of my own interest—of what pleases me. In a lucid essay on the subject of "community," Robert Paul Wolff has shown that several states of being with which we are all familiar, such as taking joy in the shared experience of communal activities or of work, cannot be so reduced, in that the condition of my personal enjoyment is that someone else is sharing it, so that without the pleasures of others my own pleasure would cease to exist.[9] But we do not even need to argue that much to see how silly absolute egoism is. We need only note that if some people satisfy themselves by satisfying their own wants and perceived personal needs and others by satisfying the wants and expressed personal needs of others—kin, friends, neighbors—then we are dealing with two entirely different kinds of people; to describe both kinds as "selfish" is to destroy the meaning of the adjective, since it is then being applied to contrary states of mind.

A political egoist like Nozick cannot have it both ways. If the hypothetical social contract from which he proceeds to an individualistic, inegalitarian polity is supposed to be a legitimate intellectual construct because it is somehow based on human reality, on an accurate psychological depiction of real people, then it is a useless falsehood: no such contract could ever be agreed to unanimously, and we cannot find a distinctive justification for the minimal state in it. On the other hand, if this social contract is intended merely as a guide to the moral imagination, then, as Mill would suggest, it is a guide to a bad moral imagination. Whether from the standpoint of how people have actually conducted themselves in history, or of what we think a decent way for people to conduct themselves, the narrowly materialistic view of people on which the free-market theorists stand is either false or obnoxious. It was no utopian radical but rather that noted neo-Hobbesian Justice Holmes who remarked, about a case dealing with the question of restrictions on trade union activity, that one of the things "freely contracting" individuals might reasonably be expected to do with their individual rights was to give them up to a collective body that might protect those rights better than they could themselves.[10] And that is as true of our joint right to secure the health of workers, the conservation of resources, or the welfare of children as of the right to own *and dispose of* productive equipment. The concerns of the factory inspector, the ombudsman or ombudswoman, the works committee, the family visitor, the economic planner, and even the tax collector are every bit as universal, to the sensitive imagination, as are the concerns of the policeman. We need only note that, for example, there is a far lower rate of industrial deaths and accidents in those European welfare states with intrusive safety agencies than in the United States with a complaisant one. Are death and disfigurement to be somehow equated with liberty? And is it coincidental that there has never been any popular opposition to industrial safety enforcement in the United States, but merely a successful industry lobby? What kind of liberty is it that most people do not want? The anti-statists are in the impossible position of first justifying the free market on the grounds that it maximizes political liberty and then decrying almost everything people normally do with that liberty. In truth it is private privilege, not public liberty, that they yearn after.

III.
The minimal state, then, cannot deliver what most people mean by "liberty." Moreover, the "liberty" it does promise is betrayed and destroyed at the very moment of its inception: the moment at which, under the guise of liberating individuals, the corporate concentration of capital is liberated (or unleashed) instead.

The anti-statist opposition to the public control of enterprise is invariably based on the initial assumption that whereas public intervention in or prohibition of "capitalist acts among consenting adults" (Nozick's phrase) is *ipso facto* an invasion of liberty, those acts themselves are always the acts of free men and women. Indeed, the anti-statists write as though "consent" and "freedom" are the same thing, leaving one baffled as to what they would say if they found out that some or even most of those Soviet citizens who troop to the polls to vote for their "representatives" actually believe in what they are doing, that a great many Paraguayans actually want General Stroessner to be their permanent dictator, or that many of the millions of Spaniards who cried when Generalissimo Franco died cannot reconcile themselves to any democratic replacement. But the psychology of consent is not the real issue in any event.

The question of "public" versus "private" arises in the economic sphere only when ownership of productive property is defined in such a way that there are adverse interests created by the definition. On an anarchist commune, where everyone owns the means of production equally (not an equal share of them, but an equal share in the total ownership of them), there would indeed be no reason to prohibit, regulate, or supersede "capitalist acts among consenting adults," for they would take place, if at all, only in the sphere of consumption. In that sphere the number of your Coca-Colas worth my pack of cigarettes (or even the number of your work hours worth my pack of cigarettes, if work is arranged in that way) is decided only by our personal tastes, and the trade we arrange is truly "free." That stops being the case if one of us owns productive property and the other does not—that is, if capitalism exists. Of course, we can imagine a form of primitive capitalism (what Marx called "simple commodity production") in which everyone owns his or her tools of production and land to produce on, there being, therefore, no corporations, no labor market, and no exchange of labor at all. But in the present context that would be a state of economic affairs so primitive that (leaving aside whether it would be humanly desirable) there is no point in considering it. Certainly it is not what Friedman, Nozick, Hayek, and the other ideologues of market capitalism have in mind; they are not making an argument against interference with personal producers by the state, but against interference with corporations or other forms of extended enterprise.

Given any form of enterprise which transcends in its scope the labor of a small group of people, the question of ownership becomes crucial. It must be either by all jointly or by a few; it cannot be by each individual separately. Capitalism is the system in which ownership is the purview of a few; or, to put it another way, capitalism is the economic system in which the wages of labor are separated from the rewards (profits) of ownership. The latter are expected to produce reinvestment; the former are not. It is certainly possible to imagine a system in which all returns from sales are distributed as wages to all employees (rather than to shareholders), who then decide as individuals how much of their wages to reinvest—or decide as a community by majority vote. In such a system (perhaps we should call it "socialism") it would seem that there could be no interference by "government" with "property," since people would only be interfering with themselves and their own rights. By contrast, the whole purpose of the free-market approach to politics is rather to argue that the "majority," whoever they are, should not interfere with the few. Free-market ideology, that is, necessarily postulates means of production, whether in the corporate or some other mode, that have the legal form described so sharply by Hegel: "[I]t consists of external objects with the special character of being property, the embodiment of the free will of others, and hence from [this] point of view its recalcitrance is absolute."[11]

This "absolute recalcitrance" is what Nozick and Friedman mean by the "rights of property." But is a "free man" who owns large-scale means of production the same kind of "free man" as one who does not, who owns nothing but his own body and its ability to do labor? The answer was made clear by Marx over a century ago. The owner of a mere body is "free" to sell labor at its price, and gets the returns on that sale from his or her employer. The latter sells *products*, the price of which includes the price of the employed labor *plus* profit. But whereas the employee can bargain with the employer about the rate of pay for labor, there is no bargaining about the disposition of profit: that belongs entirely to the employer; it is the "property right" of ownership of productive property. (Without it, to repeat, we have "socialism" rather than "capitalism.") What is the particular and unequal freedom that is given, for no apparent moral reason, to the employers of labor and not to the sellers of labor? It can be described very simply by way of an example.*

---

*This discussion of what is in effect Marx's notion of surplus value proceeds without any judgment as to whether Marx was correct in his assertion that labor creates all value. It is not necessary for egalitarians to concur in that judgment, nor in the particular judgments which Marxists are prone to make as to whether managers, middlemen, and other "nonproductive" workers deserve a living wage for their efforts, or the suppliers of capital (be they individuals or collectives) some return for the benefits they have forgone by supplying finance to

We can begin this homely, even trivial example by imagining a family who live in a house near a lake, the use of which they easily enjoy only because a neighbor whose property abuts on the lake gives them access through his property, for no return other than friendship. The members of the family all work at a nearby industrial plant. They contracted freely to work there, agreed quite cheerfully to the contractual terms of employment, and consider themselves free agents still. However, because of its ability to employ them and their fellow workers at average wages lower than the average revenue it earns from the workers' total contribution to the sale of the product they help make (even after reasonable returns to investors, contributions to sinking funds, royalties to inventors, and reasonable wages for management are subtracted), the corporation is enabled to make a profit—to realize an investable surplus. With this investable surplus, which over time becomes immense, the company buys the neighbor's lakefront property for expansion purposes. It promptly closes down the family's access to the lake. Of course, the lake has a circumference, not all of which is taken over by the company; with some trouble, the family can still find a public beach. But then the company, which manufactures chemicals, begins to discharge their residues into the lake, polluting it so badly that the lake will be unusable for years, though not so badly that the society at large has a burning interest in bringing about an immediate halt to the discharge. (This fable is not exactly a fable.) The family decides to take its freely earned wages and move. At this point, however, the company uses its surplus funds to contract with a road-building company to drive a giant highway from its expanded operation to the outside world—a sloping downhill road on which giant trailer trucks reach a double-clutched climax about ten feet from the family's front door. Their property has become worthless; they can no longer sell it at a price that will enable them to replace it with

---

others. To understand the *political* significance of surplus value, we need only look at what happens after the reasonable rewards of all labor however defined have been paid, a "rainy-day fund" for the maintenance and replacement of plant and equipment has been replenished, and investors have been repaid at a (unanimously) agreed-on "reasonable" rate of interest. What is left over—"undistributed" or "retained" profit, amounting to hundreds of billions of dollars annually in the United States economy—is what we are talking about.

a similar abode. The company, of course, will buy it from them
—for a song.

What has happened, then? This imaginary (not very) family
have lost their property and concomitantly much of their sav-
ings, been deprived of the major amenity of their lives, and been
forced to move—quite possibly into housing owned by the company or one of its agents, so that they will now be dealing with
an impersonal absentee landlord who is trying to make a further
profit from their very living arrangements and will continue to
do so unless they actually leave the neighborhood and seek employment elsewhere. (Given what was in the past the normal
operations of unfettered "private" enterprise, they may also
have to buy provisions from the company at its prices, and be
forbidden to attend meetings with—or receive in their homes—
labor organizers or other opponents of "capitalist acts among
consenting adults." This kind of arrangement still exists in East
Kentucky coal fields.) Everything about their lives, in fact, has
been destroyed; and it has been destroyed by the normal operations of a "private" contract, respecting the rights of "property," to which they "freely consented." They had intended
merely to make a living out of a "fair" exchange of their labor
for wages; they may even (it is stretching a point to presume so)
have consented to conditions of work. But they certainly never
consented to help their employer gain almost total control over
their lives. Without ever expecting to do so in the slightest, this
family of workers have discovered the relationship between surplus value in the particular form of private profit outside their
control, and alienation: that situation in which "the object which
labour produces—labour's product—confronts it as *something
alien,* as a *power independent* of the producer."[12]

Moreover, alienation of this kind is not a psychic deforma-
tion that can be treated by a sympathetic therapist, nor is it even
merely a lack of owning one's own tools and thus missing the
joys of being a craftsperson. It is a social and a political fact: a
political fact in that any attempt by this family of workers to
rectify their situation through government intervention will require (and has required, over the past century) an uphill struggle
first to organize a mass movement, then to get it represented in
the legislative arena, then to command a majority, and finally to
pass meaningful legislation that works a real change in social

relations. None of that is necessary for the owners of capital who, as far as access to the minimal state goes, are already there. Nozick, as we have seen, posits that the state comes into existence as the outgrowth of a "dominant protective association" that is hired to enforce law by the owners of property; but how will the owners of a house attain equal protection of the laws with the owners of a factory that employs them as labor? Surely, among "consenting capitalist adults" of all people, the man who pays the piper calls the tune.

IV. The defenders of laissez faire have always replied to this kind of criticism with some kind of argument about the "natural" rights of ownership. Attractive as that approach seems at first glance, it will not do, for to sustain it requires disingenuous evasion of the plain facts of history. Those rights of ownership that we can imagine as being "natural" are not the rights that Nozick and Friedman claim for owners of the means of production under corporate capitalism; and the rights claimed for those owners are man-made rather than natural. Democrats, in fact, should be grateful to Nozick. In his development of what he calls the "entitlement theory of justice" (i.e., the theory of the rights of private property) he has shown more clearly than anyone before him (more clearly even than Locke, who maintained a careful ambiguity on the origins and rights of "entitlement") just how historically empty, though ideologically replete, that theory is. Nozick, to be sure, calls his theory an example of "historical reasoning": but that is merely an example of the ways in which ideology can substitute make-believe for reality and make words mean their opposites.

An individual is entitled to a propertyholding, Nozick claims, if it was originally acquired in accordance with what seemed at the time to be just principles and has been transferred by procedurally just means. Alternatively, an individual is entitled to a holding, even though originally acquired by unjust means, if its transfer has been intended as a rectification of past injustice in the original acquisition (and intermediate transfers), again by procedurally just means. Since state action, except for the minimal "night-watchman" function of police protection, is always coercive (if agreement were unanimous no state would be needed to accomplish it), "procedurally just means" of acquisition, transfer, or rectification cannot be accomplished by public intervention. Therefore any such intervention is unjust; and therefore we are able to distinguish the legitimate protection of freely gotten acquisition from the illegitimate rectification of inequalities.

All of this, however, has nothing to do with the world we live in. In that world, little property of note was acquired "justly," and no one ever agreed to the rules of transfer now in force. On the whole people did not enter the modern "social contract" willingly, but rather were dragged into it by force, kicking and screaming. We do not expect abstract political philosophy to tell a true historical tale, but we do have a right to expect it to be based on more than sheer fantasy. The moral rules that underpin capitalist economy—the modern reign of inequality in the economic realm—are that the means of production of goods for the use of others are both rightfully and for practical purposes best left in the hands of persons with no accountable public position; that the production process can always be thought of as decomposable into separate acts of the individuals who make it up, rather than being at heart a cooperative effort; that human labor ought to be sold by unattached individuals rather than carried on jointly by families, neighborhood groups, or other communities (the idea of labor as a commodity); and that anything produced and traded is by that fact a good—or at least not a bad —thing that ought to have been produced and traded (the fetishism of growth). If we ask how these rules came to be thought of as legitimate by most people the answer is perfectly obvious, though it is the reverse of Nozick's answer. Private property in the means of production, the "free" labor market, the workplace as an arena of individual strangers ("commodities"), and the unfettered expansion of production and trade came into being with the help, and only with the help, of massive force and violence either instituted or supported by the Leviathan state. If there is a fortune or a large-scale productive enterprise anywhere that has been built up without the coercive intervention of the state on someone's behalf to the detriment of someone else's, we will have to search long and hard for it. Whether one looks at the history of wealth and the development of industry and agriculture in the United States, or at the history of land tenure in France, of monopolies in Germany, of the "great houses" in Japan (which at times have been almost inseparable from the state); whether one looks at the peculiar development of the law of corporations in Anglo-Saxon or Continental jurisdictions, or at the legal theory of subsoil rights in the United States, one finds, *always* and *only*, the state with its laws, tariffs, subsidies, licenses, grants, and armies where Nozick speaks of "just" entitlements. Only in the offshoots of the British Empire among contemporary capitalist societies was it even a partially democratic state that helped create early capitalism: not that that makes any difference to Nozick or Friedman, both of whom emphasize (quite rightly) that the partially democratic state can be every bit as coercive of or unfair to individuals and groups as any other kind—as indeed it was when distributing legally protected land or capital to railroad barons in the United States.

"Capital," said Marx at the end of his history of primitive accumulation, *wherever* it is found, comes into the world "dripping from head to foot, from every pore, with blood and dirt." In a recent study, an economic historian describes the history of English economy since Hastings as a tale of pure and simple "looting." They both exaggerate—but only just, for an effect.[13] Where blood and dirt and loot have been absent, capital has dripped subsidies, grants, bribes, the manipulation of courts to create new legal principles, and all the other familiar public paraphernalia of "private" enterprise. That essential point has always been plain to serious students of society. Hobbes and Locke on the state of nature, Rousseau on the origins of inequality, Hegel on the absence of justice among families, tribes, or even in civil society, Weber on the foundations of economy and state: all were aware that in the order of things the appropriation and development of capital inevitably took place with the help either of force, fraud, and theft or (chiefly) of the monopolistic powers of the state. There is no other way, outside the uninhabited newfound land. Nozick himself seems to recognize this when he says that "past injustices might be so great as to make necessary *in the short run* a more extensive state in order to rectify them"[14] (my emphasis). But all he accomplishes in that passage is to show that his familiarity with the technical language of ethics does not extend to politics. States do not rectify injustice, except when *people* who have previously been excluded from the state seize and use its powers. The state, in other words, is not a neutral bestower of rewards to the just but an arena in which class and group conflict take place, and it will not "wither away" before they do.

When we turn from the question of original acquisition to that of "just transfers," the ideology of the minimal state fares no better. The mode of just transfer—that is, transfers not legitimated by the coercive powers of the state, according to Nozick—is the free market. But the most important aspect of the free market, without which fortunes could never have been built up and giant corporations could not exist, is the "free market" for *labor*. "Free labor" and the concomitant kind of workplace organization with which we are familiar are the absolute *sine qua non* of "free" capital's productivity, since capitalists are people who do not do their own work. The labor market —the institution which treats workers as commodities rather than trained people with skills, education, and professional dignity—separates what I've called the class life-styles of capitalists and their professional servants from those of workers. But far from being a natural development instituted by popular demand, the free labor market and the associated notion (which Friedman and Hayek make into the foundation stone of capitalism) that reward for work is properly distributed on the basis of individual commodity contracts have been around for only a small portion of human history, and they have not always or even often been welcomed by most people. People had to be disciplined to become what we nowadays call "workers," in effect; had, by what Max Weber describes as "a long and arduous process of education," to be broken loose from their traditional moorings. "In the past," he adds, "this was in every case an extremely difficult problem."[15] Nor did Weber mean to suggest, with his phrase about "education," the comparatively painless disciplines of compulsory public schooling, a very late development in the flowering of capitalism (though it too has usually been put to the service of worker "education"). The ways in which potential workers were "educated" to accept and endorse their new fate included—in addition to the authoritative, virtually coercive pressures of state-supported churches—new laws of vagrancy, vagabondage, and debt, the establishment of workhouses, prisons, and sanatoria, the destruction of housing for "development" and its replacement by company housing, the outlawing of workers' combinations and strikes, the forcible introduction of intense specialization of labor despite steadfast worker resistance, and the occasional bloody massacre. None of this had to do with the "natural" protection of property, but rather with enabling one small group of people to make property of another, larger group. Labor as a commodity now exists only because the allegedly dreaded state put its armed forces entirely at the disposal of private entrepreneurs for a period which in some nations lasted more than a century.[16]

Market capitalism, in short, is an episode in the history of international and civil violence. Its enabling acts were acts of war, revolution, the restructuring of political institutions, and other events in the natural history of the struggle for political power and for the "monopoly of the legitimate use of physical force within a given territory."

That was not accidental: labor had to be tamed for capitalism to exist. Workers had to be inured to the idea that for better or worse, like it or not, their kind of life was going to be different from, inferior to, that of other classes of people—and necessarily so. Without the now familiar distinctions between owners, professionals, and workers, capitalism could not exist; the accumulation of capital in private hands would not take place, as there would be no assurance of security for it, no assurance of a ready supply of wage workers, no assured loyalty from the middle class.

To deal with this problem in Nozick's own terms, we must consider his and Friedman's argument that the appropriate means of rectification of an undesired state of affairs (in a "free society") is "compensation" arranged by the market rather than interventionist public action. Capitalism can exist only when labor is treated as an interchangeable, nonhuman commodity to be sold freely on the market—as a lesser social class. (We have only to compare the way General Motors hires a sales manager with the way it hires a welder, or the way it pays them for their work, or the way their worktime is supervised, to understand "labor" as a deliberately designed system of inferiority.) But what form of compensation can be paid for being a victim of this system of enforced deprivation, for belonging to the social class "wage worker"? The only form of compensation the market can arrange, the worker already receives in the form of wages. Organized bargaining (which is, anyhow, an "interference" with the free market so beloved of the anti-statists) can produce better wages and fringe benefits. But these forms of compensation cannot change the comparative way of life of him or her who remains a wage worker. The compensation that workers really want is not to be a member of the wage-labor class, a disposable commodity, and the very principle of the free market for labor is that *that* kind of compensation never will nor can be offered to workers. It can be offered to individuals, of course, in the form of social mobility for themselves or their children, but they will have to be replaced by others who will take over their previous class position. As to that, the working class can be diminished in proportion to the other classes by technological change, but it cannot be eliminated in a capitalist society. Capitalism provides only market rather than communal incentives to work, and since the market incentives for wage labor are clearly unsatisfactory to most people, the market is cleared only because there are millions of available people who are *driven* to work at wage labor by their material circumstances. If everyone could choose his or her field of endeavor the way the average college graduate or graduate of a professional school does, few people would choose to do the really productive work of society.* Only in some different system, in which informal class barriers had been eliminated or attenuated in the way I have described earlier and entry to any career line whatsoever was truly by equal, free choice, would the principle of market compensation work: dangerous work would be paid more, wearyingly responsible work compensated for by extended summer vacations, workers given more civic rights than nonworkers, and so on. Then people might actually sort themselves into job categories according to their personal tastes, and the productive work would still get done. But that is to say that for the principle of compensation to function correctly, capitalism has to be abolished!

Moreover, even leaving aside the question of its historical origins and the impossibility of subjecting it to the principle of

---

*See my remarks on pages 82–84 above.

"compensation," it is also true that a "free market for labor" cannot be managed without a good deal of coercion from the state. Again, that is because of the nature of social classes in a capitalist system. Let us suppose, for example, that laborers working for a manufacturer think that they are being underpaid, or overworked, or overexposed to carcinogenic substances. If they were sellers of a product (that is, a manufactured thing) they would withhold it from the market until its price was met, and if their belief that the product was underpriced was correct they would clear the market at the higher price. Thus the market gives aid and comfort to mistreated sellers of goods: price rises or cutbacks in production or both are available to capitalists as a means of getting compensation from consumers who, for example, have insisted on some costly environmental reform but refuse to pay for it. As a last resort, furthermore, capitalists confronted by consumers who continue to refuse to pay the market price for a product can declare themselves unable to make a profit and shut down; society may go without a desired product, but one rarely hears of major shareholders in large corporate enterprises who suffer personally when the enterprise goes out of business (usually, in reality, closes a subsidiary). The capital remains in the owner's hands, and there is always someone else to sell it off to and then premature retirement to be enjoyed at a healthy standard of living. The ability of well-cushioned owners to withdraw their services without challenge is one of the most inalienable "rights of property."*

That is not true of workers. Their withdrawal of services is the strike; but without having means of coercion legally available to them they will be unable to make their strikes effective in a minimal (nonwelfare) state. If workers walk off a job they will be replaced by other workers willing to work in dangerous conditions, or at a speeded-up rate, or for what the strikers think to be low wages. As discussed in Chapter 4, the difference in their situation from that of the employer is immense. The workers,

---

*Throughout Western Europe social democratic legislation has modified and limited the "right" of corporations to close down plants, move operations, lay off workers, etc. The United States remains what Nozick and Friedman might call a "free society" in this regard—i.e., the right to do injury to other people is unlimited if you have the power to do it.

having lived off the proceeds of labor, which are (per capita) much less rewarding than those of capital, will be in no position to withdraw from the economy for even a short while as can the employer. They cannot simply quit work, but must force the employer to rehire them. Furthermore, the employer has available a pool of unemployed labor, or the putative support of private lending institutions to finance a period of technological improvement after which the strikers' labor will be unnecessary; or both. Thus the rationalization of class divisions which ideologues like Friedman and Nozick engage in creates a version of "Catch-22." Unlike owners, who are legally free to withdraw their services, or managers and professionals, who hardly ever need to, wage workers, by the very definition of labor as a commodity rather than a profession (and the conditions of supply and demand attached to that definition), often have to use force and violence if their withdrawal of labor is to be effective. In a nonminimal state such as the anti-statists decry, they might have informal government support in the form of unemployment compensation or "welfare" payments (where those are available to strikers), or strike funds of the kind that only the most gigantic unions are able to build up (though usually but a pittance compared with what employers of the same size have available to tide them over). But in the minimal or purely capitalist state, only coercion will help striking workers. That is because effective withdrawal of labor entails preventing others from taking the strikers' place, keeping the workplace shut, and other such tactics. But then the workers will be attacking the property the minimal state was set up to protect. Like the hypothetical family of my earlier example, they too will have discovered the iron fist in the velvet glove of the "minimal state."

Or let us imagine that, in pursuance of Nozick's principles, a budgetary or programmatic decimation of the Occupational Safety and Health Administration "releases" workers to deal with their working conditions themselves, as "free" individuals; and that the employees of the asbestos industry then demand that the collective power to make and enforce all health regulations at their place of work be vested in them. We can safely predict that the companies will refuse on the ground that the prerogatives of ownership are being invaded. Their refusal will certainly be upheld by the courts in any purely capitalist society, for their claim indeed states the common law of capitalism: the law also of Nozick's minimal state, the "mere" protection of "private property." If the workers then go on a prolonged strike, they will probably lose, because the *law*—that is, again, the *state*, as would any *minimal* state—now forbids mass picketing, secondary boycotts, and all the other tactics that might give the workers at least a small chance to overcome their lack of accumulated capital. And let us suppose at last that, having lost their strike, as they most certainly would in a minimal state, the workers then decide to sit in, to seize the plant until conditions in it are rectified: the state, the minimal state, will send in armed forces to remove them. To paraphrase a remark of Marshall Berman's: we may stop making demands on the state, but it will not stop making demands on us.

The one-sidedness of the free market is revealed: it helps the sellers and (under certain conditions in which unlimited free competition would really be possible) even the buyers of goods, but not the seller of labor. The only freedom most individuals gain from the free market is the freedom to be either rewarded or injured as the fates dictate—the "fates" including the possessors of capital who, though themselves limited as everyone is by historical chance, are much less limited in the social and political choices available to them than are the mere possessors of personal labor-power. That disparity is necessarily the greater the more minimal the state, and the more unmitigated the conditions of capitalism.*

The ideologues of inegalitarianism, it is true, deny that class distinctions under capitalism are based ultimately on the kind of "might makes right" model I have described here. Since no moral theory other than "might makes right" can explain why merely the possession of a certain kind of property should enable some people to dominate others against their will, the inegali-

---

*One day in 1977 the *New York Times* printed a story which purported to verify the old adage "As profits fall, heads roll." The story discussed the fates of six top-level executives from three low-performance corporations. Four of the six heads, it turned out, had rolled laterally to other high-level positions within the same company. A fifth head had managed the prodigious feat of rolling uphill —to a prestigious banking job. The sixth had indeed resigned his position as president of a major corporation, though nothing in the article suggested that he was about to start drawing unemployment compensation.

tarians look elsewhere than to property rights alone for their justification. Rather, like Herrnstein with his fictive "meritocracy," they purport to rest their case on an argument about moral desert, as in the phrase "Jane Doe has worked hard and *deserves* an appropriate reward." Everyone will agree to *that* formulation, of course, but it remains unexplained why the rewards of hard work of *one particular kind* (i.e., managing the deployment of capital goods) must include the appropriation of power over the lives of others.*

The prerogatives and powers of ownership, as opposed to the mere right of physical possession, are a purely social construct: there is nothing natural about them, any more than about IQ scores or political aggressiveness. Nothing in the natural order of things (Locke's or anyone else's) defines property and its rights in such a way that one can have it without being required to work on it, or that one can unilaterally set the conditions for those who do work on it and then have that settlement enforced by armed might in the name of contracts. Classes are made, not given. Nothing in the nature of making steel, say, in one's own backyard gives one a natural right to a different class position from another who works with his own tools at a local sawmill owned by some third person. Hard work is hard work wherever and however it is done; people only get divided into social classes when the state, through either its legislative or judicial bodies, enforces the rule that voters of stock in an enterprise don't have to work and workers don't get to vote on the conduct of the enterprise. Property, in other words, is only an issue at all, first, because with the help of the state it has been

---

*Milton Friedman attempts a justification:

> Individuals choose occupations, investments, and the like partly in accordance with their taste for uncertainty.... If ... a preference [for providing ourselves insurance through the pooling of risks] were widespread, large diversified corporations combining risky and non-risky ventures would become the rule. The wildcat oil prospector, the private proprietorship, the small partnership, would all become rare.

One wonders what portion of the nation's productive assets would have to be controlled by and what portion of its work force employed by "large diversified corporations" before Friedman would be willing to admit that the latter were "the rule." One also has to wonder if it is ignorance or willfulness that enables him to discuss the "taste for uncertainty" as though it were a purely individual trait rather than also, if not primarily, an aspect of one's social position.[17]

distributed so that not everybody owns some, let alone equal amounts. We need only remember that once most land in Europe was either owned by feudal lords or held in common; now hardly any is held in either way, and the existence of a powerful, centralizing state antedated the new distribution. Second, property is an issue because power over the rights of others—the taming of labor—has accrued to it in its corporate form, and these powers too have been given by, and could only have been given by, the powerful, centralizing state. People have never become wage laborers voluntarily; it is hard to believe that they ever will.

V. The redistributive and regulatory efforts of the welfare state, though they do little more than soften the harsh edges of inequality, are thus the necessary consequences of capitalism itself—the mild price that the owners of capital and their professional servants must pay for being allowed to benefit from the incredible disparities in power and wealth that have been created on their behalf. The accomplishments of the welfare state—or most often, of the workers and their representatives who fought for them—may be feeble, but they are accomplishments nonetheless. Chief among them has been acceptance of the strength of organized labor, which carries with it an extent of job security, and a capacity to bargain successfully with or strike against corporations, that could not otherwise have existed. In the society Nozick and Friedman see as "just," even that accomplishment would disappear: for though the anti-statists may not propose outlawing unions, they certainly propose outlawing the closed or union shop, which is the one form of organization that has enabled unions to build up marketplace power, and reasonable strike funds, over time.

To take another crucial example: at one time, as the history of the "fellow servant rule" in Anglo-Saxon common law makes brilliantly clear, people could be denied legal redress for injuries merely because they had been injured through the bad graces of an "owner." More generally, not only in the United States but elsewhere as well, the property rights of owners (usually corporations, of course) were held by courts or other protective institutions to override the people's potentially sovereign legislative power to implement their desire to regulate private property. That time is largely past in advanced capitalist societies (though the continued success of drug and chemical companies in avoiding serious punishment for negligently poisoning their workers and customers illustrates one limit on the progress of the welfare state). Its passing, which writers like Nozick and Friedman manage to distort into a moment of enslavement, has been a moment of liberation, however gradual and tenuous, for most people.*

In other words, the state was once hardly more than the plaything of business enterprise; the vaunted "individualism" of capitalist society consisted in a few people having that state at their command. Now the balance has been slightly righted. The vast majority of people who, even while they object to its excesses, inefficiency, and unfairness, find the regulated economy an essential part of their world are simply putting into operation the principle that what was sauce for the goose ought now to be sauce for the gander: the fundamental principle of fairness.

It must be said that Nozick, unlike most other free-market theorists (including Friedman), is aware that there is a problem here: that the capitalist class contributed at least as much to the development of the Leviathan state as did the working class, if not more. Though he never confronts this issue directly, he does remark at one point:

> Economically well-off persons desire greater political power, in a nonminimal state, because they can use this power to give themselves differential economic benefits. Where a locus of such power exists, it is not surprising that people attempt to use it for their own ends. The illegitimate use of a state by economic interests for their own ends is based upon a preexisting illegitimate power of the state to

*Anyone who believes that the people who received and continue to receive injuries from corporate enterprise have simply been suffering the expectable results of a relationship they have freely entered into, as a coal miner "freely" and "willingly" agrees to contract black-lung disease before the age of fifty, will not understand how capitalism can be said, even metaphorically, to have enslaved or mistreated anyone. But people who believe that the average person has the opportunity to make *truly* free economic choices will not balk at believing anything.

enrich some persons at the expense of others. Eliminate *that* illegitimate power of giving differential economic benefits and you eliminate or drastically restrict the motive for wanting political influence.[18]

Nozick's implication that it is possible to imagine a minimal yet capitalist state is clearly intended to suggest that the historical connection between capitalism and Leviathan is accidental: thinking systematically will presumably enable us to sever that connection, at least in our analyses. Unfortunately, the connection is not severable, and an analysis that has no possible meaning for the actual world might as well not exist. The connection is not severable because capitalism itself, in order to distribute and maintain the distribution of property, and in order to contain potential laborers in the novel status of human commodities, *demands* the more-than-minimal state, and cannot exist without it. Indeed, the whole point of social contract theory is to explain how a state is "created" by people coming together to protect their property. If the people in the state of nature have roughly equal amounts of property, there will never be capitalism, since no one will give up his property to go to work as a wage laborer for someone else. Thus we cannot imagine capitalism having come into existence in the first place except that there was an antecedent unequal distribution of property. That being the case, it is impossible to imagine (if we pursue this hypothetical condition) that the property-rich, who are going to be the most exigent seekers after statehood, should voluntarily agree to forgo the most tangible benefit they can derive from it—especially as they will be able to pay the protective agency more than will the property-poor and thereby bribe it to dispense unequal justice. Thus the only reason government ever exists in a capitalist economy is to "enrich some persons at the expense of others," and it is utterly pointless to call governmental actions "illegitimate" when they are the very actions the government was instituted to implement. Whether we think of the hypothetical state of social contract theory or the real state of modern history, the bonds between property and power are indissoluble. Rousseau's account of the passage from the state of nature, though equally false to actual history, is a lot more believable than Nozick's:

The rich above all must soon have felt how disadvantageous
to them was a perpetual war in which they alone paid all the
costs, and in which the risk of life was common to all while
the risk of goods was theirs alone. . . . All ran to meet their
chains thinking they secured their freedom, for although
they had enough reason to feel the advantages of a political
establishment, they did not have enough experience to foresee its dangers. Those most capable of anticipating the
abuses were precisely those who counted on profiting from
them. . . .[19]

VI.   The reanalysis of Nozick's model enables us to see
that the so-called trade-off between "liberty" and "equality" is
an ideological invention. Liberty for all is unattainable unless all
equally have access to control over productive property.
Throughout this discussion I have proceeded from an assumption no more radical than that the enjoyment of property and the
ability to improve our lives that possessing it gives us are good
things—the very assumption, that is, upon which the ideologues
of capitalism itself have founded their defense. And pursuing
only the implications of this assumption, we have discovered
that unfettered private property in the means of production is
the enemy not only of stable community but even of the individual's equal right, apotheosized by liberal individualism, to pursue life, liberty, and property. Until their power to dominate
society by deploying their legal rights over disposition of the
surplus realized by productive capital is taken away from owners and their nominees, so that the rights of disposition become
more equally available to all who work, then corporate liberty
and individual or communal liberty cannot coexist. "It is not
individuals who are made free by 'free enterprise,'" wrote
Marx; "rather it is Capital that is made free."

To be sure, the real historical situation has not been that
simple. Millions of individuals were indeed initially and often still
are repressed in the name of the rights of property. But the
original ideals that justified the liberation of capital were also,
however hollowly, phrased so as to justify the liberation of people, and could not in the long run be freed from that linkage.
Similarly, "The advance of industry . . . [replaced] the isolation

of the labourers, due to competition, by their revolutionary combination, due to association."[20] The "combination" may not have been revolutionary, but it has certainly changed the face and the prospects of capitalism. Trade unions and working-class parties, class solidarity, "working to rule," calling on public power for protection against private rule, are not some lingering remnant of traditionalism but are of the very essence of advance capitalism itself, and thus of "free enterprise" in its real historical development. If it is a natural right to be treated as a freely contracting, independent individual at one's place of work, it is a right which has somehow failed to commend itself to most workers. Individualism may be an effective myth of capitalism, an ideology which justifies hierarchical reward systems, to those who accept their legitimacy as the price of "liberty." But *cooperation* is the reality of the industrial labor process, as even most employers have come to appreciate, and most workers have always known that it, not individualism, produces their liberty. The contemporary version of individualism or anti-statism, then, is truly of the ivory tower—the product of men who have never worked to make their living, as most people do, in concert with others. Like the worst of the "bourgeois economists" whom Marx castigated, Nozick, on behalf of anti-statism, analyzes a fantasy world of his own creation in order to philosophize about the real social world that is wholly unlike it. Again the phantasm replaces the real thing: Crusoe without Friday becomes the typical rational actor of an economy in which he could not actually survive for a month lacking the very unindividualist institutions of the modern welfare capitalist societies.

The following relationship emerges. The incipient capitalist class spoke the language of free enterprise and political liberty, but practiced restrictionist political economy, class cooperation, and forceful suppression of personal liberties to garner and protect its capital. The many who saw themselves as victims of capitalism, and even some of those with a more hopeful view of it, understood the reality of restrictionism, state aid, and cooperation; they took seriously the potentially helpful language of political liberty and scorned the obviously ideological and hypocritical language of free enterprise. At the end of the 1970s, for example, a French government dedicated to freeing the market was attempting to rationalize the nation's sagging steel industry by cutting off all state subsidies and thus forcing the closure of a great many uneconomical steel mills. But the plan was not working, because it was proving as expensive to provide disemployed workers with the retraining and re-employment they demanded as to provide the original subsidies. The state was out of one business, but deeply into another, equally expensive business. And that was because a significant proportion of the French people, for whom liberty and rights are supposed to exist, had no interest in the Friedmanian version of that liberty and those rights. For practical policy purposes, anti-statism is an exercise in futility in any capitalist society. It can only succeed in poisoning the springs of discourse by spreading lies about the origins and nature of capitalism; it can thus short-circuit progress toward greater equality by getting some people to think that public action must always be an isolated and thus inefficient stopgap rather than a programmatic attempt at social change.

The truth about capitalism leads us in quite a different direction. In the last quarter of the twentieth century the majority of people in the capitalist democracies are far from free of repression and mistreatment at the hands of either governmental or corporate bureaucracies. But they are much freer of repression and mistreatment than they were at the turn of the century, or at the turn of the nineteenth century. There *has* been a significant extension of individual liberty during that period, and it has usually been as a result of struggle *against* market capitalism and *for* unionization, government regulation of business and working conditions, and the provision of fundamental social security. There has been a battle for power, and the state has been the necessary battleground. After a century and a half of struggle the capitalist welfare state is certainly much too far out of control, but it is not nearly as out of control for the average citizen as was the capitalist state of 1850.

Once we have seen that "liberty" and "equality" ought to be conceived of as similar rather than opposed conceptions, moreover, a certain anomaly in the libertarianism of these libertarians becomes more comprehensible. In the definition of the powers of government with which we began this discussion, it may be remembered, Friedman carefully distinguishes between the function of preserving "law and order" and the function of "protecting our freedom . . . from our fellow citizens." That distinction makes no sense except on the chilling understanding that what Friedman has in mind as the domestic enemies of freedom are *political* "subversives." The whole phraseology thus reeks of the Star Chamber, the witch-hunt, the repressive apparatus of loyalty-security programs, and the secret police with their Red Squads. Despite Friedman's self-proclaimed credentials as a friend of liberty, it is hard to see his aim here as anything but the intellectual prevention of "socialism" on the one hand and the forcible protection of corporate property against direct action by workers on the other. It is a very convenient definition of "rights" that makes it legitimate to suppress both intellectual opposition and class conflict.

Thus, critics have wondered how Friedman could have allowed himself even briefly to be consulted by one of the most barbaric regimes of the century; and some have also found it ironic that Nozick's work was talked about with great enthusiasm by the inhabitants of the most repressive White House in American history. But Pinochet and the Nixonmen understood Friedman and Nozick better than Friedman and Nozick (perhaps) understand themselves. They understood that those so-called rights of property, which are really privileges, can be defended quite adequately without any reference at all to the traditional civil liberties or rights of disobedience (which may be why those real rights receive not a single mention in either *Capitalism and Freedom* or *Anarchy, State, and Utopia*). The first thing men of violence do after they have established a repressive regime is find some philosopher to explain that any attempt to bring their powers under control—to establish both majority role *and* rights for excluded or oppressed minorities—will constitute an invasion of individual liberty. As these words are being written, for example, a war is being fought in northern Brazil to determine who shall own the resource-rich land there that is going to be developed during the next century. Indian tribes are being wiped out; armed bands of "settlers" maraud against each other; murder is the order of the day. In the absence of a Brazilian revolution, before that century is halfway over a Brazilian political economist will be explaining that attempts to redistribute the ownership and control of those resources are against natural justice, an unparalleled invasion of the free market, a violation of individual rights. He will probably quote Friedman and Nozick.

As people search for political and economic forms beyond and more truly democratic than the welfare state, the antipublic ideologues offer only to preserve the inequalities that favor the already privileged and to maintain "individual liberty" in a form such that most people can never have it. "Individuals have rights," Nozick asserts, but he does not seem to care that most people in recent history have not thought they would benefit from a strict understanding of the "rights" with which he is concerned.* As though anticipating these arguments he adds, without telling us who or what is his authority, "and there are things no person or group may do to them (without violating their rights)."[21] In his hands, therefore, the tragedy of social life becomes a conspiratorial and incomprehensible melodrama: incomprehensible in that like all bad melodramatists he never explains how or why the wicked behavior all his characters engage in (for him, depriving individuals of rights) can possibly be considered wicked if everybody does it. He is for "individuals," but against the liberty of people.

To look at the total impact of the free market, then, is to see it as a useful practical tool for finding out the real costs of products, but as a pernicious and destructive institution when taken as an overarching social philosophy. It is destructive, that is, of all chances of achieving political equality. The appropriation of the social surplus by a relative handful of people, the willingness to let private economic arrangements wreak localized or even general social havoc in the name of market rationality, and the maintenance of a commodity market for human labor—even to the somewhat limited extent that these modes of production exist in modern capitalist economies, let alone what they would be like in Nozick's uncontrolled version—together operate to create and maintain two classes of political citizenship, and thus unequal liberties, by definition.

---

*Since Nozick, unlike Rousseau, Marx, Kropotkin, and other "utopians," has no anthropology at all, it is impossible to tell what he thinks is the "natural" base of individual rights. All people surely grow up with the expectation that stringent social bonds will be placed on them—unless they are still motivated by unappeased and unappeasable infantile demands. One's unmistakable impression is that Nozick takes the standards of unsocialized infants as those of normal human expectations.

VII. To be sure, it would be politically disastrous if discredited rationales of big government were to be resurrected in opposition to the ideology of anti-statism. But a coherent understanding of the history of capitalism will prevent us from making that mistake. Aside from the national defense sector, the bloated centralized state with which we are all too familiar is the outgrowth of attempts at economic planning and control and at the provision of welfare. Both those modes of government intervention are intrinsic to the operation of capitalism (whether private or state); to that system which "has pitilessly torn asunder the motley feudal ties that bound man to his 'natural superiors,' and has left no other nexus between man and man than naked self-interest, than callous 'cash payment.' " The free market can provide neither material nor moral civilization; only the existence of some kind of public authority and spirit of community can do that. If the real thing cannot be sustained, repressed as it is by the strenuous efforts of the business class to promote the kind of asocial individualism represented by Friedman and Nozick, then we have to make do, for the moment at least, with the ersatz "statist" version. Although in principle there might be some other imaginable focus than public agencies for the energies we wish to devote to social action, in historical fact there is no other—at least not for the energies of mass movements. Labor-market anarchy permits, or rather encourages, vast disparities in income that place millions of people at a subsistence level or less; government must then step in to rectify the situation, for no one else will. Private enterprise uncontrolled by either workers or consumers wreaks the havoc that economists call "externalities," and government must then step in to prevent the deterioration of the human and physical environment—for how can unrelated "consumers," an abstract and derivative collectivity to begin with, enforce standards on multi-billion-dollar corporations without institutionalized assistance? Thus, though the free-market ideologues often try to sound as though they are simply proposing that we remove social-welfare activities of various kinds to the private sector, they are actually proposing that we give them up altogether; they propose, not that we do away with the coercive state, but rather that we give up the weapon of mass collective action—the only weapon that people have to counter the collective action engaged in by corporate managers meeting together in exclusive clubs to construct marketing, pricing, and labor market policies. What individual action will repair the ravages these absentee-owned corporations create as they move their operations about the nation or the world like pieces on a checkerboard? What voluntary, individual actions can we take to restrain the fiscal ruthlessness of the medical sector, which in the United States has so far proved impervious to every pressure from consumers and governments alike; are we, in the minimal state, to institute a boycott of our own health care? It is thus embarrassing but necessary to have to argue against the view, so prevalent in the United States, that government compulsion and government spending stifle initiative, whereas cutbacks in "big government" would release it. In simple fact, of course, it is not true that the size of the public sector is inversely related to the efficiency of the productive forces: The Federal Republic of Germany, with a considerably larger public sector than the United States (that is, a larger proportion of the national product taxed away), and with institutionalized worker "interference" in the conduct of business enterprise, is now a considerably more productive society. Similarly, Japan, usually taken as a model of free enterprise because of the relatively small size of its public sector, actually has an entire welfare-state apparatus built into the organization of private industry, so that far from being unmitigatedly capitalist, the social structure is virtually feudal; moreover, Japanese industrial planning is directed very decisively from above so as to ensure a proper national balance between exports and imports —though again, the postfeudal psychology of decision-making and obedience makes unnecessary the kind of overt, coercive mechanisms that we think of as "planning."*

---

*In his most recent political writing, *Free to Choose*, Friedman goes beyond the abstract philosophizing of *Capitalism and Freedom* to give what he calls a more "nuts and bolts" version of the comparison between "the free market" and "government interference." His strange notion is to argue that Japan, West Germany, Israel, and Taiwan have been more economically successful than, respectively, India, East Germany, Egypt, and "Red China," thus allegedly demonstrating that reliance on "the free market" is preferable to reliance on "central economic planning." This kind of inauthentic argumentation, in which

In sum, the state, though indefensible, yet has to be defended. Or rather, the idea of democratic, public control over the institutions that make a decent life for all possible has to be defended. The authority of the community over individual expressions of property right may in most cases be best expressed in other forums than the centralized, hierarchical state—but that authority, which is bound to appear to us now as public intervention, against the individual, must be asserted. During the gas crisis in the summer of 1979, the Libertarian Party ran a full-page ad in the *New York Times,* the gist of which was that the administration should "get out of our way" and let "us" deal with the energy problem by ourselves. If one turned over the page, one discovered a somewhat smaller ad paid for by the Amway Corporation, promoting the very same message—except that the "us" invoked was "private enterprise." Both ads were correct in their claim that government intervention—that is, the system for allocating fuel oil and gas during shortages—was largely responsible for those shortages in the first place. But that system only existed because both the general public and its sometime representatives in government had over the years learned the very realistic lesson that private suppliers of

---

two extreme points on a continuum are compared as though they were the only two possibilities, is known as the fallacy of the excluded middle. But as for the supposed lesson of the comparisons themselves, Robert Heilbroner has anatomized it perfectly:

> The argument sounds convincing until one begins to think about what has been left out: the long traumatic Indian experience with British imperialism for which the Japanese have no counterpart; the linguistic fragmentation of India, compared with the homogeneity of Japanese culture; the Japanese descent into dictatorship.... The huge injection of American capital into Japan after World War II.... Whatever the free enterprise talk in Tokyo, there is also the informal planning of government, banks, and corporations in Japan ("Japan Incorporated") contrasted with the sprawling chaos of Indian village life, whatever the socialist rhetoric in Delhi.... The contrast between East and West Germany makes no mention of the drain of resources out of East Germany by Russia. In discussing the difference between Israel and Egypt they do not consider the respective skills and training of the two populations or the critical infusion of philanthropic capital into Israel. The juxtaposition of Taiwan and mainland China omits the fact that the market system of precommunist China collapsed.

A more extensive and detailed demolition of Friedman's claim that high tax levels and government regulation result in inferior economic performance can be found in Lester Thurow's recently published *The Zero-Sum Society.*[22]

energy have not the slightest interest in resolving the energy-supply problems of any part of the public if to do so would interfere with profits. And though most of us reading the *Times* that day had absolutely no input into either the private or the public system of decision-making, we certainly all had and still have a much better chance of making our interests heard in the public system. That I as an individual have spent several winters with my home thermostat set at 60 degrees Fahrenheit has had no impact at all on either the supply or the price of heating oil in New England; but my representatives—the "state," a small part of the system of public agency—have made at least a modest effort to listen to my complaints and take them seriously.

Or again, the editor of an anti-statist organ recently opposed national health insurance on the grounds that "we" know how to spend "our" money better than "government" does; and he replied to an inquisitive reader that he couldn't think of a single way in which "bureaucracy" has helped us to obtain the means to a good life.[23] Superficially that is patent nonsense: as isolated pseudocitizens, none of us has the faintest idea how to spend "our" money on public health, or mental hospitals, or penal institutions, or national defense, or the construction of dams, or the provision of mass transit or workplace safety; only trained people familiar with the specific problems and paid to devote time to them can do that. Nor does the absurdity of that assertion apply only to so-called public goods. Most of us of middle or low income have no idea how to go about allocating present income for only vaguely discerned future needs—which is precisely why the citizens of every industrial society find the whole "bureaucratic" apparatus of social security, unemployment insurance, and workmen's compensation so valuable a part of "the good life," even when that apparatus is staffed, as it occasionally must be (since humans are imperfect), by "arrogant, pointy-headed bureaucrats." No one can really believe that the elderly should be without Medicare, that the safety legislation that helps make West German mines the world's safest should be repealed, that American workers were better off before the National Labor Relations Board was instituted; no state, no matter how minimal or who is in charge of it, will abolish these intrusions on the market. Or rather, no *people* will voluntarily do away with agencies to promote their own well-being. To the extent that the move for retrenchment has ideological support, rather than being merely the result of cost-consciousness in a savagely inflationary period, we must seek the reasons for that support elsewhere than in the obviously false proposition that uncontrolled capital is thought to be desirable by a majority anywhere.

In the United States at least, those reasons are not hard to find. Most people are aware that something is badly wrong with the carrying out of what we now call government regulation and control: that it is coercive and authoritarian where it ought to be supportive and democratic. Fewer people, however, are aware of the ways in which the expansion of the obtrusiveness of government is directly related to the expansion of concentrated economic power, which at the same time creates a multitude of human casualties in its wake and counsels us to treat their travail as their own fault. The alternative interpretation is so dangerous for the owners of concentrated wealth and their sympathetic functionaries in the state apparatus that they do everything possible to discourage its expression. Thus if in the United States many of us tend to think that the problem is the absence of an illusory freedom from interference rather than what it really is—the absence of political and economic democracy—that is not just because of our immersion in a liberal historical tradition but also because so many billions of dollars are spent every year to get us to think the one thought and be unaware of the other. The new free-market individualism—that is, the new corporate apologetic—is but a part of that expenditure. Just as the opponents of affirmative action misuse the language of individual liberty to justify the continued exclusion of minorities from an equal place in the commonwealth, so these new individualists misuse that language in order to justify the special privileges of the minority to which they belong against the potential claims for more equality of popular majorities.

CHAPTER

EPILOGUE:
WHO WANTS EQUALITY?

I. It is not a matter of indifference how we approach the subject of equality. Knowing is a matter of moral choice; the moral ramifications of the way in which we choose to view the supposed facts of life were brought home to me sometime after I first began, several years ago, to attempt a critical summary of Arthur Jensen's work for a planned paper on equality. The most commonly encountered liberal critique of Jensen, which I expected to verify myself, was that he took no account of all the possible cultural and environmental factors that obviously would explain the "fact" of inferior black performance on IQ tests. I soon discovered, however, that Jensen had indeed taken very careful account of all those factors and had dismissed them, apparently with reason, on the grounds that blacks even of a higher social class had IQs inferior to those of whites of a lower social class. If that were true, I realized with a jolt—if all the data reported by Jensen and his interpretations of the data were accurate—then it seemed only genetic laws could explain the discrepancy; perhaps blacks really were "by nature" inferior.

Apparently, I would have to give up a longstanding and profoundly felt belief in natural human equality. I had also to ignore my own experience, which was that the black people I had known, mostly at school or in the academic profession, were clearly as intelligent (whatever that might mean) as the average members of their own or any other social class (just as one can take Goldberg seriously on "patriarchy" only by choosing to ignore the plainly visible great number of dynamic and forceful women one knows, whose talents are being so palpably under-utilized). Alternatively, I had to assume there must be some mistake in Jensen's reporting of the data.

Chapter 3 of this book is the result of the search I then undertook. "Mistake," it turned out, was too kind a word; the data, as we have seen, had been consistently falsified by Jensen or his sources precisely on the point of the social class/IQ rela-tionship among blacks and whites. To discover this, though, it was necessary for me to distrust every piece of data that seemed to bear either way on Jensen's hypothesis: to pursue all his factual claims back to their original sources, and in some cases even to recheck the calculations or statistical manipulations of those sources. I know of other egalitarians who did this kind of work, to one extent or another, but not a single inegalitarian: every inegalitarian I know, personally or by reputation, who commented on Jensen's work assumed that he had established a bona fide, prima facie case; that some evidence at least was for now on his side; and that egalitarians would have to "face up" to the issue rather than engage in the "unprofessional" behavior of doubting Jensen's scholarly integrity and competence.

Given the shabby historical record of inegalitarianism, how-ever, egalitarians have concluded that the only professional thing to do is indeed to doubt the competence or integrity of work that claims to establish "facts" of natural inequality, until we have some minimal reason to believe the contrary. Data do not come to us out of thin air, and neither do our interpretations of their meaning nor the ethical or political theories within which we place those interpretations. In the study of human affairs a research strategy, or an intellectual strategy, is first and fore-most a political strategy. Inegalitarianism is one such strategy. The inegalitarian searches for mechanisms, no matter how ar-cane or invisible to the naked eye, that will make social inequali-ties seem to have some natural causation. The search may re-quire empirical invention, as in the sleight of hand by which the unobserved effects of unobserved genes or hormones are straightforwardly linked to actual, observed behavior; or con-ceptual invention, as when a "state of nature" opposite in every conceivable way to the real, historical state of affairs is invoked as a different kind of "natural" explanation of inequality. At the same time, the inegalitarian carefully hunts out ways to discount the visible evidence of how our own behavior toward each other brings about inequality; or else turns a bland or blind eye toward the results of that inequality as if to imply, should the "explanations" fail, that there is nothing there to be explained anyway.

Egalitarianism, of course, is an intellectual and research strategy in the same way.* The egalitarian—as I have done in these essays—casts a skeptical eye at all claims to have discovered some "natural" substratum of real and unassailable social inequality. All egalitarians take their stand on Rousseau's premise that the subject of the "causes" of "moral" or "political" inequality is fit only to be discussed by slaves in the presence of their masters—though nowadays we are forced to discuss it in the presence of our academic peers. Egalitarians recognize that the original causes of particular inequalities, or uneven development, of human groups may be purely contingent and accidental —as in Hilaire Belloc's remark that Europeans had conquered the African continent because "we have got/The Gatling gun, and they have not." But to understand what causes those inequalities to be sustained in a social order and transmitted from generation to generation, we need do nothing further than look unflinchingly at what is happening before our eyes. The only "natural" increment to social and political inequality we have ever seen convincingly demonstrated is this: that people learn to live with what they have, to prefer a bird in the hand to two in the bush; and that an inegalitarian social order can therefore be adjusted to almost as though it were natural. That is especially so if, as we have seen, a majority of the people within it benefit from one or more of the inequalities that sup-

---

*Obviously there can be better or worse strategies. In my discussion of IQ, for example, I eschewed the argument that the tests are culturally biased in their substance, since, like Jensen's contrary argument, that hypothesis is unfortunately not subject to empirical proof or disproof. I also eschewed the argument that class structure, not the existence of some real thing which we should call "cognitive ability," gives IQ tests their social significance, since this approach settles the hash of IQ by definition, and important theoretical disputes should not be settled by definition.

port it and that it supports in turn. Our assumption, though, is
that a majority of people will recognize, when the case is put to
them properly and under appropriate historical circumstances,
that the marginal privilege of being a white male, or a tradition-
al-minded white female, is a poor recompense for the more profound, more decisive exclusion from full participation in self-
governance that the inegalitarian way of life entails; that they
will benefit more than they will lose from the pursuit of an order
in which *no* group is victimized; and that not only their interests
but their fundamental morality dictates their participation in
that pursuit.

   To restate the theme with which I introduced these essays,
two centuries of industrialization have witnessed a massive advance, even if there have been setbacks here and there, in the
pursuit of both civic and social equality. If, in the middle run,
that pursuit is taken up once again, then the assumptions of
egalitarians will to that extent be vindicated.

II.
To be sure, equality does not seem to be on the immediate agenda in most advanced capitalist or social democratic nations today. How can it be in the *sauve qui peut* atmosphere of
inflation and over-all productivity crisis that marks contemporary capitalism? In that atmosphere, and especially in a nation
with the individualist political traditions and fragmented political institutions of the United States, the idea of collective action
for collective improvement and self-government languishes. But
the crucial question is, Who really wants more equality? Is that
nothing more than a dream of disenchanted intellectuals, on
which "the people" regularly turn their backs? Are the neoconservatives whose arguments I have been discussing in these
pages spokesmen for the true popular philosophy?

   At one level, it might be claimed that we need only look to
our ubiquitous public-opinion polls to find the answer to that as
to any question about what the majority really wants. Indeed,
the contemporary polling of public opinion offers at least as
much solace to egalitarians as to inegalitarians. Aid to racial
minorities aside, the people who answer the pollsters' questions
consistently favor more, not less, governmental intervention of
the kind designed to improve the material lot of the majority by

regulating the conduct of private enterprise, or redistributing income in the form of providing certain kinds of public services (such as prepaid health care); it is *Public Interest,* the *Wall Street Journal,* and the American Enterprise Institute that enthuse over "deregulation," not the ordinary consumer or worker.[1] But that is the least interesting form of evidence. If one chooses to believe the results of such polls, then one must believe the results of all polls: and somewhere there are equal and opposite answers for every question that we can conceive of asking. Furthermore, it is doubtful whether people really believe, in any fundamental way, what they tell the pollsters they believe, for in fact the polls report our most cheaply held beliefs: nothing at all depends on what we say to them; no reflection is required, for no action has to follow. It is a much more useful approach to think about the demands that a majority of us actually make on our political and economic institutions, and to compare our knowledge of those demands with what is said about them by those inegalitarians who propose to speak for the "real majority."

Perhaps the most articulate of all spokesmen for the new inegalitarianism is Irving Kristol, who in various essays has mounted an all-out attack on the notion that egalitarianism wears a popular face. The most comprehensive of those essays is entitled "Utopianism, Ancient and Modern."[2] It begins with the perceptive argument that earlier utopias such as Plato's *Republic* were meant only as dreams, and as such added to the dignity of human longing. Modern utopias, however, are essentially insane expressions of a desire to realize what Kristol calls an unrealizable dream on earth: the dream of equality. And it is a dream, not of "the people" or the working class, but of irresponsible intellectuals, to whose credit (or discredit) all the evils of modernity accrue.

> [G]rowth and decay are precisely what most offend the utopian cast of mind, for which time is an enemy to be subdued. And this is why the dimension of time is so rigorously excluded from modern city planning—and from modern architecture too, which derives from the same utopian tradition.

Although that passage has to do only indirectly with egalitarianism, it marks a useful starting point in our considera-

tion of the question Who wants (more) equality? For in it we
begin to see the strategy of those who argue that "the people"
are really inegalitarian. That strategy, simply, requires a massive distortion of the history of capitalism—a distortion related
to that practiced by the free-market theorists whom I discussed
in the previous chapter.

Reading Kristol's prose, with its seductive air of sagacity,
we must pause to remember, for example, that not Fourier or Le
Corbusier but a long line of oligarchs, speculators, and servants
of corporate capitalism and the state, from Baron Haussmann
to Georges Pompidou, were the architects of modern Parisian
order; or to look elsewhere, that Reston, Virginia was created to
make a corporate profit, not to fulfill a utopian dream. Does
Kristol really not know that the planned obsolescence of modern
urban architecture derives from the imperative of profit and the
special-interest nature of tax laws and building codes? It is difficult to believe that this cavalier attitude toward history is not
deliberate; it becomes more difficult as we continue. "[C]ertain
identifiable trends of thought," Kristol asserts, contributed to
the emergence of the utopian mode of thought.

> These trends can be identified as millenarianism, rational-
> ism, and . . . "scientism." . . . What makes modern millenar-
> ianism so powerful—one is tempted to say irresistible—is
> its association with modern scientific rationalism and mod-
> ern technology. Scientific rationalism . . . came to mean—it
> is, indeed, the essential meaning of that period we call the
> Enlightenment—that existing institutions could be legiti-
> mized only by reason. . . .

Again, Kristol carefully obscures the historical reality: it
was not primarily Enlightenment *philosophes* but rather the
rise of the capitalist free-market spirit and the political liberalism associated with it that produced legitimation through reason, and thus subverted traditional sentiments of loyalty, obligation, and human attachment. Obviously such a change in
intellectual temper could not have taken place if the precarious
religious unity of the Middle Ages had not been breaking down
at the same time, but it was circumstances, not merely ideas,
that destroyed that unity. Hobbes did not write the *Leviathan*
because he was a rationalist contaminated by millenarianism but

rather because he correctly perceived that the controlled pursuit of domestic economic betterment by individuals would be the surest way to produce social cohesion out of the chaos around him. Somewhat later his insight would be systematized by a rising capitalist class and its philosophers, not because they were rationalists, but because they were engaged in making a world which had to be rationalized.

Thus Kristol stands history on its head with a vengeance—but not without purpose. What he has done, in sum, is to attribute the destructive element of capitalist development ("All that is solid," Marx wrote about the bourgeois revolution, "melts into air, all that is holy is profaned") to an allegedly adversary class of intellectuals—a tactic borrowed from Daniel Bell, who does the same thing at greater length in *The Cultural Contradictions of Capitalism.*[3] This is the purpose of the new inegalitarians: to discredit the very source of egalitarianism itself. We are being instructed to forget that the modern egalitarian spirit is a logical response to the havoc wrought by the untrammeled market forces of capitalism (untrammeled, that is, from the standpoint of the ordinary worker or citizen); instead, we are advised to hold marginal intellectuals responsible for that havoc. From this point on in Kristol's argument anticapitalism itself will seem irrational: a choosing of sides with destructive "rationalists" who were and are somehow external to the capitalist system, rather than a reasoned response to the excesses of the system itself.

Having thus told us that "the people" advisedly should be opposed to egalitarian intellectuals rather than to the capitalist class, Kristol is now prepared to assure us that in any event popular sentiment merely replicates his own.

> Modern conservatism found it necessary to argue what had always been previously assumed by all reasonable men: that institutions which have existed over a long period of time have a reason and a purpose inherent in them, a collective wisdom incarnate in them. . . .

If we take its superficial content seriously, this too is a very puzzling notion. Not capitalism but feudalism and Roman Catholicism hold the track record for sheer longevity in European civilization. If Kristol thinks there was a collective wisdom incarnate in *them*, why does he so laud the bourgeois parvenus who destroyed the power of both those institutions? It begins to seem that "all reasonable men" are simply any handful of men who are able to justify the appropriation of power by a minority at one time or another. The German barons no doubt thought their power had a reason and a purpose to it, but the peasants who kept revolting against them did not: perhaps they were not reasonable. But of course it was not the rebellious peasants who finally destroyed the feudal version of community; it was capitalists and the aggrandizing central state. One would think, then, that modern conservatism should be *anti*capitalist; should defend, both retrospectively and immediately, the yeomen against the gentry, the Chartists and the Luddites and their descendants against the industrialists and corporate rationalizers, the people of Appalachia against the absentee coal-mine operators, the family farm against corporate farming, and so on. But it does none of these things; instead, it defends the economically powerful, attacking the rationalist character of capitalism (as though that had some purely extrinsic cause) rather than the way it actually distributes power. Apparently the power relationships of capitalism are the kind of "institution" that "all reasonable men" in their "collective wisdom" think of as having "a reason and a purpose."

But is that the case? In an earlier essay, Kristol asserts directly that the working class in capitalist societies is never really anticapitalist; only radical intellectuals are. He provides absolutely no evidence for that assertion.[4] Still, is he really a closet populist defending the collective wisdom of the procapitalist, anti-egalitarian people? As it turns out, not exactly.

> Most ordinary people, most of the time, intuitively feel the force of this conservative argument. But these same ordinary people are defenseless intellectually against the articulated and aggressive rationalism of our intellectual class—and this explains why, when modern men do rebel against the unreasonableness of modern rationalism, they are so likely to take refuge in some form of irrationalism. The 20th-century phenomenon of fascism is [such] an expression. . . .

Aside from a sinister treatment of the "intellectual class" that seems little more than a justification for repression, the most striking aspect of this passage is Kristol's implicit view of anti-egalitarian fascism as the only truly popular rebellion of our time: in his perspective, the class "ordinary people" apparently does not include the organized working classes of Italy and Germany, fascism's initial—and egalitarian—victims. Almost as striking is his expression of contempt for those "ordinary people" whose "collective wisdom" is supposed to be the repository for (among other sentiments) inegalitarianism. The poor defenseless people would be procapitalist most of the time if only they weren't so easily victimized by rational intellectuals; their collective wisdom is seemingly of a much lesser order than his more resistant intelligence. When people take a wrong turning it is because they are dupes, not because they are driven there by the activities of those ruling groups against whose power many people genuinely *are* defenseless. Conservative "populism" is patronizing indeed.

But what about egalitarianism? Is "fascism" instead the only recourse of popular sentiment? Here his argument dovetails neatly with all those defenses of the existing social order we have been analyzing in these pages:

> The tremendous expansion of government during these past three decades has not obviously made us a happier and more contented people . . . yet the response to this state of affairs among our educated classes is to demand still more governmental intervention. . . .

On the other hand,

> the ordinary people, whose common world always anchors them more firmly in common sense, are skeptical of such a prescription. . . .

When Kristol wants to uphold his devil theory of radical intellectuals, the people are intellectually hapless and subject to the appeals of fascism; but when he wants to pose as an inegalitarian populist, their intellects are suddenly firmly resistant to nefarious influence. However one turns this coin, the people are never on the side of egalitarian change: that is his consistent theme. What, then, are we to make of the fact that almost everything capitalist governments do even today is *demanded* by some very large number of "ordinary people" (or else it wouldn't be done)? The only visible disagreement among most people in capitalist societies is, still, not *whether* government should intervene but how, and more important, on whose behalf. Farmers, for example, may be "skeptical" about the usefulness to them of further advances in the welfare state, but everywhere in the capitalist world they remain extraordinarily credulous about the social virtue of crop price supports. Moreover, it is not merely logrolling self-interest that inflates the role of the capitalist state. For reasons I have suggested earlier, a majority of people in all the advanced capitalist nations taken together are undoubtedly "procapitalist" from the standpoint of a committed socialist or anarchist. But are all "ordinary people" attached by the force of real belief, as Kristol alleges, to the primary institutions of capitalism: the free market for pricing goods, the commodity market in labor, the authoritarian structure of employment, the unalloyed right of corporate property to do what it wishes with itself, and political rule on behalf of corporate wealth?

On the contrary, every one of those institutions has been under massive attack from "ordinary people" since the dawn of capitalism itself. Even while accepting capitalism, even sometimes while aggressively defending it in argument, even while scorning "utopian" alternatives to it and having no intention of pursuing them, millions of people in all capitalist societies work effectively to resist its sway and to undermine it; they organize to demand policies and changes that, if adopted wholesale, would be incompatible with the continued existence of what Kristol means by "capitalism." It is in order to accommodate such continual resistance that capitalist states have been forced to create reformist institutions and programs (or at least institutions and programs that look reformist) that are inconsistent with the more productive working of capitalist economy. On the one hand, popular demands have bloated the state, supported endemic inflation, and generated a realm of institutional and moral incoherence that it becomes harder and harder to defend.

(Is it really *all right* for chemical plants to poison the environment at will? Is it really *all right* for people to be disemployed and productive plants shut down in order to maintain profit levels? Do "ordinary people" think so?) On the other hand, large numbers of people have also made more directly political demands—for control of their workplaces, restrictions on unfettered corporate activity, defense of communities threatened by speculative growth, job rights and insurance cushions—that if adopted make capitalism less and less what it is supposed to be: that attempt to make it more egalitarian.

Kristol himself really is aware of that, much as he tries to hide social reality from our eyes. As we pursue the thread of his argument that massive inequality is somehow humanly "natural," it unravels before our eyes.

> The transformation of the bourgeois citizen into the bourgeois consumer has dissolved that liberal-individualist framework which held the utopian impulses of modern society under control. One used to be encouraged to control one's appetites; now one is encouraged to satisfy them without delay.

The defense of inequality turns out, unsurprisingly, to lead to nothing more than a legitimation of domination: with "ordinary people" very clearly in the subordinate position, apparently because they are not really satisfied with the results of capitalist inequality after all. Again the conservative version of history is bizarre: even in the United States, Kristol's "bourgeois citizen" was always in a minority; and at all times here, as in England and on the Continent, it has been poverty, powerlessness, and oppressive force as well (as visited, for example, upon strikers) that have enforced the "control of appetite" for millions. But Kristol's only complaint about that domination is that it wasn't successful enough. The ordinary people, once so beloved, are suddenly a ravening wolf battering at his door—why can't they learn to live within their means, just as he presumably lives within his? Kristol may have only two cheers for capitalism, as the title of his collected essays indicates, but as it turns out, that is more than he has for democracy. The reason he, like most neoconservatives, opposes both reformist "government intervention" *and* radical prescriptions for self-government is that they are both too democratic for him; ordinary people should stay in their place.

> The modern world, and the crisis of modernity we are now experiencing, was created by ideas and by the passions which these ideas unleashed. To surmount this crisis, without destroying the modern world itself, will require new ideas—or new versions of old ideas—that will regulate these passions and bring them into a more fruitful and harmonious relation with reality.

An English counterpart of Kristol puts this argument more succinctly, making it even clearer that the case against more equality is simply a case against more popular democracy as well.

> The political and economic organization of modern liberal democracies is dedicated, above all, to the satisfaction of individual wants. How are we to establish what individuals want? By asking them. How are we to ensure that they get what they want, at least so far as possible? By letting them make the decisions. How do we arrange that? By letting them elect their governments and by letting them spend their money in a free competitive marketplace.
>
> This engagingly simple political philosophy may indeed have been a useful antidote to the depredations practiced on mankind by authoritarian and paternalist regimes in the name of higher values. But, alas, it already has built into it the tension—historicists might say the contradiction—that lies at the root of our present troubles. . . .
>
> . . . Indeed, the essence of democratic politics is a gigantic celebration of the fact that you *can* get something for nothing, or at least that *you*—the individual voter—can get something for nothing. . . . for government, with its legalized powers of coercion, can award benefits here while it charges costs there. That indeed is the whole nature of the redistribution of wealth and income, an almost universally accepted function of government.[5]

"Almost universally accepted"—so much for the notion that the desire for more equality is a desire foisted on the duped people by scheming intellectuals. In the end the anti-egalitarian attack on "intellectuals" is an attack on the majority of "ordinary people" as well. It is wholly fitting, then, that the public-television series speaking for the new conservatism, Ben Wattenberg's "In Search of the Real America," was paid for by Mobil Oil, Bethlehem Steel, AT&T, and tax-exempt foundations dispensing the Olin, Annenberg, Richardson, and Scaife fortunes.

How then can we answer our question, Who wants more equality? Beyond any doubt there is a momentary turning against the politics of equality, but on the historical record we have little reason to believe it is more than momentary. In part (and here Kristol's argument about the "new class" may be turned against itself), the new public mood simply responds to the ideological predominance of that class of people, or rather an important segment of it, who get relatively little help from the welfare state or the regulated economy—small businesspeople, professionals, junior executives. Of course they get much more help than they are willing to admit: from the licensing and professional-school admissions procedures that make a closed shop of law and medicine, to the defense contracts and other government expenditures that have stimulated the American economy so munificently over the past three decades, to the aid-to-education and mortgage-insurance programs that have done so much to generate the way of life of the educated middle class in America. No one, it must be noted, proposes to turn back these benefits to the general public, let alone turn back that class position which the legal structure of state-supported capitalism itself has made possible. But since these are the people most able to obtain access to the various mass media of communication and to use that access intelligently, their ideology thrives.

We must not, however, fall into the trap (as does Kristol) of attributing all mass ideas to the subversive influence of others. An ideology only takes hold outside the relatively small group of those who promulgate it because it seems to provide an answer to the real social needs of large numbers of people. Thus in times of crisis the so-called inefficiency of public enterprise (as though any collective enterprise were ever unwasteful) comes to the fore of public consciousness for the simple reason that we are unable to vent our anger effectively on other, more fundamental sources of the crisis. Ironically, the tighter the stranglehold of private enterprise on our lives (and in few places is it tighter than in the United States), the more the public sector and public agencies must bear the burden of public unhappiness —not because they are less responsive than private enterprises, but because they constitute the only social sector that is responsive to any extent at all.

At the same time, outbursts of antigovernment sentiment are also partly genuine responses to the fact that public power, though far more responsive than private power, is still too much out of the control of most of us. Recognition of this simple truth becomes an ideology of privilege only when the divorce between "us" and "government" is seen as a static principle of life rather than a condition to be rectified. The most telling phrase in Milton Friedman's indictment of government is that *"government* may enable *us* at times to accomplish jointly what *we* would find it more difficult or expensive to accomplish severally" (my emphasis). To posit (as Kristol does also) an inherent division between "us" and "it"—which is to say, between people and the public of which they are a part—is to ensure that we can never turn pseudodemocracy into the real thing. The best we can do, this message tells us, is to trade in irresponsible government authority for irresponsible corporate authority: a corporate state without a state which, the facts of social life being what they are, will simply be a corporate state.

Thus, the elaboration of the new individualist ideology serves a useful purpose in the end: it shows us how to think more clearly about democracy and the state. Our problem (except for those among us who wish to experiment in the creation of truly anarchist communities outside the mainstream) is not to find ways to annihilate the state, let alone turn it into a free-market police state, but rather to find ways to make self-governing publics into real entities. Our need is to get Leviathan—the modern corporate economy in whose service so much of the state apparatus at present exists even when its masters attempt to act independently—under our real and equal mastery; to scale down productive activity, wherever feasible, to a more humanly accessible, less demonically uncontrolled size: to remake the capitalist state into a democratically controlled institution by remaking capitalism into a democratically controlled set of productive institutions.*

Finally, any assessment of the demand for equality must recognize one undeniable condition. In the United States (and elsewhere too), the idea of public agency is partly a victim of its association in the minds of many with preferential aid to minorities of the kind I have justified earlier. In a society where especially racial differences are the visible source of a constant, irritating tension, government or any other institutionalized system for dealing with problems of race (that is, for "helping" black people) comes to be perceived as though that were its sole and (to many) discreditable function. That is especially true, moreover, in a time of persistent economic crisis, when scapegoating becomes a regularized activity (not least because ideologues of "less government" constantly make use of it as a campaign technique). If there is any realm in which the ideals of egalitarianism seem to confront intractable social facts, it is that of race relations, for in that realm the egalitarian principles of majority rule and minority representation collide head-on. Thus it is always necessary for egalitarians to engage, as I have done, in an apparently paradoxical activity: to discuss inequality as a system of minority privilege *and* inequality as a system of majority privilege (though to a much lesser extent) under the same rubric. The struggle for democratic self-government in a plural society has that painful duality at its heart. We may conceivably never overcome that duality. For the reasons I have given earlier (see Chapter 6), the strategy of formally "equal opportunity" is a strategy for maintaining the position of blacks, women, and similar minorities in their existing condition of stigma and relative exclusion; it is a strategy for keeping a plural society unequally plural. On the other hand, no amount of Supreme Court rulings on behalf of "affirmative action" nor of philosophical argument such as that offered here will do anything but raise the

---

*A more extensive discussion of this prospect, as well as of the case for democratic representation touched on in Chapter 6, will be contained in my *Political Equality* (forthcoming from Pantheon Books). An important recent statement about the relationship between capitalism and democracy is Martin Carnoy and Derek Shearer, *Economic Democracy.*[6]

level of social anger if they are not tied to a plausible general strategy for redistributing power, wealth, and privilege throughout the social order. The completion of the liberal revolution must proceed hand-in-hand with the broader search for equality; neither can succeed without the other.

No one has shown us a plausible strategy for accomplishing that dual purpose. But it is only egalitarians who are trying. And at least, in confronting these massive political problems egalitarians, unlike inegalitarians, need not stoop to manipulating the facts, distorting history, or turning their backs on the idea of social justice.

APPENDIX

ARTHUR JENSEN'S
METHODOLOGY

For those interested in some of the more technical criticisms of Jensen's work, I have relegated certain detailed analyses to this appendix so as not to interfere with the flow of the main argument of Chapter 3. The list that follows is indicative and abbreviated, as are the critiques; an exhaustive account of Jensen's methodological errors would require another book.

1. *Heritability and race.* The "heritability" of a trait refers to the extent to which variations in measurement from the average value of the trait may be traceable to genetic variations in the measured population. The key word here is "population," for heritability statistics apply only to a specific breeding and rearing population (as geneticists put it). Thus, for a population that has regularly inbred to the exclusion of outsiders, a heritability of, say, 0.50 would mean that half of the total variation from the mean (average) would be accounted for by genetic differences in the population.

We have already seen that such a figure can also be conceptualized as nothing more than the obverse of the extent to which salient features of the population's environment account for expressed behavioral differences. Suppose, then, that two environments are very much alike regarding those aspects that have the strongest impact on measured intelligence within a given population. Then, obviously, genetic variations will *seem* to account for most of the variance in a variable trait that is manifested within those environments. But the variations may themselves be trivial, and the genetic "imprint" on the trait very weak, or very malleable, or both. On the other hand, if the members of a measured population grow up in sharply unlike environments, then the heritability of the very same trait will seem to be very low. Therefore, the heritability of a trait in (inbreeding) population X is wholly irrelevant to knowledge of its heritability in population Y. The members of population X may live in environments that are on the average pretty much like each other compared to the more dissimilar environments that members of population Y live in, and in that case the genetic variance for the particular trait would seem to be greater.

Now let us suppose that groups X and Y live together in a single society, and we are trying to determine the heritability of a trait like intelligence for the whole population $(X + Y)$, so that we can determine whether manifest average differences between X and Y (if there are any) are the result of genes or environment. Unless the two populations are so inbred that we can no longer distinguish between them (rendering the original question meaningless), *it is impossible to do this.* It is easy to see why. In the two populations, we may under ideal experimental conditions (which never exist for social research) be able to say what causes variation *within* each population, but the methods for doing this have no applicability to the prospect for determining the causes of variance *between* populations. What Jensen is doing is analogous, therefore, to a geneticist's arguing about the causes of variance in the average different size of wild sheep in the Scottish Highlands and domestic sheep in an English meadow. Geneticists, as their texts reveal, do not do that sort of thing; they could not. For example, if size were not a valuable economic characteristic, then breeders of domestic sheep would not breed for it, and most variation in size would seem to be accounted for by nongenetic factors. If it were a valuable economic characteristic and bred for in a carefully controlled environment, then genes would seem to account for most of the variance in size of domestic sheep. If size were a survival factor and thus selected for within populations of wild sheep, genes would again appear to account for most of their variance in size. On the other hand, if size were not a survival factor, or if it were so in some natural environments but not in others, then environment would appear to account for more of the variance in the size of wild sheep. The genetic variance would be the same for the two different populations only if size had the same (economic or survival) value for each, *and* the environments of each were similarly controlled or uncontrolled (that is, invariably similar or dissimilar from one generation to the next or for different members of the same generation). In other words, the genetic variance would be the same only if there were no difference between the wild and domestic breeds with respect to the impact of size on each of them. Thus we cannot even test a comparative hypothesis about the genetic "imprint" for size on the different breeds unless we have already decided on the answer to begin with! That is exactly Jensen's procedure with respect to race and intelligence. Having decided to begin with, against every bit of informed knowledge we possess, that there is no substantial socio-logical difference between whites and blacks and that they can thus be treated as one population, he then is able to engage in countless and pointless statistical exercises which discover that, lo, there is no socio-logical difference between them . . .

There is, in fact, only one way we could determine the extent to which genes account for the IQ variance in population $X + Y$, where X are American whites and Y American blacks. That would be if the two races had thoroughly interbred; some parents then had genetically identical twins except that one of them was genetically "white" and the other was genetically "black"; the twins were separated at birth, the black twin moving into an environment significantly above the mean environment (a mansion) and the white twin remaining in an environ-ment significantly below the average environment (a slum); and the black twin never encountered any discriminatory or otherwise derogat-ing behavior. If in those circumstances the black twins' IQs were consis-tently the same as or lower than those of the white twins—even though they were receiving significant social advantages, including most prominently the noticeably higher IQs of their foster parents, un-matched by the white twins—*then and only then* could we say that the hypothesis of the genetic inferiority of average black cognitive ability had been supported, or even tested. No other evidence having to do with the statistical study of trait variance is at this point even remotely relevant to Jensen's proposition. As one researcher has put it: "Only if black children could be reared as though they were whites, and vice versa, could the effects of different rearing environments on the geno-type distribution of the two races be estimated."[1]

Thus the entire discussion of heritability studies in the context of racial IQ differences is a foolish waste of time, made necessary only by Jensen's original (and incredible) error in asserting their relevance. Jensen himself, oddly enough, offers a somewhat similar analysis in chapter 5 of his *Educability and Group Differences*, and then adds that "the higher the within-group heritability, the greater is the *plausi-bility,* or the *a priori* probability, that genetic differences exist be-tween the groups. Plausibility is a subjective judgment of *likelihood.*" So it is, but italicizing words does not increase their truth-value, and it must be repeated that nothing in the literature of within-group herita-bility has the slightest bearing on an informed estimate of that "likeli-hood." On the contrary, because the genes for intelligence are undoubt-edly so many and so diverse, there is no conceivable reason why the original gene pools for intelligence should have had, over all, different genetic value in any of the human "races."

As we have noted, the "plausibility" of Jensen's "hypothesis" really has nothing at all to do with the literature of human genetics but rather with the entirely unrelated question, discussed further below, whether *environmental* effects can plausibly be said to account for the known IQ difference between the races. Indeed, the only factor that could legitimately cause us to give a high *a priori* probability to the notion that significant genetic differences in intelligence exist between racial groups would be not the logically pointless piling up of heritability figures, but rather the general existence of significant genetic differences between the human races, especially regarding behavioral traits heavily implicated in social interactions. We have no knowledge of human genetics with respect to such traits—period. But we do know a fair amount about the genetics of what seem to be more strictly biological traits among both animals and humans. Among domestic animals, for example, the heritability of traits having to do with size is generally quite low, even though these are economically valuable traits. And among humans, though there is much within-population variance for most traits, we have no evidence for anything but marginal racial variations except as regards certain trivial matters of physical appearance. Some races or cultural groups might be said to be averagely of different stature or strength, but except perhaps with respect to height no human group falls outside the normal ranges for such traits or is deficient in significant physical talents. Moreover, what differences do exist seem to diminish with changes in diet and health care, and this is true even of within-population variances (e.g., the difference in size between social classes in Great Britain has apparently almost been eliminated over the past century and a half). The only kind of evidence, in other words, which would be relevant to the plausibility of Jensen's hypothesis makes it seem, on its face, totally implausible.

2. Environment and IQ. The full flavor of Jensen's method for handling embarrassing evidence can only be hinted at: three examples must suffice. In discussing—and discounting—the potentially differential effects of early brain damage on white and black children, Jensen relies heavily on a pioneering and questionable study of "development quotients" (DQs). This study purported to show that black infants initially are physically more precocious than whites, but later fall behind white children. According to Jensen:

> Such findings would be compatible with a markedly higher incidence of neurological damage in Negro infants only if it is argued that the Negro infants are normally so very advanced over white

infants in psychomotor development that even with a high incidence of brain damage the mean Negro performance is still above
the white mean. *But this possibility should result in a larger
variance of Developmental Quotients for Negroes as compared
to whites,* and Bayley's data show no significant racial difference
in the variance of DQs.[2]

The italicized clause is false, and it seems deliberately false. Given all
the statistical work Jensen has done (his most recent book contains,
inter alia, a primer in psychostatistics), he must know that there is no
relationship at all between the size of means and the size of variance,
which measures *deviation* from the mean. If the mean of one set of
measurements is 998, and of another 7, but the distance from the means
to the various other measurements is the same, then the variances will
be the same (see the footnote discussion on page 24 above).

On another occasion a discussion about the *total* variance in IQ
measurements for blacks and whites seems to be leading Jensen in a
discomfiting direction: he has found that IQ variance among whites is
greater than among blacks, which would seem to indicate that the two
populations are not comparable (or, in the terms I have used above, that
blacks live in more similar—more uniformly depressed—environments
than whites). Jensen handles this embarrassment by suddenly switch-
ing to a discussion of *genetic* variance: "Why should two populations
have different genetic variances?" he asks; and answers: "Differences
in gene frequencies and in the degree of assortative mating are the
chief causes." At worst the question is an outright lie, softened only by
the question mark after it. At the very least, he has not only changed
the topic of discussion from total variance to genetic variance, but in
so doing has implicitly made a claim for which there is not an iota of
evidence: that blacks' *IQs* are, one might say, *genetically* and uniformly depressed—which is in fact the "hypothesis" that he has supposedly been trying to establish all along. The object of investigation,
again, becomes the means of verifying itself.

Neither of these examples of "Jensenism" is very significant by
itself: the study by Bayley is unbelievable in any event, and since the
relationship between total and genetic variance to begin with is derivative, the data which Jensen is trying to obscure by distortion could
themselves be no more than mildly suggestive. But together these
examples suggest an animus and a method which tell us accurately that
Jensen has no intention of ever treating any data on the differential
lives of blacks and whites in the United States with honest respect. A
final note on this subject highlights that comment: Jensen always reports the major sociological studies in the field of environmental depri-

vation as supporting his claims, so that we have to go to the original sources to find out that they do not. Thus, from the use he makes of a summarizing article about the interrelation between nutrition and intellectual performance, one would never know that its authors conclude:

> Children from underprivileged families in the United States exhibit growth characteristics resembling those of children in less developed countries, where inadequate nutrition has been shown to retard physical health. . . . In short, the information available at present about the distribution of malnutrition and retardation in the United States suggests that it resembles the distribution in other areas of the world [being found] among other groups who are vulnerable not only because of food deprivation but as part of the whole culture of poverty.[3]

The authors go on to find strong suggestions of a linkage between poor nutrition, infectious disease, and low IQ—all unremarked or at least unreported by Jensen. It is the cumulative pattern of these occurrences that matters: one or two could be mistakes; all together they are a scandal.

3. *SES.* The core of Jensen's approach to race, as we saw in Chapter 3, is neither the hypothesis about heritability nor his dismissal of environment as a causal agent, but rather his treatment of the data on class and caste, or socioeconomic status. Before turning to his use of Audrey Shuey's research, we should look at some other examples of his handling of this issue which show that his treatment of Shuey's data is again part of a pattern of scholarly malfeasance on the one hand and incredible ignorance on the other.

As to malfeasance, two comments are in order. In the text, I have referred to his treatment of a study of Australian Aborigines (a study no longer taken seriously by anthropologists, if it ever was). Jensen reproduced a table titled "Comparison of the number of part-Aboriginal and full-Aboriginal children showing Conservation."[4] What he did, however, was to suppress the most important part of the original evidence by leaving out the parenthetical phrase "(Herrmansburg Group)" after "children" in the table title—a parenthesis that appears in the original of the table. There were, in reality, *two* mission schools, at Herrmansburg and at another village called Elcho, and the Elcho group were all (allegedly) full-blooded Aborigines. A trial-and-error analysis of the original data from both missions shows that no matter how we reanalyze the data to make all measurements as comparable as possible, the part-Aboriginals at Herrmansburg did indeed do better than the full-Aboriginals there, *but among the older age groups the full-blooded*

Aboriginals at Elcho did better than or equal to the part-Aboriginals on at least four of the six Piagetian tests. (The original article provided no such analysis, and our own must be trial-and-error because it does not provide the same kinds of data about age or test-score distribution for the two missions.)

That the full-Aboriginals at Herrmansburg did not do as well as either of the other groups is a matter of mild intellectual interest—and there are several obvious explanations—but it has no relevance for "genetic" interpretations of the test-score difference. "Caucasian genes" either add something that non-Caucasian genes lack, or they do not: the performance of the Elcho children is sufficient evidence that they do not. In fact, if we were to take this absurd study seriously as evidence for a genetic interpretation of IQ differences, it would actually show that full-blooded Aborigines at the ages Piaget considers close to intellectual maturity, and living in their own community, are slightly superior!

Second, we cannot pass over Jensen's attempt, in his original *Harvard Educational Review* article, to give a genetic explanation of the allegedly much greater incidence of subnormal IQ (below 75) among blacks than among whites. In his later works Jensen dropped all reference to this point, perhaps because the "science" and "scholarship" contained in that passage are so wretchedly shoddy as to be beyond defense. Still, he has never repudiated this particular argument, and it stands as an example of his need to distort data to uphold his thesis—and of his sociological ignorance as well.

What Jensen does is to present a table that compares blacks and whites in five SES quintiles (top 20 percent in socioeconomic status, next 20 percent, etc.) for below-75 IQ rates.[5] The table reads as follows:

SES	White	Negro
High 1	0.5	3.1
2	0.8	14.5
3	2.1	22.8
4	3.1	37.8
Low 5	7.8	42.9

It is of some interest to note that Jensen's table (adapted from the work of another researcher, to be sure) compares a 1963 sample of blacks from five Southeastern states where IQ scores, white and black, are generally lower than elsewhere in the United States, with a sample of whites from all over the United States in 1937.[6] (In that earlier year, moreover, IQ testing had not penetrated as deeply into educational systems as it had by 1963, so that rates may well have been understated especially in the lower quintiles.) But that is a minor problem compared to the use Jensen then proceeds to make of this table.

"In the two highest SES categories," Jensen writes,

> the estimated proportions of Negro and white children with IQs below 75 are in the ratio of 13.6 to 1. If environmental factors were mainly responsible for producing such differences, one should expect a lesser Negro-white discrepancy at the upper SES levels. Other lines of evidence also show this not to be the case. A genetic hypothesis, on the other hand, would predict this effect, since the higher SES Negro offspring would be regressing to a lower population mean than their white counterparts in SES, and consequently a larger proportion of the lower tail of the distribution of genotypes for Negroes would fall below the value that generally results in phenotypic IQs below 75.[7]

If we assume for the sake of argument that causation really can be measured in this way, and that filial regression to the mean really does exist in human populations, then we discover, astonishingly, that the exact opposite of what Jensen claims is actually the case. In amalgamating, with no methodological warrant whatsoever, the top *two* quintiles into one for the purpose of this "analysis," he has concealed the true relationships expressed by the table. In the *five* (not four) SES categories the ratios of black "subnormality" to white "subnormality" are (roughly) 6.2, 18.1, 11.3, 12.2, and 5.5. Note that there *is* a "lesser Negro-white discrepancy at the upper SES levels"—exactly what we should expect, according to Jensen, "if environmental factors were mainly responsible." His argument is based on simple falsification. Moreover, he misuses the concept of "filial regression to the mean." We don't need Galton to tell us that if it works for populations with an *above*-average incidence of a trait, it must also work in the same way for populations with a *below*-average incidence of that trait. The *lower* "SES Negro offspring" should be "regressing to a lower population mean than their white counterparts in SES," and consequently (if genetic laws are operative) the black/white "subnormal" ratio should be *higher* in the lowest quintile; more blacks will have started farther below the 75 cutoff line, and fewer of their children will escape above it through mere regression to the mean. Thus Jensen can salvage his genetic hypothesis here only by misusing both data and concept. On the contrary, these data, were they real, would be explicable only on an environmental hypothesis. We would note that between the lowest and highest SES quintiles the subnormality ratio is similar for each race taken by itself (15.6 for whites, 13.8 for blacks), whereas in every such comparison not involving the highest quintile, the black interclass ratio is much foreshortened compared with the white. (E.g., between class 3 and 2 the ratio for blacks is about 1.6, whereas for whites it is about 2.6; between class 4 and class 2 it is about 2.6 for blacks and about 3.9 for whites; between class 5 and class 2 it is about 3 for blacks and about 10 for whites.) Were we to take this seriously, it would suggest that at the time the data were gathered only a small proportion of blacks as compared with whites (mostly those in the upper SES quintile) had really escaped the stultifying aspects of "lower-class" life (in Banfield's sense). The data, which show that the black/white subnormality ratio falls sharply in the lowest quintile (to 5.5), would also suggest that the rate of "subnormality" in blacks has already reached diminishing returns in the population well before one gets to the lowest quintile of blacks, whereas "subnormality" among whites is just beginning to take off in the lowest quintile. In other words, the table as a whole suggests, or even shouts, that if the data are accurate and meaningful, and to the extent that class is associated with IQ score owing to environmental reasons, the black lower class begins higher up on the SES scale than the white lower class—which of course we know to be true. Thus our sociological knowledge and an *environmental* hypothesis support each other; the genetic hypothesis can only be supported by falsification of the data. Finally (with respect to this table) a genetic hypothesis can make no sense of the correlative fact that according to the table the subnormality ratio differs in the various quintiles, for if subnormal intelligence really were carried racially, then that ratio would always be roughly the same for any two similar breakdowns of the two populations. How could there be such a disproportionately immense difference between the incidence of low IQ for blacks and whites at SES level 2, unless blacks at that level have already begun to be affected by the penalties of caste? Thus this table, for all its faults, clearly suggests that dividing the two racial populations up into the same SES quintiles does *not* truly equate them with each other socially. But Jensen resolutely fails to notice the suggestion, and acts so as to hide it.

As to ignorance, in *Educability* Jensen argues that the lower average SES of black people cannot account for the over-all strikingly higher incidence of prematurity and pregnancy complications among them.[8] Referring to a widely cited study from Baltimore in the early 1950s, he expresses doubt that "the average Negro SES is below the lower tenth or lower fifth of the white population in Baltimore," as the comparative rates of reproductive casualty would suggest. He goes on to give a most *outré* genetic explanation of reproductive casualty itself, relating it "to the genetic heterogeneity of the ancestral gene pools of the American Negro." Demographers will be interested if not shocked to learn that American whites have relatively homogeneous "ancestral gene pools" compared to African blacks, and geneticists, one imagines, may be a bit surprised to learn that homogeneous gene pools—inbreeding!—are a good thing. In any event, not the "average SES" was in question in the Baltimore study, but rather average health care and general maternal and infant welfare in a border city, in a period well before the rise to middle-class status of a significant proportion of American blacks. Moreover, SES in that study was defined by average census-tract characteristics, and it is quite possible that the average black census tract in that segregated city at that time was indeed in roughly the state, relative to indices of social welfare, of the worst white census tracts.[9]

Finally, with this introduction in mind, we should now look closely at Jensen's use of the Audrey Shuey data, specifically, the six studies which purport to show that upper-class blacks have lower average IQs than lower-class whites.

A 1940s study from Winston-Salem, North Carolina, is perhaps the most interesting of the six, though Shuey and Jensen fail to find the points of most interest in it. When blacks and whites were matched by occupational title, there was a great disparity (more than 1 standard deviation) between black and white "salesmen," and between black and white "railroad workers." There was a lesser disparity between black and white "factory workers," and only one-half of an SD between black and white "barbers and beauticians" or "truck drivers." The real lesson of this study is thus the opposite of the one Shuey and Jensen drew from it. *The more alike the actual work done by the subjects, the closer their average IQs; where whites tend to be supervisors and blacks laborers, the spread gets greater.* All of this supports the egalitarian/environmental interpretation of the sources of group inequality.

There is also a category for blacks called "professionals," which indeed shows a lower mean IQ than white factory workers—but a lower mean also than that of black butchers and bakers. White professionals are described as "accountants, auditors, bookkeepers, managers, clerks, engineers," in a city in which the blacks were still concentrated "in the simpler tasks" and had in their homes "few of the appurtenances of our modern culture." Occupations, as it turns out, were specified by the children themselves, and it is perfectly clear from the internal evidence that in that segregated Southern city few of the many black people described as professionals could possibly have been professional at all in the sense described by the professions listed in the quotation above. That black butchers should have had higher average IQs than black professionals—a complete and (if true) inexplicable reversal of the pattern for whites—should have alerted any disinterested or unbiased reader to the spuriousness of the comparison. Shuey and Jensen were quite evidently neither.

(Jensen's lack of scrupulousness about his data is revealed even more strikingly by the fact that he also enlisted in his cause a study for the Civil Rights Commission,[10] despite the fact that the author of that study made this very same point about his own characterization of blacks as "professionals," pointing out as an example that blacks in his segregated city who listed themselves as "ministers" routinely did manual labor. The author of that study also noted that SES differences among blacks are considerably less than among whites, and suggested that this is because there are far fewer genuinely middle-class blacks in the community.)

The other studies follow this pattern. One unpublished master's thesis is from another segregated Southern school system in the 1940s and contains no occupational comparisons at all, the children being identified instead as from "superior" or "inferior" backgrounds by their teachers, "the ratings in each case to be relative to the particular classroom group"(!) The study thus completely falsifies Shuey's and Jensen's account of it, and it seems almost superfluous to add that it also falsifies their conclusion: the black students described by their teachers as being of "superior" background, compared to other black students, outdid the analogously described "inferior" white students by 6 IQ points on the average.

A third study, from a Southern city in the late 1950s, assigned SES solely on the basis of formal educational attainment of parents, thus again completely missing the real points of comparison. A fourth study from the only junior high school of a Northern industrial city attributed status solely on the basis of "occupational level of father"—a categorization that is virtually meaningless since, as Jencks points out, there is almost as much income (and thus social-class) variation within as there is between occupations. Moreover, internal evidence again reveals that more than 10 percent of the black subjects exceeded the white mean by about 1 SD, which is just about what we would expect on the basis of a comparative class analysis from that period, thus demonstrating further that "mean IQ by occupational title" (which fails to turn up this 10 percent) is or at least was a futile rubric for ranking the IQs of blacks.

Worst of all, a fifth study, from St. Louis in the 1950s, made comparisons between black children from schools "serving the best residential area of appreciable size available to St. Louis Negroes," and white children from three schools serving "the downtown, river-industrial areas." In a moment of incredible forgetfulness, Shuey lets us know that, based on census data given in the original (unpublished) study, "the high socio-economic group of the Negroes would be equivalent to some point between the low and middle socio-economic groups of the whites but nearer the former."[11] Their mean IQ is also nearer that of the "low" whites—only *1 IQ point* away, in fact. The only surprising thing about this study, then, is that Shuey and Jensen could bring themselves to use it as an argument for the genetic superiority of whites! One can only conclude that biological inegalitarians are unwilling to pay attention even to their own data when these fail to support their prejudices.

The sixth study, finally, from a Northern elementary school in the early 1960s, makes a more determined effort at matching class characteristics, though relying on the very dubious measures of the prestige ratings of occupations and education of the "main breadwinner" in a family. This study, on reanalysis, shows the top 15 percent of blacks having a mean IQ at about the national average, 5 points above that of the bottom 45 percent of whites in the study, and slightly above that of the bottom 80 percent of whites in the study. Shuey "hid" its findings, as Jensen did after her, by amalgamating them with the other five studies, some of which had been of much larger sample populations, as though the data and control methods were comparable; that act served the purpose of freeing Shuey and Jensen from having to pay real attention to an embarrassing datum.[12]

In sum, Jensen (again) simply did not allow himself to notice what we should expect anyone writing about race in American society to know almost as second nature: to say that blacks are in the "second 20 percent" does not make it so. To clarify this point, finally, "SES" ordinarily refers to a specific index, which is composed of points equally gained for income, occupation, and years of education. But the latter two categories especially (even the first to some extent) are meaninglessly abstract unless we know they are measuring the same thing all the time. For members of low-caste groups, those indices do not measure the same thing as they measure for whites. That is, at a given occupational "rank" blacks in the past almost certainly have been lower down within the particular occupation, and therefore earning a good deal less income; at a given educational level (years of schooling), blacks with the same formal attainment as whites were almost certain to have received an inferior education which would pay off less well for them than similar education would for whites, especially as they would be discriminated against in job markets. We might best conclude this appendix, therefore, by reiterating what was said in the text: Jensen can only make his case by resting it entirely either on the proposition that discrimination against blacks does not exist in the United States, or that, if it does, it has no effects.

APPENDIX

THE BELL-SHAPED CURVE

I. The normal or bell-shaped curve represents a distribution of observations in which a few measurements are located at either extreme but most bunch toward the average value of whatever is being measured, there being also an equal number of cases on either side of the average or mean value; moreover, the mean, median, and modal value are identical. For IQ tests, of which the mean value (of most of the well-known ones) is 100 with a standard deviation of 15 points, a normal distribution entails that approximately 68 percent of observed cases fall equally within plus or minus 1 standard deviation (SD) from 100. That is, 34 percent fall from 85 to 100, and 34 percent from 100 to 115; an additional 27 percent fall plus or minus 2 SD from the mean (between 15 and 30 points above or below it); and most of the remaining 5 percent fall plus or minus 3 SD from the mean (between 55 and 70, or 130 and 145).

For knowing what the scores mean humanly, it is clear that the really significant element in a normal distribution is the *size* of the standard deviation of the population sample. We have noted that virtually all the cases for a normal distribution fall within plus or minus 3 SD from the median/mean: we can divide the area enclosed by a normal curve on a graph into six equal parts (equal in horizontal distance covered along the graph, that is), which will contain most of the cases in the proportion stated above. But the size of the deviation units is given by the standard deviation, that is, the distance from one deviation point (separating those six blocks of space) to the next. If the absolute size of those deviation units and thus of the standard deviation is very small as compared with the mean size of whatever is being measured, we are given a totally different impression of the phenomenon than we would obtain if the deviation units were comparatively large: we obtain a relatively "egalitarian" normal curve in which the existing, proportional inequalities do not amount to very much in real terms.

To return to the case of human height, if we were told that the height of adult males in a certain society showed a midpoint of 5 feet, 9 inches (about what it is in the United States today), and an SD of 6 inches, then we would know that about 95 percent of those males were between 4 feet, 9 inches and 6 feet, 9 inches. We would think to ourselves that male height in that human group was extremely unequal, and it would never occur to us to adopt policies for equalizing it, such as the mass production of elevator shoes or crash programs of research into the nutritional deficiencies of short people. Contrarily, if the SD were 2 inches, it would seem a fairly egalitarian society to us by comparison with the other one—though the proportional distribution of heights would be *exactly* the same—and if it were found that short men were, for example, less attractive to women than tall men, innovation with elevator shoes might become a serious issue.

IQ tests purport to measure a phenomenon that is obviously much more subject to reform and equalization through conscious policy-making than is height. But for IQ tests, 100 has been set as the midpoint (mean, mode, and median) and the SD *has been set* at 15 points. Thus two people with IQs 1 SD above and below the mean differ in their IQs by almost one-third of the social mean (30/100). This is a considerably greater degree of absolute inequality than even that given in my first height example (12/69). It is as though 32 percent of all American men were either shorter than 4 feet or taller than 7 feet, 5 inches! Do the psychometrists really believe that something similar is true of human intelligence? If so, why have they offered no explanation for this astonishing condition?

Again, a person with an IQ of 80 is separated from one with an IQ of 130 (2 SDs above and below the mean) by 50 points, or *half* the mean. This is a most substantial difference. To say that you have an IQ of 50 points less than another, when for more than 99 percent of the population the entire range itself contains only 90 IQ points, is clearly to suggest that there is a great variation in "innate" intelligence (the + 3 SD score of 145 is more than two and a half times as large as the −3 SD score of 55). It is also clearly suggested thereby that someone at or near the lower end of the scale must be decisively incompetent by comparison with someone at or near the upper end. Moreover, the extensiveness of the range enables us to make very fine comparisons among these apparently "innate" values, comparisons that seem to carry their own aura of reality with them. No one, after all, would think to make statements about the intelligence of A versus B if their IQ scores were respectively 120 and 118. But if one score is 120 and the other 110 (or "two-thirds of an SD" apart) then comparisons begin to suggest themselves; it even begins to seem feasible to make requirements out of them, formally or informally, so that we begin to want our managers to have IQs of 120 and our foremen IQs of "only" 110.

All of these comparisons and assessments are functions entirely of the size of the standard deviation. Suppose the IQ SD were set at 3 points. Then the difference of two-thirds of an SD between A and B would be a mere 2 IQ points rather than 10, and only psychometric pedants would dream of making competence comparisons between them. Even the distance from -3 SD to $+3$ SD would be only the distance from an "IQ" of 91 to an "IQ" of 109. In that case, in fact, we would not bother to have IQ testing at all—a fact which reveals to us, again, that the purpose of such testing is precisely to discover "significant" differences.

My counterexample, of course, would be meaningless or dishonestly evasive if the standard deviation of 15 points on IQ test scores were a natural or random phenomenon; that is, if we had set out to "measure" intelligence according to some objective baseline standard and discovered, to our surprise, that our sample showed a means score of 100 and an SD of 15 points. But IQ is not like height, which will be the same when measured against a common reference point such as a tree or a wall, regardless of who is measuring it or for what purposes. As to IQ, that is not what happens methodologically, and as we have seen, that is not what happened historically. On the contrary, IQ tests consist of questions selected precisely in order to produce a mean of 100 and an SD of 15. When either of those values shows signs of a drift away from the norm, the tests are rewritten to make them "harder." The questions, in other words, exist to produce scores that the testmakers think will be an appropriate collection of scores, and there were and are no other, "objective" grounds at all on which the appropriateness of the questions could be demonstrated. In the sense, therefore, in which statisticians say a measurement is valid—truly measuring what is supposed to be measured—IQ tests and measures (such as the 15-point SD) associated with them cannot possibly be said ever to have been validated.

What all this means (aside from telling us something about the social power of the test-makers) is that there is nothing inherently "natural" about the great spread of intellectual capacities which, according to our social mythology, IQ tests uncover. Did they wish it, the testers could equally well design tests showing that most people are very close to average intelligence, or alternatively that there are millions upon millions of submorons or geniuses: "Any distribution of I.Q. test scores can be skewed to the right by making the test questions more difficult, or to the left by making them easier," and thus the results "tell us nothing about the actual shape of mental-ability distribution."[1] (In fact, the very first tests showed men to be more intelligent than women, and since nothing in the psychometrists' arsenal of prejudices explained this "fact," eventually they restandardized the tests so that they would *not* show that difference systematically.)

On the basis of the work that has been done so far, and owing to the fact that most of our mental testing is norm-referenced—purely comparative—rather than skill-oriented, no one can say with even a glimmer of certitude what the "real" distribution of "innate intelligence" is in our society. The fit between IQ scores and job performance is the only indicator we have: thus the significance of Herrnstein's inability to offer any but fatuously insignificant correlations between the two, and conversely, of Jencks's finding that among people who have managed to be admitted into a given field of work, IQ is not a predictor of income.

II.

Herrnstein, of course, is a trained behavioral scientist who should know better; given his failure to use statistical concepts intelligently, we should not be surprised that the same kind of statistical superstition also afflicts untrained observers. Thus in his essay on equality Irving Kristol, arguing that income distribution is similar in all industrial societies and *must* be similar, refers to "the tyranny of the bell-shaped curve." Factually he is quite wrong. Even more so than is the case for IQ, the shape of the income distribution curve in most nations is badly skewed at the lower end of the distribution: too much poverty, not enough riches. If the bell-shaped curve which Kristol alleges to discover looks somewhat like a humpbacked whale, the actual shape of the income distribution in, say, the United States more closely resembles that of an anteater with its tail hacked off. More to the point, though, than the inaccuracy of Kristol's data is the misappropriated statistical conception. In the first place, as we have just seen in the case of Herrnstein, he confuses the shape of an (income) distribution with the actual size of the dispersion, which is a much truer index of "egalitarianism"; with respect to the absolute distance between the worst-off and the best-off, or between particular occupational groupings, all industrial societies are far from being identical. But above all, he makes a claim about the alleged "facts of life" that is spurious. In plain English, Kristol has merely said that all industrial societies to now are hierarchical, and that the hierarchy consists of a few bosses, a larger number of underlings, a much larger mass of average laborers, and (had he stated the data correctly) a somewhat smaller mass of unskilled or unemployable people. In even plainer English, he tells us that social classes exist in all industrial societies, including the state socialist societies. Surely we already knew that. The only question we are interested in is, Can that condition be changed, in what ways, and to what extent? By speaking glibly of "the tyranny of the bell-shaped curve," Kristol has given what may be, but also may not be, an organizational necessity the undeserved aura of a "natural" fate.

Chapter 1. Introduction: The Equality Debate

1. John Rawls, *A Theory of Justice* (Cambridge, Mass.: Harvard University Press, 1971), pp. 14–15. See also Herbert J. Gans, *More Equality* (New York: Pantheon Books, 1973).

2. The most notorious proponent is Irving Kristol; see his collected essays in *Two Cheers for Capitalism* (New York: Basic Books, 1978), especially pt. 1. See also Daniel Bell, *The Coming of Post-Industrial Society* (New York: Basic Books, 1973), chap. 3; B. Bruce-Briggs, ed., *The New Class?* (New Brunswick, N.J.: Transaction Books, 1979); and the discussion of Daniel Patrick Moynihan (chap. 6) and others in Peter Steinfels' *The Neo-Conservatives* (New York: Simon & Schuster, 1979).

3. See, for example, Studs Terkel, *Working* (New York: Pantheon Books, 1974); Patricia Cayo Sexton and Brendan Sexton, *Blue Collars and Hard Hats* (New York: Random House, 1971); Jonathan Cobb and Richard Sennett, *The Hidden Injuries of Class* (New York: Random House, 1972); and Lillian Breslow Rubin, *Worlds of Pain: Life in the Working Class Family* (New York: Basic Books, 1976).

4. The best statement of this position is still Max Weber's, as first brought to the attention of American social scientists in Talcott Parsons' translation of *The Theory of Social and Economic Organization* (New York: Free Press, 1947), especially pt. 3. The mainstream of modern American sociology has for the most part restated his argument. See, e.g., Suzanne Keller, *Beyond the Ruling Class: Strategic Elites in Modern Society* (New York: Random House, 1963); Talcott Parsons, *The Social System* (New York: Free Press, 1951), pt. 5, and "The Distribution of Power in American Society," *World*

Politics (10 October 1957), pp. 123–42; and Kingsley Davis and Wilbert E. Moore, "Some Principles of Stratification," *American Sociological Review* 10 (April 1945): pp. 242–49. On the development of that position in modern American political science, see Robert A. Dahl, *A Preface to Democratic Theory* (Chicago: University of Chicago Press, 1956), and *Who Governs?: Democracy and Power in an American City* (New Haven, Conn.: Yale University Press, 1961), and Peter Bachrach, *The Theory of Democratic Elitism* (Boston: Little, Brown & Co., 1967).

5. The manifestos of this intellectual counterrevolution in the realm of biology are Arthur R. Jensen, "How Much Can We Boost IQ and Scholastic Achievement?" *Harvard Educational Review* 39 (Winter 1969): 1–23 (hereinafter referred to as *HER*); and Richard J. Herrnstein, "IQ," *Atlantic Monthly*, September 1971, pp. 43–64 (hereinafter referred to as *Atlantic Monthly*). On equality generally, see also Kristol, *Two Cheers*; Bell, *Post-Industrial Society*; Nathan Glazer, *Affirmative Discrimination: Ethnic Inequality and Public Policy* (New York: Basic Books, 1975); Aaron Wildavsky, "Government and the People," *Commentary*, August 1973, pp. 25–32; Robert A. Nisbet, *Twilight of Authority* (New York: Oxford University Press, 1975), and "Where Do We Go from Here?" in Colin D. Campbell, ed., *Income Redistribution* (Washington, D.C.: American Enterprise Institute, 1977) pp. 179–96; Michel Crozier, Samuel P. Huntington, and Joji Watanuki, *The Crisis of Democracy: A Report on the Governability of Democracies to the Trilateral Commission* (New York: New York University Press, 1975); and generally the pages of *Commentary, Public Interest,* and the *Wall Street Journal.* These are only a few of the important statements, however. To *feel* the shift, one has to have been reading such organs of establishment liberalism as the *New York Times* during this period.

6. Herrnstein, *Atlantic Monthly*.

7. Steven Goldberg, *The Inevitability of Patriarchy*, 2nd ed. (New York: William Morrow & Co., 1974). This line of argument begins in the contemporary period with Lionel Tiger, *Men in Groups* (New York: Random House, 1969). See Chapter 5 below for some illustrative statements of this position from other well-known sociobiologists.

8. For an extended discussion, see Steinfels, *Neo-Conservatives.*

PART ONE. THE RATIONALIZATION OF INEQUALITY

Chapter 2. Sociobiology and Inequality

1. See Oliver Gillie, *Who Do You Think You Are?* (New York: Saturday Review Press, 1976).

2. See note 12 below, and the remarks of Arthur R. Jensen and Hans J. Eysenck quoted in D. D. Dorfman, "The Cyril Burt Question: New Findings," *Science* 201 (September 29, 1978): 1177–86. Jensen's performance is truly astonishing. In his latest book, *Bias in Mental Testing* (New York: Free Press, 1980), he refers to the work of Sir Cyril Burt on a dozen separate occasions without once acknowledging the by now obvious truth that Burt consistently fabricated and falsified evidence.

3. The quotation in the text is from Lord Alexander of Potterhill, General-Secretary of the Association of Educational Committees (Great Britain), and appeared on the front page of the *Times* of London, October 28, 1976; it was called to my attention by Leon Kamin. Also see R. L. Dugdale, *The Jukes*, 4th ed. (New York: G. P. Putnam's Sons, 1888), and Henry H. Goddard, *The Kallikak Family* (New York: Macmillan Co., 1912; reprinted 1939), and the discussion of those works in Gillie, *Who Do You Think You Are?;* Edward O. Wilson, *On Human Nature* (Cambridge, Mass.: Harvard University Press, 1978), p. 43, and Gillie's discussion of the XYY chromosome controversy in chap. 10 of his book.

4. Stephen T. Emlen, "An Alternative Case for Sociobiology," in Arthur L. Caplan, ed., *The Sociobiology Debate* (New York: Harper & Row, 1978), pp. 338–39.

5. Wilson, *On Human Nature*, p. 13. For a detailed presentation of the resort to fanciful and unwarranted assumptions and self-confirming hypotheses in the work of Wilson and other sociobiologists, see pts. 5 and 6 of Caplan, ed., *The Sociobiology Debate*, especially Sociobiology Study Group of Science for the People, "Sociobiology—Another Biological Determinism," pp. 280–90; Joseph Alper *et al.*, "The Implications of Sociobiology," pp. 333–36; Stephen Jay Gould, "Biological Potential vs. Biological Determinism," pp. 343–51; and Lawrence G. Miller, "Fated Genes," pp. 269–79.

6. Wilson, *On Human Nature*, p. 78.

7. See *ibid.*, pp. 67–68. In addition to works by Wilson and Tiger already cited, see Richard Dawkins, *The Selfish Gene* (New York: Oxford University Press, 1976), with a foreword by Robert L. Trivers; David P. Barash, *Sociobiology and Behavior* (New York: Elsevier North-Holland, 1977), with a foreword by Wilson; and *Exploring Human Nature* (Cambridge, Mass.: Education Development Center, 1973), a high school curriculum prepared by Irven DeVore and Trivers. Generally, see the articles mentioned in note 5 above for citations to some of the more flagrantly inegalitarian statements in the works of these sociobiologists.

8. This analysis is presented in Jensen's *HER* article (see note 5 to Chapter 1).

9. See Lloyd G. Humphreys, "Theory of Intelligence," in Robert Cancro, M.D., ed., *Intelligence: Genetic and Environmental Influences* (New York: Grune & Stratton, 1971), p. 34.

10. Jensen, *HER*, pp. 43, 50–51.

11. Arthur R. Jensen, *Educability and Group Differences* (New York: Harper & Row, 1973), hereinafter cited as *Educability*. See the "Appendix on Heritability."

12. L. S. Hearnshaw, *Cyril Burt, Psychologist* (Ithaca, N.Y.: Cornell University Press, 1979); Leon J. Kamin, *The Science and Politics of IQ* (New York: John Wiley & Sons, 1974); Dorfman, "The Cyril Burt Question," and reply to critics, *Science* 206 (October 2, 1979): 142–43.

13. See Kamin's reanalysis of these studies in *The Science and Politics of IQ*, and Harry Munsinger, "The Adopted Child's IQ: A Critical Review," *Psychological Bulletin* 82 (September 1975): 623–59.

14. John C. Loehlin and Robert C. Nichols, *Heredity, Environment, and Personality: A Study of 850 Sets of Twins* (Austin: University of Texas Press, 1976), p. 94; Sandra Scarr and Richard A. Weinberg, "Attitudes, Interests, and IQ," *Human Nature* (April 1978): 29–36.

15. Adrian M. Srb, Ray D. Owen, and Robert S. Edgar, *General Genetics*, 2nd ed., rev. (San Francisco: W. H. Freeman & Co., 1965), pp. 491–92; italics added. Approximately 225 words are omitted by the ellipsis.

16. Jensen, *Educability*, p. 57.

17. Human height is the best-known case; see L. L. Cavalli-Sforza and Walter F. Bodmer, *The Genetics of Human Populations* (San Francisco: W. H. Freeman & Co., 1971), pp. 609–10.

18. Alfred Binet, *Les Ideés modernes sur les enfants* (Paris: Flammarion, 1909), p. 143. Jerry Hirsch called this passage to our attention in "Jensenism: The Bankruptcy of 'Science' Without Scholarship," *Educational Theory* 25 (Winter 1975): 3–27.

19. Zena Stein and Mervyn Susser, "Mutability of Intelligence and Epidemiology of Mild Mental Retardation," *Review of Educational Research* 40 (February 1970): 64; see also the excellent summary (from which I take the term "ecological intervention") by Urie Bronfenbrenner, "Is Early Intervention Effective? Some Studies of Early Education in Familial and Extra-Familial Settings," in Ashley Montagu, ed., *Race and IQ* (New York: Oxford University Press, 1975), pp. 287–322. The most dramatic studies are by H. M. Skeels, *Adult Status of Children with Contrasting Early Life Experiences*, Monograph #31, no. 3, Society for Research in Child Development (Washington, D.C., 1966); and R. Herber *et al.*, *Rehabilitation of Families at Risk for Mental Retardation*, Regional Rehabilitation Center of the University of Wisconsin (Milwaukee, 1969). The Mil-

waukee Project (as Herber's work is known) is described by Stephen P. Strickland, "Can Slum Children Learn?" in Carl Senna, ed., *The Fallacy of IQ* (New York: Third Press, 1974). An equally dramatic account concerning individuals rather than structured learning groups is that of Robert B. McCall *et al.*, *Developmental Changes in Mental Performance*, Monograph #38, no. 3, Society for Research in Child Development (Washington, D.C., 1973). That monograph and Bronfenbrenner's article both have full-length bibliographies; see also B. S. Bloom, *Stability and Change in Human Characteristics* (New York: John Wiley & Sons, 1964), and Martin Deutsch and Associates, *The Disadvantaged Child: Studies of the Social Environment and the Learning Process* (New York: Basic Books, 1967). See the migration study by Otto Klineberg, *Negro Intelligence and Selective Migration* (New York: Columbia University Press, 1935); it was replicated fifteen years later, with similar results, by E. S. Lee, "Negro Intelligence and Selective Migration: A Philadelphia Test of the Klineberg Hypothesis," *American Sociological Review* 16 (April 1951): 227–33.

20. *New York Times*, June 29, 1978.

21. Gene V. Glass and Mary Lee Smith, *Meta-analysis of Research on Class Size and Achievement*, Far West Laboratory For Educational Research and Development (San Francisco, September 1978); Michael Rutter, *Fifteen Thousand Hours: Secondary Schools and Their Effects on Children* (Cambridge, Mass.: Harvard University Press, 1979); *New York Times*, April 27, 1975, and April 10, 1979 (C5). See also Carol Tavris, "Compensatory Education: The Glass Is Half Full," *Psychology Today*, September 1976, pp. 63–74; "Schools Do Make a Difference: The Philadelphia Federal Reserve Bank Study," *Today's Education* 64 (November–December 1975): 24–31; and Herbert H. Hyman, Charles R. Wright, and John Selton Reed, *The Enduring Effects of Education* (Chicago: University of Chicago Press, 1975).

22. Barbara Bowen Doak, "Life Out There Is Good," *Swarthmore College Bulletin* (July 1975): 22.

23. Christopher Jencks, *Inequality* (New York: Basic Books, 1972), p. 255.

Chapter 3. Rationalizing Inequality: Race

1. See U.S. Department of Commerce, Bureau of the Census, *Current Population Reports*, "Consumer Income," Series P–60, no. 120 (November 1979), table C, "Selected Characteristics of Persons, Families, and Unrelated Individuals, by Poverty Status in 1978."

2. Jensen, *HER*, p. 82; Herrnstein, *Atlantic Monthly*.

3. See Gillie, *Who Do You Think You Are?* for a description of Eysenck's strange career.

4. Audrey M. Shuey, *The Testing of Negro Intelligence,* 2nd ed. (New York: Social Science Press, 1966); Henry Garrett, *Statistics in Psychology and Education,* 5th ed. (New York: Longmans, Green & Co., 1960); Nathaniel Weyl, *The Negro in American Civilization* (Washington, D.C.: Public Affairs Press, 1960); Weyl and Stefan T. Possony, *The Geography of Intellect* (Chicago: Henry Regnery Co., 1963). William Shockley's campaign to bring racial comparisons to the forefront of American scientific discussion is typified by his talk given in the spring of 1967, quoted in *Science* 158 (1967), p. 892, and his address, "Human Quality Problems and Research Taboos," given to the National Academy of Sciences, Washington, D.C., in the spring of 1968.

5. Note how few of the commentators on Jensen's initial statement in the *HER* reprint question his comments about race, though many take aim at his conclusions about heritability. See, as late as 1978, Brigitte Berger's willfully inaccurate remark in *Public Interest* that "name-calling has failed to evaporate the data on which the 'bad guys' [Jensen, Shockley, and Herrnstein] base their arguments." ("A New Interpretation of the IQ Controversy," Winter 1978, p. 30). Berger's article contains no citations to any sources whatsoever.

6. See, e.g., Kamin, *Science and Politics of IQ;* N. J. Block and Gerald Dworkin, eds., *The IQ Controversy* (New York: Pantheon Books, 1977), the best collection of essays on the subject; *Race and IQ,* edited by Ashley Montagu; David Layzer, "Heritability Analyses of IQ Scores: Science or Numerology?" *Science* 183 (March 29, 1974): 1259–66; the various articles in *Science, Heritability, and IQ, Harvard Educational Review* Reprint Series, no. 4 (1969); James M. Lawler, *IQ, Heritability and Racism* (New York: International Publishers, 1978); Jeffrey M. Blum, *Pseudoscience and Mental Ability* (New York: Monthly Review Press, 1978); Hirsch, "Jensenism"; and Senna, *Fallacy of IQ.* The article by Jane R. Mercer and Wayne Curtis Brown in the Senna book, "Racial Differences in IQ: Fact or Artifact?" offers an effective critique of Jensen's argument about race. An earlier version of the detailed critique contained in this chapter appeared in Philip Green, "The Pseudoscience of Arthur Jensen," *Dissent* 23 (Summer 1976): 284–97.

7. Jensen, *HER,* p. 81.

8. *Ibid.,* pp. 111ff.

9. Edward C. Banfield, *The Unheavenly City Revisited* (Boston: Little, Brown & Co., 1974).

10. On pp. 87, 95, and 99 of Banfield's *Unheavenly City Revisited,* one

finds examples of his self-contradiction on this fundamental point. See also William Muraskin, "The Moral Basis of a Backward Sociologist: Edward Banfield, the Italians, and the Italian Americans," *American Journal of Sociology* 79 (May 1974): 1484–96.

11. Banfield, *Unheavenly City Revisited*, p. 113.
12. See "The Widening Economic Gap," a report of the National Urban League, summarized in the *New York Times*, July 24, 1979.
13. Ernest A. Haggard, "Social Status and Intelligence," *Genetic Psychology Monographs* 49 (1954): 141–86.
14. Fascinating examples of the kinds of materials to be found on allegedly objective standard IQ tests can be seen in Kamin, *Science and Politics of IQ*, Clarence Karier, "Testing for Order and Control in the Corporate Liberal State," *Educational Theory* 22 (Spring 1972): 154–80; and especially Mercer and Brown, "Racial Differences in IQ."
15. Jensen, *Educability*, pp. 186–87.
16. Compare the table in Srb, Owen, and Edgar, *General Genetics*, p. 490. It is instructive to contrast the presentation of the idea of "heritability" in this standard textbook with Jensen's. The authors of the text emphasize, not deductions about "nature" and "nurture" which the concept allegedly enables us to make (according to Jensen and Herrnstein), but the limited and controlled circumstances under which geneticists are able to make any statements at all about heritability in animals. Their cautious treatment of that topic leaves a strong impression that Jensen has confused people with fruit flies.
17. Jensen, *Educability*, p. 316.
18. Jensen, *HER*, p. 84; Shuey, *Testing Negro Intelligence*, p. 520.
19. Shuey, *Testing Negro Intelligence*, pp. 516–20 and *passim*.
20. S. R. Tulkin, "Race, Class, Family, and School Achievement," *Journal of Personality and Social Psychology* 9 (September 1968): 31–37. Jensen's performance in concealing the nature and impact of Tulkin's findings is almost brilliant (see *Educability*, pp. 237–38). The Coleman Report is *Equality of Educational Opportunity*, prepared for the U.S. National Center for Educational Statistics by James S. Coleman *et al.* (Washington, D.C.: U.S. Government Printing Office, 1966), vol. 2. Only one carefully controlled study ever unambiguously showed the effect that Shuey and Jensen describe, for young children: Sandra Scarr-Salapatek, "Race, Social Class, and IQ," *Science* 174 (December 24, 1971): 1285–95. However, the author of this study comments that "social-class groups of children were far more differentiated among whites than among blacks, despite the same criteria for assignment," a comment which lets us know that the careful controls have revealed (rather than compensated for) the disparate

meanings of "class" for blacks and whites in the United States. In any event, Jensen would have been much wiser not to refer to this study at all, since it also reports a generally low proportion of genetic variance among its black subjects in comparison with that shown by its white subjects: a contrast which, when put together with the comment about social class (and assuming one takes the entire enterprise of twin studies, etc., with more seriousness than it deserves), can only be explained by the kind of environmentalist explanation outlined on pages 58–61 above.

21. John R. Baker, *Race* (New York: Oxford University Press, 1974).
22. David K. Cohen, "Immigrants and the Schools," *Review of Educational Research* 4 (February 1970): 13–28; Karier, "Testing for Order and Control," especially p. 163.
23. Berger, "A New Interpretation of the IQ Controversy."

Chapter 4. Rationalizing Inequality: Class
1. See Jensen, "Reducing the Heredity-Environment Uncertainty," and Carl Bereiter, "The Future of Individual Differences," both in *Environment, Heredity, and Intelligence, Harvard Educational Review* Reprint Series, no. 2, pp. 209–43 and 162–70. In addition to Herrnstein's *Atlantic Monthly* article, see his *IQ in the Meritocracy* (Boston: Little, Brown & Co., 1974), and an elaboration of his position in "More About IQ," *Atlantic Monthly*, December 1971, pp. 101–10. An exchange between Herrnstein and Noam Chomsky, in which Chomsky presents an argument similar to that made here, may be found in *Cognition* 1, nos. 1, 2, 4 (1972–1973): 11–46, 301–10 and 407–18. Chomsky's critique originally appeared in *Social Policy* 3 (May–June 1972) pp. 19–25.
2. Davis and Moore, "Some Principles of Stratification"; Bell, *Post-Industrial Society*, p. 454.
3. Melvin M. Tumin, "Some Principles of Stratification: A Critical Analysis," *American Sociological Review* 18 (August 1953): 387–94; reply by Davis and Moore, *ibid.*, pp. 394–97; see also Walter Buckley, "Social Stratification and Social Differentiation," *American Sociological Review* 23 (August 1958): 369–75, and Dennis H. Wrong, "The Functional Theory of Stratification," *American Sociological Review* 24 (December 1959): 772–82.
4. Bell, *Post-Industrial Society*, p. 414.
5. See Herrnstein's exchange with Philip Green, "An Exchange on IQ," *Dissent* (Summer 1977): 297–306.
6. See, among others, Harry Braverman, *Labor and Monopoly Capital* (New York: Monthly Review Press, 1974), especially p. 445; Martin Carnoy and Derek Shearer, *Economic Democracy: The Challenge of*

the 1980s (White Plains, N.Y.: M. E. Sharpe, 1980); Gerry Hunnius, G. David Garson, and John Case, eds., *Workers' Control: A Reader on Labor and Social Change* (New York: Vintage Books, 1973); Michael Walzer, "In Defense of Equality," *Dissent* 20 (Fall 1973): 399–408; Gar Alperovitz, "Notes Toward a Pluralist Commonwealth" in Staughton Lynd and Gar Alperovitz, *Strategy and Program: Two Essays Toward a New American Socialism* (Boston: Beacon Press, 1973), pp. 49–110; Murray Bookchin, "Toward a Liberatory Technology" and "The Forms of Freedom" in C. George Benello and Dimitrios Roussopoulos, eds., *The Case for Participatory Democracy* (New York: Viking Press, 1971); Carole Pateman, *Participation and Democratic Theory* (Cambridge: Cambridge University Press, 1970); and Gans, *More Equality*.

7. Kristol, *Two Cheers*, chap. 23. This essay was originally published in *Commentary* as "About Equality," November 1972.

8. Cf. David Lane, *The End of Inequality?: Stratification Under State Socialism* (Harmondsworth, Eng.: Penguin Books, 1971); and see Michael Don Ward, *The Political Economy of Distribution* (New York: Elsevier North-Holland, 1978), for a recent assessment of income inequality worldwide.

9. The basic discussion can be found in Charles A. and Mary R. Beard, *The Rise of American Civilization* (New York: Macmillan Co., 1933), vol. 2; also in William Appleman Williams, *The Contours of American History* (Chicago: Quadrangle Books, 1966). See also Matthew Josephson, *The Robber Barons: The Great American Capitalists, 1861–1901* (New York: Harcourt, Brace & Co., 1934), and among many other relevant case studies, Louis Hartz, *Economic Policy and Democratic Thought* (Cambridge, Mass.: Harvard University Press, 1948); Grant McConnell, *The Decline of Agrarian Democracy* (Berkeley: University of California Press, 1959); Norman Ware, *The Labor Movement in the United States, 1860–1895* (New York: D. Appleton & Co., 1929; reprint ed., New York: Vintage Books, n.d.); and Morton J. Horwitz, *The Transformation of American Law, 1780–1860* (Cambridge, Mass.: Harvard University Press, 1977).

10. Generally, see Karl Marx, *Capital* (Chicago: Charles H. Kerr), vol. 1, pts. 3, 4, and 8; Karl Polanyi, *The Great Transformation: The Political and Economic Origins of our Time* (Boston: Beacon Press, 1944), pt. 2; and Christopher Hill, *Reformation to Industrial Revolution* (New York: Pantheon Books, 1968). On the United States experience, see among others Braverman, *Labor and Monopoly Capital;* Stephen A. Marglin, "What Do Bosses Do? The Origins and Functions of Hierarchy in Capitalist Production," and Katherine Stone, "The Origins of Job Structures in the Steel Industry," both in

Review of Radical Political Economics 6 (Summer 1974): 60–112 and 113–73.

11. Herrnstein, *Atlantic Monthly,* p. 63.

12. Bell, *Post-Industrial Society,* chap. 3.

13. Jencks, *Inequality,* p. 220.

14. Compare Herrnstein in *Atlantic Monthly,* pp. 50–53, and in *IQ in the Meritocracy,* chap. 3, and Jensen in *HER,* pp. 13ff.

15. Jencks, *Inequality;* Samuel Bowles and Herbert Gintis, *Schooling in Capitalist America* (New York: Basic Books, 1976), pt. 2; and U.S. Department of Health, Education and Welfare, *Socioeconomic Background and Occupational Achievement, Final Report,* Project no. S–0074 (EO–191), prepared for the Office of Education by Otis Dudley Duncan, D. C. Featherman, and Beverly Duncan (Washington, D.C.: Government Printing Office, 1968).

16. Jencks, *Inequality,* pp. 186–87.

17. Philip Green, reply to Herrnstein, *Dissent* 24 (Summer 1977): 301–6.

18. Braverman, *Labor and Monopoly Capital,* p. 81.

19. Herrnstein, *IQ in the Meritocracy.* Compare pp. 118–22 (and fig. 3) with p. 51 of *Atlantic Monthly,* and both of them with the original sources: T. W. and M. S. Harrell, "Army General Classification Test Scores for Civilian Occupations," *Educational and Psychological Measurement* 5 (1945): 229–39, and Naomi Stewart, "A.G.C.T. Scores of Army Personnel Grouped by Occupation," *Occupations* 26 (1947): 5–41.

20. Herrnstein, *Atlantic Monthly,* pp. 51, 53.

21. Braverman, *Labor and Monopoly Capital,* p. 239.

22. Herrnstein in *Dissent,* p. 300.

23. See my comments in *Dissent,* pp. 301–2.

24. Herrnstein in *Dissent.*

25. See Gans, *More Equality,* chap. 4.

26. Compare Robert Heilbroner, "Benign Neglect in the United States," *Transaction* 7 (October 1970): 15–20; Eli Ginzberg, "Sweden: Some Unanswered Questions," in Daniel Bell and Irving Kristol, eds., *Capitalism Today* (New York: New American Library, 1971), pp. 187–98; and Morton Kondracke, "The German Challenge to American Conservatives," *New Republic,* September 29, 1979, pp. 16–21.

27. Michael Burawoy, "Toward a Marxist Theory of the Labor Process: Braverman and Beyond," *Politics and Society* 8 (1978): 247–312, especially p. 277.

28. David F. Noble, "Social Choice in Machine Design: The Case of Automatically Controlled Machine Tools, and a Challenge for Labor," *Politics and Society* 8 (1978): 318–48, especially pp. 334ff.

29. Braverman, *Labor and Monopoly Capital,* p. 370.

30. *Ibid.*, pp. 355, 384.

31. See Edgar K. Browning, "How Much More Equality Can We Afford?" *Public Interest* 43 (Spring 1976): 90–110, for a typical statement.

32. Jencks, *Inequality*, p. 262. For his complete analysis of the extent to which inheritance has an independent effect on income, see chap. 7. His findings there are not greatly modified by his later study, *Who Gets Ahead? The Determinants of Economic Success in America* (New York: Basic Books, 1979).

33. On this point, see Walzer's discussion in his 1973 *Dissent* article, "In Defense of Equality."

Chapter 5. Rationalizing Inequality: Sex

1. The passages quoted are, respectively, from Edward O. Wilson, *Sociobiology: The New Synthesis* (Cambridge, Mass.: Harvard University Press, 1975), p. 569 (the interior quotation is from Robin Fox, "Alliance and Constraint: Sexual Selection in the Evolution of Human Kinship Systems" in B. G. Campbell, ed., *Sexual Selection and the Descent of Man, 1871–1971* [Chicago: Aldine-Atherton, 1972], p. 291); Wilson, "Human Decency Is Animal," *New York Times Magazine*, October 12, 1975, p. 48; *ibid.;* Wilson, *Sociobiology*, table 27–1, p. 552; Barash, *Sociobiology and Behavior*, pp. 194–95; Wilson, *On Human Nature*, pp. 91–92; *ibid.*, pp. 128, 132, 147; and Robin Fox, "The Cultural Animal," in J. F. Eisenberg and W. S. Dillon, eds., *Man and Beast: Comparative Social Behavior* (Washington, D.C.: Smithsonian Institution Press, 1971), p. 284.

2. See Goldberg, *Inevitability of Patriarchy;* George Gilder, "The Case Against Women in Combat," *New York Times Magazine*, January 28, 1979, pp. 29–30, 44–46, and *Naked Nomads: Unmarried Men in America* (New York: Quadrangle Books, 1974); Wilson, *On Human Nature*, pp. 128, 241.

3. Susan Brownmiller, *Against Our Will: Men, Women and Rape* (New York: Simon & Schuster, 1975); C. A. Tripp, *The Homosexual Matrix* (New York: McGraw-Hill Book Co., 1975).

4. Goldberg, *Inevitability of Patriarchy*, pp. 256–61.

5. *Ibid.*, p. 85.

6. *Ibid.*, pp. 86–90.

7. See the critique of animal studies by Donna Haraway, "Animal Sociology and a Natural Economy of the Body Politic," pts. 1 and 2, *Signs: Journal of Women in Culture and Society* 4 (Autumn 1978): 21–60. Also see Ruth Bleier, "Bias in Biological and Human Sciences," *ibid.*, pp. 159–62.

8. On Geddes and other Victorian theorists of sexuality, see Jill Ker

Conway, "Stereotypes of Femininity in a Theory of Sexual Evolution" in Martha Vicinus, ed., *Suffer and Be Still: Women in the Victorian Age* (Bloomington, Ind.: Indiana University Press, 1973).

9. See Helen H. Lambert, "Biology and Equality: A Perspective on Sex Differences," *Signs* 4 (Autumn 1978): 97–117.

10. Abraham Kaplan, *The Conduct of Inquiry: Methodology for Behavioral Science* (San Francisco: Chandler Publishing Co., 1964), p. 61.

11. Goldberg, *Inevitability of Patriarchy*, pp. 264–66. Italics added.

12. *Ibid.*, pp. 112–14.

13. Gilder, "Women in Combat"; Eleanor E. Maccoby and Carol N. Jacklin, *The Psychology of Sex Differences* (Stanford, Cal.: Stanford University Press, 1974).

14. Maccoby and Jacklin, *Sex Differences*, chap. 7.

15. *Ibid.*, pp. 271–73.

16. On the recruitment of women into politics and the corporate structure, see Berenice A. Carroll, "Political Science, Part I: American Politics and Political Behavior," *Signs* 5 (Winter 1979): 289–306; Rosabeth Moss Kanter, *Men and Women of the Corporation* (New York: Basic Books, 1977); and Susan Welch, "Women As Political Animals? A Test of Some Explanations for Male-Female Political Participation Differences," *American Journal of Political Science* 21 (November 1977): 711–30, and "Recruitment of Women to Public Office: A Discriminant Analysis," *Western Political Quarterly* 31 (September 1978): 372–80.

17. The literature on dominance in families is summarized by Maccoby and Jacklin, *Sex Differences*, p. 262.

18. Goldberg, *Inevitability of Patriarchy*, p. 112.

19. Virginia Sapiro, "Women's Studies and Political Conflict" in Julia A. Sherman and Evelyn T. Beck, eds., *The Prism of Sex* (Madison, Wis.: University of Wisconsin Press, 1979), p. 262.

20. See L. E. Kreuz and R. M. Rose, "Assessment of Aggressive Behavior and Plasma Testosterone in a Young Criminal Population," *Psychosomatic Medicine* 34 (July/August 1972): 321–32.

21. See John Money and Anke A. Ehrhardt, *Man and Woman, Boy and Girl* (Baltimore: Johns Hopkins University Press, 1972). Wilson's reference to their work is on p. 132 of *On Human Nature*.

22. For a description of this development, see, e.g., Kathleen McCourt, *Working-Class Women and Grass-Roots Politics* (Bloomington, Ind.: Indiana University Press, 1977); Susan Tolchin and Martin Tolchin, *Clout: Womanpower and Politics* (New York: Capricorn Books, 1976); and Jane S. Jaquette, ed., *Women in Politics* (New York: John Wiley & Sons, 1974).

23. *New York Times*, June 17, 1979. Part of this development is a tendency toward redefinition by various interest groups, such as women, of what constitutes the political realm—the realm in which we try to make our influence felt publicly. On the definition of the "political," see Susan C. Bourque and Jean Grossholtz, "Politics As an Unnatural Practice: Political Science Looks at Female Participation," *Politics and Society* 4 (Winter 1974): pp. 225–266; and Jean Bethke Elshtain, "Methodological Sophistication and Conceptual Confusion: A Critique of Mainstream Political Inquiry on Women, Politics and Values," in Sherman and Beck, eds., *Prism of Sex*, pp. 229–52.

24. Michel Crozier *et al.*, *Crisis of Democracy*.

25. Eleanor Leacock, "On Goldberg's Response," *American Anthropologist* 77 (March 1975): 73–75.

26. The role of women in hunter-gatherer societies is discussed most extensively by Nancy Tanner and Adrienne Zihlman, "Women in Evolution, Part I: Innovation and Selection in Human Origins," *Signs* 1 (Spring 1976): 585–608.

27. The quotation is from Elise Boulding, *Women in the Twentieth Century World* (New York: Halsted Press, 1977), pp. 211–212. Her *The Underside of History: A View of Women Through Time* (Boulder, Col.: Westview Press, 1977) is a massive and magisterial compendium of the public activities of women in all recorded civilizations; it does not so much refute Goldberg's contentions about the constancy of patriarchy as annihilate them. And see also Mary R. Beard, *Woman As a Force in History: A Study in Traditions and Realities* (New York: Macmillan Co., 1946).

28. See Sherry B. Ortner, "Is Female to Male As Nature Is to Culture?" in Michelle Zimbalist Rosaldo and Louise Lamphere, eds., *Woman, Culture and Society* (Stanford, Cal.: Stanford University Press, 1974).

29. See Carolyn T. Adams and Kathryn T. Winston, *Mothers at Work: Public Policies in the United States, Sweden and China* (New York: Longman, 1980).

30. Gilder, "Women in Combat."

PART TWO. THE PREVENTION OF EQUALITY

Chapter 6. The New Individualism:
Keeping Them in Their Place

1. Bell, *Post-Industrial Society*, p. 438; Earl Raab, "Quotas by Any Other Name," *Commentary*, January 1972, pp. 41–45.

2. See, e.g., Robert Calvert, Jr., *Affirmative Action: A Comprehensive*

Recruitment Manual (Garrett Park, Md.: Garrett Park Press, 1979); Nijole V. Benokraitis and Joe R. Reagin, *Affirmative Action and Equal Opportunity: Action, Inaction, Reaction* (Boulder, Col.: Westview Press, 1978); Phyllis A. Wallace, *Equal Employment Opportunity and the AT&T Case* (Cambridge, Mass.: MIT Press, 1975); Phyllis A. Wallace and Annette M. LaMond, eds., *Women, Minorities and Discrimination* (Lexington, Mass.: Lexington Books, 1977), especially Wallace's essay, "A Decade of Policy Developments in Equal Opportunities in Employment and Housing"; Harrell R. Rogers, Jr., and Charles S. Bullock III, *Law and Social Change: Civil Rights Laws and Their Consequences* (New York: McGraw-Hill Book Co., 1972); and Ronnie Steinberg Ratner, ed., *Equal Employment Policy for Women: Strategies for Implementation in the United States, Canada, and Western Europe* (Philadelphia: Temple University Press, 1980).

3. G. W. F. Hegel, *A Philosophy of Right*, trans. T. M. Knox (London: Oxford University Press, 1967), secs. 257–70.

4. Examples of this literature are Joseph Adelson, "Living with Quotas," *Commentary*, May 1978, pp. 23–29; Daniel Bell, "On Meritocracy and Equality," *Public Interest* 29 (Fall 1972): 29–68 (this essay is also reprinted in Bell, *Post-Industrial Society*, pp. 408–55, as sec. 3 of the Coda); William J. Bennett and Terry Eastland, "Why Bakke Won't End Reverse Discrimination," *Commentary*, September 1978, pp. 29–35; John H. Bunzel, "Bakke v. University of California," *Commentary*, March 1977, pp. 59–64; Carl Cohen, "Why Racial Preference Is Illegal and Immoral," *Commentary*, June 1979, pp. 40–52; James S. Coleman, "Rawls, Nozick, and Educational Equality," *Public Interest* 43 (Spring 1976): 121–28; James S. Coleman, "Disadvantaged Groups, Individual Rights," *New Republic*, October 15, 1977, pp. 5–9; Terry Eastland and William J. Bennett, *Counting By Race: Equality from the Founding Fathers to Bakke* (New York: Basic Books, 1979); Nathan Glazer, *Affirmative Discrimination*, and "Why Bakke Won't End Reverse Discrimination: 2," *Commentary*, September 1978, pp. 36–41; Alan H. Goldman, *Justice and Reverse Discrimination* (Princeton, N.J.: Princeton University Press, 1979); Donald L. Horowitz, "Are the Courts Going Too Far?" *Commentary*, January 1977, pp. 37–44; "The Pottinger Papers: HEW, Affirmative Action and the Universities," *Commentary*, May 1972, pp. 10–30; Bradley R. Schiller, "Equality, Opportunity, and the 'Good Job'," *Public Interest* 43 (Spring 1976): 111–20; Paul Seabury, "HEW and the Universities," *Commentary*, February 1972, pp. 38–44, and "The Idea of Merit," *Commentary*, December 1972, pp. 41–45; Thomas Sowell, "'Affirmative Action' Reconsidered," *Public Interest* 42 (Winter 1976): 47–65, and *Affirmative Action*

Reconsidered: Was It Necessary in Academia? (Washington, D.C.: American Enterprise Institute for Public Policy Research, 1975). A good compendium of the views of professional philosophers on both sides of this question is Marshall Cohen *et al., Equality and Preferential Treatment* (Princeton: Princeton University Press, 1977).

5. See, e.g., Carl Cohen, "Why Racial Preference Is Illegal and Immoral," and "Justice Debased: The Weber Decision," *Commentary*, September, 1979, pp. 43–53.

6. Regents of the University of California v. Alan Bakke, 438 U.S. 265 (1978); Steelworkers v. Weber, 443 U.S. 193 (1979), 61 L. Ed. 2d 480. For Fullilove v. Klutznick, see note 11 below.

7. A sampling of the arguments on this matter will be found in the journal *Philosophy and Public Affairs*. See, e.g., Michael Slote, "Desert, Consent and Justice," 2 (Summer 1973): 323–47; Alan Zaitchik, "On Deserving to Deserve," 6 (Summer 1977): 370–88; Norman Daniels, "Merit and Meritocracy," 7 (Spring 1978): 206–23; and George Sher, "Effort, Ability, and Personal Desert," 8 (Summer 1979): 361–76. See also Robert Goodin, "How to Determine Who Should Get What," *Ethics* 85 (July 1975): 310–21. The essays of Joel Feinberg, *Doing and Deserving: Essays in the Theory of Responsibility* (Princeton, N.J.: Princeton University Press, 1970), are especially thoughtful.

8. I am indebted to an unpublished analysis by Thomas M. Divine of Northampton, Massachusetts, for the distinction between the "ordinal ranking" model and the "skill pool" model.

9. Cohen, "Why Racial Preference Is Illegal and Immoral," pp. 42, 44. This argument is presented at greater length in Goldman, *Justice and Reverse Discrimination*.

10. Glazer, *Affirmative Discrimination*, p. 201.

11. Fullilove v. Klutznick, 65 L. Ed. 2d 902 (1980). Mr. Justice Stewart, dissenting, at pp. 954–55. *U.S. Law Week*, 48(50), June 24, 1980 (Washington, D.C.: Bureau of National Affairs), pp. 4999–5002; p. 4999.

12. Cohen, "Why Racial Preference Is Illegal and Immoral."

13. Craig v. Boren, 429 U.S. 190 (1976); Califano v. Goldfarb, 430 U.S. 199 (1976). For a complete account of the prior case law on gender discrimination (as of 1974), see Barbara Allen Babcock *et al., Sex Discrimination and the Law: Causes and Remedies* (Boston: Little, Brown & Co., 1975).

14. Harris v. McCrae, 65 L. Ed. 2d. 784 (1980); Mr. Justice Stewart's remark about "indigency" is on p. 804 of his majority opinion. *U.S. Law Week*, 48(50), June 24, 1980 (Washington, D.C.: Bureau of National Affairs), pp. 4942–49; p. 4948.

15. This argument is made, with complete inattention to the meaning

and interpretation of the questions that make up such polls, in Thomas Sowell, "Are Quotas Good for Blacks?" *Commentary*, June 1978, pp. 39–43.

16. On racial discrimination, see Dorothy K. Newman *et al., Protest, Politics, and Prosperity: Black Americans and White Institutions, 1940–1975* (New York: Pantheon Books, 1978); Raymond S. Franklin and Solomon Resnik, *The Political Economy of Racism* (New York: Holt, Rinehart & Winston, 1973); George E. Simpson and Milton Yinger, Jr., *Racial and Cultural Minorities: An Analysis of Prejudice and Discrimination,* 4th ed. (New York: Harper & Row, 1972); Thomas R. Pettigrew, ed., *Racial Discrimination in the United States* (New York: Harper & Row, 1975); Robert Blauner, *Racial Oppression in America* (New York: Harper & Row, 1972); Derrick A. Bell, Jr., *Race, Racism and American Law* (Boston: Little, Brown & Co., 1973); Joseph Feagin and Clairece Feagin, *Discrimination American Style: Institutional Racism and Sexism* (Englewood Cliffs, N.J.: Prentice-Hall, 1978); and John H. Franklin, *Race Equality in America* (Chicago: University of Chicago Press, 1976). On sexual discrimination, see Joan Abramson, *Old Boys—New Women: The Politics of Sex Discrimination* (New York: Praeger Publishers, 1979); Martha Blaxall and Barbara Reagan, eds., *Women and the Workplace: The Implications of Occupational Segregation* (Chicago: University of Chicago Press, 1976); Jessie Bernard, *Academic Women* (Cleveland, Ohio: World Publishing Co., 1964); Mary Roth Walsh, *"Doctors Wanted: No Women Need Apply": Sexual Barriers in the Medical Profession, 1835–1975* (New Haven, Conn.: Yale University Press, 1977); Kirsten Amundsen, *A New Look at the Silenced Majority: Women and American Democracy* (Englewood Cliffs, N.J.: Prentice-Hall, 1977); and Sara Ruddick and Pamela Daniels, eds., *Working It Out* (New York: Pantheon Books, 1977), especially Evelyn Fox Keller, "The Anomaly of a Woman in Physics," pp. 77–91.

17. See, e.g., *New York Times*, July 15, 1980, for an account of recent cases and settlements in the field of higher education.

18. This argument about the "demeaning" quality of affirmative action has been made by Thomas Sowell and, most strongly, by Midge Decter on the Op-Ed page of the *New York Times*, July 6, 1980. It should occasion no surprise that the opposition to affirmative action is spoken for on this particular point by a black man and a white woman; those who have "made it" through conventional channels are often the most upset by proposals to extend different rules to others like themselves. In no way, however, can they purport to speak for all those equally qualified blacks and women who have not been so

fortunate, and who quite accurately foresee nothing but a future of exclusion in the perpetuation of traditional procedures. The phrase "blaming the victim" is from the justly influential book of that title by William Ryan (New York: Pantheon Books, 1971).

19. See, e.g., Michael Novak, *The Rise of the Unmeltable Ethnics* (New York: Macmillan Co., 1972).

20. Personnel Administrator of Massachusetts v. Feeney, 442 U.S. 256 (1979).

21. Michael Young, *The Rise of the Meritocracy* (Harmondsworth, Eng.: Penguin Books, 1961).

22. On the question of "credentials," see Ivar Berg, *Education and Jobs: The Great Training Robbery* (New York: Praeger Publishers, 1970), Colin Greer, *The Great School Legend* (New York: Basic Books, 1972), Randall Collins, *The Credential Society* (New York: Academic Press, 1979); and also see Jencks, *Inequality* and *Who Gets Ahead?*

23. See E. J. Mishan, *The Costs of Economic Growth* (Harmondsworth, Eng.: Penguin Books, 1969), and his latest book, *The Economic Growth Debate* (London: George Allen & Unwin, 1977); and Fred Hirsch, *Social Limits to Growth* (Cambridge, Mass.: Harvard University Press, 1978).

24. The literature of discrimination in specific fields, how it affects blacks, women, and other minorities, and how alternatively they might reorganize the delivery of services to themselves is so immense that we can only scratch the surface of it here (perhaps that says something about the nature of the problem). On blacks and the police, see Robert Wintersmith, *Police and the Black Community* (Lexington, Mass.: Lexington Books, 1974); Arthur Waskow, "Community Control of the Police," *Trans-Action*, December 1969, pp. 4–7; Robert Lefcourt, ed., *Law Against the People: Essays to Demystify Law, Order, and the Courts* (New York: Random House, 1971); and Jerome H. Skolnick, *Justice Without Trial: Law Enforcement in Democratic Society*, 2nd ed. (New York: John Wiley & Sons, 1975). On women, minorities, and health care, see Jerry Weaver, *National Health Policy and the Undeserved: Ethnic Minorities, Women, and the Elderly* (St. Louis: C. V. Mosby Co., 1976); Claudia Dreifus, ed., *Seizing Our Bodies: The Politics of Women's Health Care* (New York: Random House, 1978); Sheryl B. Ruzek, *The Women's Health Movement: Feminist Alternatives to Medical Control* (New York: Praeger Publishers, 1978); Barbara Ehrenreich and Deirdre English, *For Her Own Good: 150 Years of Experts' Advice to Women* (New York: Doubleday & Co.; Old Westbury, N.Y.: Feminist Press, 1979); Gena Corea, *The Hidden Malpractice: How American Medicine*

Treats Women as Patients and Professionals (New York: William Morrow & Co., 1977); and Sue-Ellen Jacobs, "Our Babies Shall Not Die: A Community's Response to Medical Neglect," *Human Organization* 38 (Summer 1979): 120–33. On blacks, women, and the legal system, see Clarice Feinman, *Women in the Criminal Justice System* (New York: Praeger Publishers, 1979); Jerold S. Auerbach, *Unequal Justice: Lawyers and Social Change in Modern America* (London: Oxford University Press, 1977); Charles E. Owens and Jimmy Bell, eds., *Blacks and Criminal Justice* (Lexington, Mass.: Lexington Books, 1977); and C. B. Jones, "Critical Equal Employment Issues in Criminal Justice," *Journal of Police Science and Administration* 7 (June 1979): 129–37.

25. This story is recounted by Donald Allen Robinson in his article "Two Movements in Pursuit of Equal Employment Opportunity," *Signs* 4 (Spring 1979): 413–33.

26. A revealing study of the ways in which an elite can surmount the limitations of "objective" standards of "merit" is a British study by Graeme Salaman and Kenneth Thompson, "Class, Culture, and the Persistence of an Elite: The Case of Army Officer Selection," *Sociological Review* 26 (May 1978): pp. 283–304. Salaman and Thompson were allowed access to tape recordings of conversations between candidates and selection boards, and among the members of the boards themselves. The tapes show the boards reinterpreting performance on the "objective" tests and field exercises to accord with traditional elite expectations, so that "performance" in such categories as "natural leadership ability" and "coolness under stress" is used to overturn rankings based on the tests and exercises. The word "performance" is advisedly in quotes, as the selecting officers, all from a public school, upper-class background simply find that their own typical behavior patterns are the desirable ones. Thus, e.g., "keeping a stiff upper lip," the emotionally unresponsive demeanor which is a norm at the upper-class public schools, is interpreted as "coolness under stress." (This is a clear instance of discrimination according to class background. In Britain, especially in the armed forces and certain sectors of the civil service, class background is still an important factor in selection and advancement. In most advanced industrial societies, though, that particular kind of discrimination, which is essentially a pre-capitalist relic, has become attenuated or even vanished. That is certainly true of the United States—see the discussion below.)

27. I have elaborated further on this point in "What Is Political Equality?" *Dissent* 26 (Summer 1979): 351–63.

28. Although I do not follow her usage precisely, I am indebted to

Kathryn Pyne Parsons for the concept of "moral revolution," specifically the notion that such revolutions are based on the creation of new "social facts." See Parsons, "Moral Revolution," in Sherman and Beck, eds., *Prism of Sex*, pp. 189–229, and "Nietzche and Moral Change" in Martha Lee Osborne, ed., *Women in Western Thought* (New York: Random House, 1979), pp. 235–48.

29. On the perception of women during the early period of American capitalism, see Nancy F. Cott, *The Bonds of Womanhood: "Woman's Sphere" in New England, 1780–1835* (New Haven, Conn.: Yale University Press, 1977). Jill Ker Conway, in "Women Reformers and American Culture, 1870–1930," *Journal of Social History* 2 (Winter 1971–72): 164–77, has noted the extent to which even female reformers such as Jane Addams accepted the "controlling power of the stereotype of the female temperament" (p. 166): a stereotype which comes, of course, from the "domestic sphere."

30. It is fitting that this argument about "woman's place" should have been put most sharply by the greatest democratic theorist of them all, who thereby illuminates for us just how dependent is "democracy" on a prior, theoretical determination of who shall constitute the citizenry. See Jean-Jacques Rousseau, *Emile*, trans. Allan Bloom (New York: Basic Books, 1979), bk. 5.

31. The unhappy relationship between white and black workers in the United States is well known. Recent scholarship on women in work has brought to light a similar story of what has taken place between the sexes. See especially Heidi Hartmann, "Capitalism, Patriarchy, and Job Segregation by Sex," *Signs* 1 (Spring 1976): 137–70, and Ruth Milkman, "Organizing the Sexual Division of Labor: Historical Perspectives on 'Women's Work' and the American Labor Movement," *Socialist Review* 10, no. 49 (January–February 1980): 95–150.

32. Their review of all the available literature on "the psychology of sex differences" leads Eleanor Maccoby and Carol Jacklin (*Sex Differences*, chap. 8) to conclude that a dearth of credible adult role models is the single most important factor explaining the relative lack of accomplishment by women in those areas in which, according to Goldberg, they fall short for lack of sufficient testosterone.

33. Edwin Dorn, *Rules and Racial Equality* (New Haven, Conn.: Yale University Press, 1979), p. 147.

34. Christian Bay, *The Structure of Freedom* (New York: Atheneum Publishers, 1965), p. 7. The implications of this stance are also developed in Philip Green, "Decentralization, Community Control and Revolution: Reflections on Ocean Hill–Brownsville," in Philip Green and Sanford Levinson, eds., *Power and Community: Dissenting Essays in Political Science* (New York: Pantheon Books, 1969); and in Mi-

chael Walzer, "The Obligations of Oppressed Minorities," in his *Obligations: Essays on Disobedience, War, and Citizenship* (Cambridge, Mass.: Harvard University Press, 1970). The stringency of the conditions which would allow us to agree that a given exercise of majority rule was fair is spelled out, of course, in Jean-Jacques Rousseau's *The Social Contract;* see *On the Social Contract,* ed. Roger D. Masters, trans. Judith R. Masters (New York: St. Martin's Press, 1978). The other classic statement of this position, from within a much different philosophical position, is in chap. 5 of John Stuart Mill's "On Utilitarianism," *Collected Works of John Stuart Mill,* ed. J. M. Robson and F. E. L. Priestly (Toronto: University of Toronto Press, 1965), vol. 10. The best-known and most carefully thought out attempt to explain why "underdogs" must come first in a "just society" is John Rawls's elaboration of the "difference principle"; see Rawls, *Theory of Justice.*

Chapter 7. The New Individualism: The State, the Public, and Liberty

1. On that point, see Mark Green and Norman Waitzman, "Cost, Benefit, and Class," *Working Papers,* May/June 1980, pp. 39–51.
2. Robert Nozick, *Anarchy, State, and Utopia* (New York: Basic Books, 1974), and Milton Friedman, *Capitalism and Freedom* (Chicago: University of Chicago Press, 1962).
3. Friedman, *Capitalism and Freedom,* p. 2.
4. Nozick, *Anarchy, State, and Utopia,* p. 26.
5. Edward Hallett Carr, *The New Society* (Boston: Beacon Press, 1951).
6. Friedman, *Capitalism and Freedom,* p. 165.
7. John Stuart Mill, "Principles of Political Economy," in *Collected Works,* vols. 2 and 3.
8. See Mill's essay "Bentham," in *Collected Works* 10: 99–100.
9. Robert Paul Wolff, *The Poverty of Liberalism* (Boston: Beacon Press, 1968), chap. 5.
10. Coppage v. Kansas, 236 U.S. 1, 46–47 (1915).
11. G. W. F. Hegel, *Philosophy of Right,* sec. 195, p. 128.
12. Karl Marx, *Early Writings,* trans. T. B. Bottomore (New York: McGraw-Hill Book Co., 1964), p. 122.
13. See Marx, *Capital,* vol. 1, pts. 7 and 8; W. G. Hoskins, *The Age of Plunder: The England of Henry VIII, 1500–1547* (New York: Longman, 1976); also see the works cited in note 9 to Chapter 4.
14. Nozick, *Anarchy, State, and Utopia,* p. 231.
15. Max Weber, *The Protestant Ethic and the Spirit of Capitalism,* trans. Talcott Parsons (New York: Charles Scribner's Sons, 1958), p. 62.

16. The richest literature on this development is that pertaining to the English experience. See especially E. P. Thompson, *The Making of the English Working Class* (New York: Vintage Books, 1966); *Whigs and Hunters* (New York: Pantheon Books, 1976); "Eighteenth Century Crime, Popular Movements and Social Control," *Bulletin of the Society for the Study of Labour History* 25 (1972): pp. 133–65; "Patrician Society, Plebeian Culture," *Journal of Social History* 7 (Summer 1974: pp. 382–405); and "Eighteenth Century Society: Class Struggle Without Class," *Social History* 3 (1978). See also Christopher Hill, *Reformation to Industrial Revolution;* E. J. Hobsbawm, *Labouring Men: Studies in the History of Labour* (Garden City, N.Y.: Doubleday & Co., 1967), and "Social Criminality," *Bulletin of the Society for the Study of Labour History* 25 (1972).

17. Friedman, *Capitalism and Freedom*, p. 163.

18. Nozick, *Anarchy, State, and Utopia*, p. 272.

19. Jean-Jacques Rousseau, "Discourse on the Origin and Foundations of Inequality" in *The First and Second Discourses*, ed. Roger D. Masters (New York: St. Martin's Press, 1964), pp. 159–60.

20. See Marx, "The Communist Manifesto," in *Karl Marx and Frederick Engels: Selected Works* (Moscow: Foreign Languages Publishing House, 1962), 1: 43.

21. Nozick, *Anarchy, State, and Utopia*, p. ix.

22. Milton and Rose Friedman, *Free to Choose: A Personal Statement* (New York: Harcourt Brace Jovanovich, 1980). See Robert Heilbroner's review "The Road to Selfdom," *New York Review of Books*, April 17, 1980, p. 4; Lester Thurow, *The Zero-Sum Society: Distribution and the Possibilities for Economic Change* (New York: Basic Books, 1980). And also see the brilliant review of the Friedman book, exposing falsification after falsification, by Gus Tyler, "The Friedman Inventions," *Dissent* 27 (Summer 1980): 279–90.

23. See *Inquiry*, September 4, 1978.

Chapter 8. Epilogue: Who Wants Equality?

1. See, e.g., Curtis B. Gans, "Conservatism by Default," *The Nation*, October 14, 1978, pp. 372–74.

2. Kristol, *Two Cheers for Capitalism*, chap. 22.

3. Daniel Bell, *The Cultural Contradictions of Capitalism* (New York: Basic Books, 1976). Bell's confessed inspiration for the thesis that capitalism's major defect is the tendency of intellectuals to become disaffected from it is Joseph Schumpeter, *Capitalism, Socialism and Democracy* (New York: Harper & Row, 1950), especially pt. 2.

4. Kristol, *Two Cheers*, chap. 1.

5. Peter Jay, "Englanditis," in R. Emmett Tyrell, Jr., ed., *The Future That Doesn't Work: Social Democracy's Failures in Britain* (Garden City, N.Y.: Doubleday & Co., 1977), pp. 167–85. I have commented at greater length on the antidemocratic tendencies of this kind of argument in "Social Democracy and Its Critics: The Case of England," *Dissent* 25 (Summer 1978): 334–40.
6. See also my "What Is Political Equality?" *Dissent* 26 (Summer 1979): 351–63.

Appendix A. Arthur Jensen's Methodology

1. See Sandra Scarr-Salapatek, "Race, Social Class, and IQ," *Science* 174 (December 24, 1971): 1287.
2. Jensen, "Educability and Group Differences," p. 243. The original study by Nancy Bayley, "Comparisons of Mental and Motor Test Scores . . . ," appeared in *Child Development* 36 (1965): 379–411.
3. See Zena A. Stein and Hannah Kassal, "Nutrition," in Joseph Wortis, ed., *Mental Retardation* (New York: Grune & Stratton, 1970), 2: 110–11.
4. Table 17.1 in Jensen, *Educability*, p. 316.
5. Jensen, *HER*, p. 83.
6. The noncomparability of these data was first called to our attention by Jerry Hirsch, "Jensenism: The Bankruptcy of 'Science' Without Scholarship," *Educational Theory* (Winter 1975): 3–27.
7. Jensen, *HER*, p. 83.
8. Jensen, *Educability*, pp. 343ff.
9. See B. Pasamanick and Hilda Knobloch, "Retrospective Studies on the Epidemiology of Reproductive Casualty: Old and New," *Merrill-Palmer Quarterly of Behavior and Development* 12 (1966): 7–26.
10. See Jensen, *HER*, p. 84; *Educability*, p. 240.
11. Shuey, *Testing of Negro Intelligence*, p. 114.
12. See Arthur M. Jordan, "Efficiency of Group Tests of Intelligence in Discovering the Mentally Deficient," *High School Journal* 31 (1948): 73–94; Alan B. Wilson, "Educational Consequences of Segregation in a California Community," *Racial Isolation in the Public Schools*, Report of the U.S. Commission on Civil Rights, 1967, appendices, 2, especially p. 174; Ruth C. Wylie, "Children's Estimates of Their Schoolwork Ability, As a Function of Sex, Race and Socioeconomic Level," *Journal of Personality* 31 (1963): 203–24; and Martin Deutsch and Bert Brown, "Social Influences in Negro-White Intelligence Differences," *Journal of Social Issues* 20 (1964): 24–35.

Appendix B. The Bell-Shaped Curve

1. See Martin Bronfenbrenner, *Income Distribution Theory* (New York: Aldine Publishing Co., 1971), p. 57.

INDEX

About the Author

Philip Green received his B.A. from Swarthmore College and a Ph.D. in politics from Princeton University. He is currently chairman of the government department at Smith College and a member of the editorial board of *The Nation* magazine. He is the author of *Deadly Logic: The Theory of Nuclear Deterrence* and numerous articles, and the editor of *Power and Community: Dissenting Essays in Political Science* (with Sanford Levinson) and *The Political Imagination in Literature* (with Michael Walzer).